THE CHINESE LIFESTYLE

The research presented in this book explores the formation of the middle class in contemporary urban China.

Including case studies on middle-class professionals living in Beijing, this book analyses how social and economic changes to Chinese society created a middle-class lifestyle and new forms of distinction with a particular focus on the social construction of identity. Looking through the lens of individuals' perception of life trajectories and ideological taxonomies generated within the framework of post-Maoist China, the book uncovers the role that the Chinese middle class play in a state-sponsored discourse and where the distinctions identifying the middle-class lifestyle produce inequality, transfer privilege, and disadvantage in contemporary urban China. It goes on to question hegemonic discourses on class, arguing that a middle-class identity is progressively constructed in urban China not only though consumption practices, but through the experience of non-individualistic activities in both the public and private spheres.

Analysing how social distinctions are performed contributes to the under-standing of the Chinese middle class pre-pandemic, as well as the continual chal-lenges this social group shall face in the years to come. As such, this is a must read for those interested in the Chinese middle-class, Chinese politics, and gender studies.

Alfonso Sánchez-Romera is a researcher at Universitat Autònoma de Barcelona (InterAsia Research Group) and postdoctoral fellow at Freie Universität Berlin. He graduated in Humanities and East Asian Studies and holds a PhD in Intercultural Studies. His research interests include middle class, Chinese society, and discourse analysis.

ROUTLEDGE CONTEMPORARY CHINA SERIES

The Pulse of China's Grand Strategy
Jean Kachiga

Chinese Regionalism in Asia
Beyond the Belt-Road Initiative
Tiang Boon Hoo and Jared Morgan Mckinney

Sensing China
Modern Transformations of Sensory Culture
Shengqing Wu & Xuelei Huang

Chinese Modernity and Socialist Feminist Theory
Song Shaopeng, Edited by Sharon R. Wesoky

China's Provinces Go Global
Internationalization under Guided Autonomy
Wiebke Antonia Rabe

Premarital Abortion in China
Intimacy, Family and Reproduction
Ruby Y. S. Lai

The Chinese Lifestyle
The Reconfiguration of the Middle Class in Contemporary China
Alfonso Sánchez-Romera

Red Tourism in China
Commodification of Propaganda
Chunfeng Lin

Human–Animal Interactions in Anthropocene Asia
Victor Teo

Deliberation with Chinese Characteristics
A Tale of Two Chinese Cities' Participatory Budgeting Experiences
Su Yun Woo

For more information about this series, please visit: https://www.routledge.com/ Routledge-Contemporary-China-Series/book-series/SE0768.

THE CHINESE LIFESTYLE

The Reconfiguration of the Middle Class in Contemporary China

Alfonso Sánchez-Romera

Routledge
Taylor & Francis Group

LONDON AND NEW YORK

First published 2023
by Routledge
4 Park Square, Milton Park, Abingdon, Oxon OX14 4RN

and by Routledge
605 Third Avenue, New York, NY 10158

Routledge is an imprint of the Taylor & Francis Group, an informa business

British Library Cataloguing in Publication Data
A catalogue record for this book is available from the British Library

ISBN: 978-1-032-28955-7 (hbk)
ISBN: 978-1-032-28957-1 (pbk)
ISBN: 978-1-003-29930-1 (ebk)

DOI: 10.4324/9781003299301

Typeset in Bembo
by Taylor & Francis Books

A Agustina y José, mis padres.

CONTENTS

ILLUSTRATIONS

Figure

Tables

ACKNOWLEDGEMENTS

This book is the product of many motivations. I would like to take this opportunity, however, to thank at least some of the many people who have supported and accompanied me in the researching and writing. As empirical research, special thanks go to all those people who shared their stories with me during my time in China. I am indebted to their patience and kindness. They have all been anonymized; fictious names are used here, none of the informants are named in this book. The names of their hometowns have also been replaced with fictious ones, and personal details of little relevance to this study have been modified or omitted to prevent the identification of the informants.

I would especially like to thank Dr. Joaquín Beltrán Antolín and Dr. Amelia Sáiz López, my mentors and friends, for their indispensable advice, trust, generosity, as well as many other conversations in Barcelona, and many dinners and jokes; our friendship has been and still is one of the most cherished outcomes of this research project.

In Beijing, I am deeply indebted to Renmin University of China, which hosted me during fieldwork and eventually became a second home for me. Many people at Renmin University have helped me in many ways. In particular, I am grateful to Dr. Tang Kuang for their enlightening guidance and support for my research, and Dr. Zhang Jing for her openness, kind assistance, and advice. In Taipei, Dr. Lin Thung-hong in Academia Sinica, for providing me with precious suggestions and kindly offering me his help in Taiwan during the COVID-19 pandemic. I completed the last stage of writing in Berlin, where Dr. Katrin Gengenbach welcomed me as a postdoctoral fellow at Graduate School of East Asian Studies (GEAS) at Freie Universität Berlin; I am deeply grateful for her hospitality, generosity, and support in the writing.

I save the last thanks to those whom I owe the most: my family and friends. I would like to thank my parents, José and Agustina, and my brothers and sisters,

Tomás, Tensi, Anna, and Víctor, and my nephews Biel and Víctor, and my niece Nora, for the boundless support and goodwill offered during the six years that this project has lasted and throughout my life so far. I owe immeasurable gratitude to my entire family and friends, close or far away, for their unconditional love and support in many different ways accumulated over the years. Thank you all.

The research presented in this book is part of the Spanish R & D project "New socio-cultural, political and economic developments in East Asia in the global context" (PID2019–107861GB-I00, MINECO/FEDER, EU) with professor Amelia Sáiz López and professor Joaquín Beltrán Antolín at Universitat Autònoma de Barcelona, as main researchers of the InterAsia Research Group.

This ethnographic research would not have been possible without the financial support of a number of organizations. These include:

2017/2018 – China Confucius Studies Program, Joint PhD fellowship (孔子新汉学计划),
2019 – Taiwan Fellowship (臺灣獎助金),

as well as support from the Universitat Autònoma de Barcelona postdoctoral Margarita Salas Grant, funded by the European Union-Next Generation EU, and the Ministerio de Universidades (Ministry of Universities), which founded the writing stages of this book at Freie Universtät Berlin.

INTRODUCTION

The paradigm of the middle class in contemporary China

This is a book on class in contemporary urban China. Since the middle of the 1990s, class has been an ongoing process of reconfiguration of the unequal distribution of material, cultural, and symbolic rewards in the People's Republic of China (PRC). The second and more ambitious wave of market reforms implemented in the 1990s led to the rise of living standards, and new social practices and representations emerged in urban China. Not only the improvement of living conditions, but also China's economic growth, globalization, and the acceleration of industrialization and urbanization changed previous class structure in large cities. The PRC transformed from a modern industrial society to a post-industrial society with a distinctive lifestyle linked to the middle class. Therefore, the lifestyle of the post-reform middle class was related more to experiences associated with cultural consumption, leisure, and nonmaterial concerns than to experiences linked to productive activity and material grounds. The post-reform era thus provides a unique opportunity to investigate and discuss the emergence and development of new social relations and class distinctions, and the role of Party-state, market forces, and social groupings in the reconfiguration of inequality and privilege in urban China today.

The Chinese middle class is increasingly playing a decisive role in public debate both inside and outside China. It is presented as the "largest middle-class consumption market segment in the world and a priority market for major multinational firms" (Kharas and Dooley 2020). Further, the middle class is also said to be an essential element in the economic development strategy of the Dual Circulation (*shuang xun huan*) designed by the Chinese government and based on reliance on domestic demand and development through domestic innovations for the next twelve years (Yasinskii and Kozhevnikov 2022). After the tremendous achievements of the poverty elimination campaign, the Chinese government reintroduced the "common prosperity" (*gongtong fuyu*) in 2021 to increase the size of

DOI: 10.4324/9781003299301-1

the middle class and thus expand domestic demand by "raising the earnings of low-income groups and reduce excessive incomes" (Dunford 2022). Additionally, given that the knowledge and ability to implement innovation in the PRC are in the hands of the middle class —researchers, scientists, managers, technicians, etc.—this group will play an essential role in the next decade, not only as potential consumers—economic capital—but also as generators of innovation—cultural and human capital.

Through case studies of middle-class professionals residing in Beijing, this book examines the formation of the urban middle class, with a particular focus on the social construction of identity by analysing lifestyle and social distinctions in contemporary urban China. Based on Pierre Bourdieu's class theory, "class" here will be discussed relationally in terms of lifestyle and capital possession. For Bourdieu (1987), class was "characterized in a certain way as sets of agents who, by virtue of the fact that they occupy similar positions in social space" (6), given the distribution of the various forms of capital, namely economic, cultural, social, and symbolic capital (4), "are endowed with similar dispositions which prompt them to develop similar practices" (6), and thus produce "practices and representations of a similar kind," that is, a class lifestyle (5). Thus, in this study class is understood as the result of "the relationships between the universe of economic and social conditions and the universe of lifestyles" (Bourdieu 1984, *xii*). However, Bourdieu added that class only existed as "a real class" in social space "by asserting and manifesting themselves as such, can become political forces capable of imposing their own vision ... and ensuring the triumph of such dispositions and interests as are associated with their position in social space" (13). On that basis, lifestyles reflect not only class location and capital possession but also social identity as the political expression of collective visions of change.

These observations underline that class as lifestyle, class as social structure, and class as social consciousness, are all involved in the formation of class in post-industrial societies (Crompton 1998) —that is, societies characterized by a transition from industrial production to service provision under advanced capitalism, and whose occupational structures denoted the creation of a service-based economy, the pre-eminence of the professional and technical class, and the centrality of theoretical knowledge as the source of innovation and policy formation (Bell 1976; Esping-Andersen 1999; Lin 2008). Firstly, class lifestyle can be understood as a set of configurations that explain the way in which a particular social group performs and understands how the social space works at a particular time. Lifestyle manifests a set of social practices (behaviours) and representations (attitudes and discourses) specific to a social group (Mauger, in Rocca 2017, 6). In global societies, "with the rise in standards of living, it is argued that issues related to *consumption*, rather than production, are becoming more relevant" (Crompton 1998, 166). Thus, the pervasive links between systematic structures of inequality and varying patterns of consumption appears obvious in post-industrial societies.

Secondly, class is one manifestation of social inequality, but not the only one. As Kirk (2007) suggested, class is "a social relation constituted dialogically and relationally, cast within the shadow of structures and processes which create and reinforce inequalities" (5). Under these conditions, class is an organizing and systematic structure of production and reproduction of inequality that acts both potentially and hierarchically in the social space. And class analysis is a methodological tool to gauge the lack of legitimized reciprocity in social relations considering material, cultural and symbolic rewards. However, class analysis cannot only be reduced to hierarchical systems based on different objective and subjective variables such as income, education attainment, or political ideas. Rather, what is needed is the detection and recognition of class inequality and oppressive classifications as dynamic structures based on gender, sexuality, and race, and how they are constituted in the discursive and the material sense. Under these conditions, class has to be with positioning and recognition, with displacement and context. That is why, class is understood here as "a *well-founded historical artefact*" (Bourdieu 1987, 8–9, emphasis in original), a continual reconfiguration of inequalities and capital in a world in constant transformation.

Thirdly, class also exists as social identity and representative organizations who proffer a properly political expression on the basis of interests of class. Modernization theorists associate the middle class with the concept of "civil society" and democratization. The term civil society comes from anti-dictatorial movements that emerged in East Central Europe, Latin America, and South Africa in the 1980s, but it also reflects a new kind of critique of neoliberal and interventionist social state in terms of discourse and conflict in global societies. To a large extent, Modernization theorists, both Chinese and foreign, assumed that due to a higher standard of living among the urban dwellers in the post-reform era, they would build a civil society movement to challenge the Party-state and facilitate democratization. However, this did not happen, and scholars began to use other concepts such as subjective social status and sense of distinction to explore social identity in post-reform China. The aim was to understand "how people see themselves as being located in the social hierarchy" (Chen and Fan 2015, 1) and how they see the interrelationship between politics, community and the self in neo-authoritarian China.

In line with the goal of approaching the social construction of identity through lifestyle and social distinction in urban China, the specific objectives of this study are formulated as follows:

a   To define the space in which the cluster of intellectual narratives about the middle class are generated in China studies
b   To do a critical review of pertinent literature on the debate concerning the standard criteria for defining the Chinese middle class
c   To elucidate middle class as "a *well-founded historical artefact*" before and after the establishment of the PRC in 1949
d   To examine in detail the construction and development of the official discourse on the middle class through the content of articles on middle class published on *Renmin Wang* during the period 2000–2015

e   To analyse in-depth the ethnographic materials collected by fieldwork conducted in Beijing between 2017 and 2018
f   To formulate a critical synopsis of the main features on which the social construction of identity within the Chinese middle class in the context of the pandemic times

Framed by this theoretical and methodological design, this analysis of the social construction of identity of the middle class in urban China today is based on the theoretical assumption that the post-reform middle class can be understood as a transhistorical social construct that is impossible to define but has been captured by a distinctive lifestyle. Additionally, the social phenomenon of the Chinese middle class has been the result of an ongoing process of reconfiguration of social, material, and cultural differences since the second stage of reforms was implemented in the 1990s. Relations among urban dwellers are understood and enacted through "a sense of distinction" in the form of a post-industrial lifestyle that serves to produce and reproduce hegemonic discourses and inequalities in everyday life in urban China today.

Thus, the leading argument proposed by this study is that the conceptualization of the Chinese middle class as a social identity can be considered to relate more to cultural consumption than to production. On that basis, and using Bourdieu's theoretical schema, the members of the Chinese middle class, therefore, would not only be inclined to develop a unitary lifestyle, a set of dispositions and a tacit sense of their place in the world, but also they would be "placed in homogeneous conditions of existence imposing homogeneous conditionings and producing homogeneous systems of dispositions capable of generating similar practices," and consequently, "a class habitus (and, in particular, systems of classificatory schemes)" (Bourdieu 1984, 101). Consequently, class analysis in the PRC needs to ask how and when classificatory schemes and social hierarchies have been established, how class positions produce conflict at the level of the symbolic, why the Chinese middle class is so present in the public debate today, and "why it is that classification is the mechanism by which we know the contemporary" (Skeggs 2004, 4–5). The development of this position is used to examine not only class formation but also the role of the Party-state and market forces in the construction of social identity and inequality in the PRC.

These observations underline the limits of the paradigm of the Chinese middle class in the post-reform era. On the one hand, the main problem when analysing the phenomenon of the Chinese middle class is definitional; there is no unified consensual system of criteria for identifying Chinese citizens as middle class. The size and consumption capacity of this social group can vary significantly depending on the defining criteria used. That is why, behind every definition of middle class lies political, economic, and business expectations (Guo 2008). However, as Rocca (2017) noted, despite differing perceptions of the topic of the Chinese middle class among scholars, journalists, Party-state leaders, and the urban middle class for a variety of reasons, "the size and the precise characteristics of the Chinese middle class do not matter per se because they have no inherent signification in themselves beyond social imaginaries and hidden agendas." Rather, the crucial aspect is to understand the social construction and the ways the issue of the middle class emerged among the public (5).

On the other, the lifestyle associated with the urban middle class is the paradigm that explains social relations in China today. Paradigms are social representations, or "ways of world making" (Moscovici 1988, 231), that are developed "at the societal, contextual and individual level." At the societal level, paradigms are established through media communication and institutions, at the contextual level through communication with and action upon others, and at the individual level through internal debate and dialogical selves (Castro and Batel 2008, 479). In the case of the paradigm of the Chinese middle class, and similarly to Solé-Farràs's (2014) definition of discourse, interdependent representations intellectually structure both the determining of diverse desires for living in a certain way, often employing imprecise conceptions associated with certain behaviours and values, but not others, and the contingency of unintentional attitudes and actions benefiting this ideal.

The paradigm of the Chinese middle class suggests that the city is the "civilizing space" that allows Chinese citizens to develop into "their own person," becoming modern, well-educated and "civilized citizens" (Schein 2001, 237), and competent consumers with a high human quality (suzhi) (Zavoretti 2017, 4). In this context, suzhi appears in new representations of social distinction and the discursive production of middle classness by extending its sense from a discourse of backwardness (the countryside) and development (the civilized city) "to encompass the minute social distinctions defining a 'person of quality' in practices of consumption and the incitement of a middle-class desire for social mobility" (Anagnost 2004, 190). Regarding the lifestyle of the Chinese middle class, cultural consumption and leisure are the obvious while suzhi is the discursive. Although this paradigm is a collective creation, it is a prominently urban, hierarchical, and class-based representation upheld by specific policies and binary narratives of social distinction and meritocracy. Under these conditions, paradigms in this book can be understood as social representations and discourses on the "common sense" that, together with social practices, shape lifestyles. Thus, by exploring the post-industrial lifestyle of the urban middle class in Beijing, this book simultaneously explores the limits of the paradigm of the Chinese middle class and presents a more nuanced account of the phenomenon of class formation in China.

This is a quantitative and qualitative research study on class in post-reform China. Two methods are adopted for data collection: documentary analysis and semi-structured interviews. The intellectual debates in China studies in the existing literature, the PRC's constitutional amendments, speeches, and ideological programmes of Party-state leaders, and the content of articles on middle class published on digital media are critically evaluated from a discourse analysis approach. Following the goals and arguments of approaching class location in general and specifically, this study adopts an inter- and transdisciplinary perspective which brings together separate disciplines and methodologies such as sociology, historiography, discourse analysis, and so on, a common theme to create a holistic approach. Indeed, different from those normative ethnographies that focus on the definitional and ontological aspects of the middle class, the investigation presented here explores the Chinese middle class through a multidimensional analysis, from Party-state-promoted discourses in digital media to the voices of protagonists, complementing all this with participant and non-participant observation, which provides an exhaustive, comprehensive, and intersectional account for understanding the Chinese middle class of the 2020s.

As this investigation is ethnographically framed, the core data of this book come from interviews with middle-class individuals in field sites. I spent 16 months in Beijing where I conducted semi-structured interviews as well as participant and non-participant observation. In order to ensure comparability, informants were considered middle class if they fulfilled four objective criteria: they reside in Beijing; they have educational qualifications including college, undergraduate, and above; their age is between 25 and 65 years; and finally, their occupational activity is accordance with the occupational model developed by Lu Xueyi (2002) and his colleagues at the Chinese Academy of Social Sciences (CASS) Institute of Sociology, and which is drawn from the work of Giddens (1973) and Wright (1997). Salary has not been a decisive criterion because urban residents have substantial unreported (hidden) income, in particular operating income and property income have high omission rates and distort China's household income (Wang and Woo 2011; Zhang and Zhao 2019).

Most of the participant observations and conversations with informants came from two major and very rich sources: working with colleagues in their thirties and forties as a visiting doctoral student in Beijing, and spending leisure with friends in their twenties and thirties, and occasionally colleagues, shopping in malls of Haidian, and eating out in traditional restaurants and in the increasing number of fashionable themed or "ethnic" and international cuisine restaurants. Further, I undertook other kinds of participant and non-participant observation by visiting "middle-class" coffee shops in business districts, 798 Art Zone and Wangfujing, gated community areas all over Beijing, art galleries, concert halls (European classical music, traditional Chinese operas) such as the National Centre for the Performing Arts (NCPA), and alternative music venues in Gulou. The sample of interviewees conducted in 2017 and 2018 includes 20 middle-class urban dwellers, professional and technical staff, white collar workers, professors, professionals, managerial staff, entrepreneurs, and a local official.

As we have seen, class is a major analytical tool in the exploration of inequality and the understanding of the Chinese society in the 21st century. In the conception of this book there is an attempt to contribute new perspectives to the debate about class in the PRC and to explain the social construction of the Chinese middle class by considering testimonies of Beijing's middle class immediately before the COVID-19 pandemic. In order to understand urban society in China today, it is essential not only to know the middle class before the pandemic, but also to understand the continuity and challenges that this social group will face in the post-pandemic future. In addition, considering the growing literature based on various aspects of the middle class over the last two decades in China studies, this study also updates all the intellectual debates on the middle class and social inequality in urban contexts up to the present day through the integration of objective and subjective criteria. While bearing this complexity in mind, the methodological combination employed in this investigation provides a rich account of the intellectual debate about class in China studies, hegemonic discourses on middle class created by the Party-state and market forces, and the voice of the protagonists.

This book consists of five chapters. Chapter 1 investigates the formation of the Chinese middle class by assessing class as "a *well-founded historical artefact*" from the late Qing era to the COVID-19 pandemic, and analysing the discursive construction of the concept of "middle class" in Chinese digital media. The first part of Chapter 1 aims to understand China's structural history, that is, historical processes and power relations, and the systematic structures of inequality created before and after the establishment of the PRC in 1949, and assess the role of the Party-state and market forces in the construction of the post-reform middle class in urban China. After the historical review of class formation in China and discussion on how a middle-class lifestyle in the PRC has been shaped by state intervention, the second part of this chapter is a quantitative and qualitative analysis of the content of 427 articles on middle class published between 2000 and 2015 on *Renmin Wang*, the digital version of the newspaper *Renmin Ribao* (considered the mouthpiece of Central Committee of the CCP).

Chapter 2 offers a glance on the intellectual debate on the Chinese middle class that includes a literature review of class theories in China studies and a critical analysis of the various criteria for defining the concept of "Chinese middle class." It reflects the diversity of thought and vested interests both outside and inside China. Economic expectations, political considerations, and the ideological agenda of most scholars addressing the issue of the middle class have added a complex discursive dimension to the description of social groupings and structures in the PRC. This chapter sheds light on the formative process of the Chinese middle class from an epistemological perspective by identifying the underlying forces in intellectual debates on class in China studies and estimating their legitimation in bringing about new imaginaries and representations in the post-reform era. In any case, these aspects are all involved in the public debates on China's urban society in which the middle class plays a prominent role.

Based on empirical data, Chapters 3, 4, and 5 examine in depth the ethnographic work conducted in Beijing in 2017 and 2018 and argue that the middle-class lifestyle that emerged in the post-reform era can be considered to relate not only to experiences associated with productive activity, but also, increasingly, to experiences related to post-industrial practices and representations based on cultural consumption, non-material concerns, and Western and traditional Chinese values. To be more specific, Chapter 3 addresses the social trajectories of Beijing's middle-class dwellers and how they are marked by a distinct cultural consumption. On the one hand, the questions of social distinctions and boundaries between classes included in this chapter consider the main dimensions of class formation in urban China, that is, the amount, proportion, and evolution of capital, and the evolution of the historical track of status position. On the other, by using the social space as a framework and the methodological lens of lifestyle, this chapter also evaluates the cultural consumption practices of the Chinese middle class as class-based consumption and manifestations of class hierarchies, in particular those practices associated with online and offline shopping, high culture aspirations, and lifestyle mobility in Beijing.

By considering social representations within the middle-class lifestyle, Chapter 4 looks at the relevance of the motivations to achieve by urban dwellers in terms of social success (celebrities), happiness, and loving relationships. Whereas the evaluation of social figures reveals social change and new interactions between the individual and the community identity, the analysis of the conceptualization of happiness and romantic love uncovers the emergence of post-material concerns and ideals of long-lasting committed and heteronormative relationships. As a result, Chapter 4 not only indicates ideological narratives as support for hegemonic representations within the lifestyle of the post-reform middle class but also explores notions of class, gender, individualization, and nationalism in everyday life in Beijing before the COVID-19 pandemic.

Chapter 5 completes the methodological plan of the study of the lifestyle of the post-reform middle class by exploring the interactions between the public and private spheres after the dismantling of the *danwei* system in the late 1990s. This chapter focuses mainly on gender asymmetries through the notion of *haoyong* ("useful") women that imposes a binary social stratification among middle-class women in the professional sphere, and the intergenerational relationships around the indigenous concept of filial piety (*xiao*). Additionally, an assessment is made of the nature of friendship networks, the validity of the concept of *guanxi* between friends, and variations in sociability by analysing instrumentality, affection, and identity construction (social distinction). Finally, the involvement of the urban middle class in residents' committees and homeowners' associations in neighbourhood governance is also evaluated, as well as expressions of a probable civil society, grassroots democracy, class segregation, and self-governance under the Party-state's authoritarian rule.

The epilogue, beyond drawing certain general conclusions from this study in the form of observations, addresses the significance of this research in the context of the pandemic times. It is found that the Chinese middle class can be understood as a heterogeneous phenomenon that goes beyond the validity and the reactionary configuration of the concept of class. In the midst of the current global crises, class is an accurate manifestation of the institutionalization, legitimatization, and reproduction of social inequality in contemporary urban China.

Bibliography

Anagnost, Ann. 2004. "The Corporeal Politics of Quality (*suzhi*)." *Public Culture* 16: 189–208. doi:10.1215/08992363-16-2-189.

Bell, Daniel. 1976. *The Coming of Post-industrial Society: A Venture in Social Forecasting*. New York: Basic Books.

Bourdieu, Pierre. 1984. *Distinction. A Social Critique of the Judgement of Taste*. Translated by Richard Nice. Cambridge, MA: Harvard University Press.

Bourdieu, Pierre. 1987. "What Makes a Social Class? On Theoretical and Practical Existence of Groups." *Berkeley Journal of Sociology* 32: 1–17.

Castro, Paula, and Susana Batel. 2008. "Social Representation, change and Resistance: On the Difficulties of Generalizing New Norms." *Culture & Psychology* 14 (4): 475–497. doi:10.1177/1354067X08096512.

Chen, Yunsong, and Xiaoguang Fan. 2015. "Discordance between Subjective and Objective Social Status in Contemporary China." *The Journal of Chinese Sociology* 2 (14): 1–20. doi:10.1186/s40711-015-0017-7.

Crompton, Rosemary. 1998. *Class and Stratification*. Cambridge: Polity Press.

Dunford, Michael. 2022. "The Chinese Path to Common Prosperity." *International Critical Thought* 12 (1): 35–54. doi:10.1080/21598282.2022.2025561.

Esping-Andersen, Gøsta. 1999. *Social Foundations of Postindustrial Economies*. New York: Oxford University Press.

Giddens, Anthony. 1973. *The Class Structure of Advanced Societies*. London: Hutchinson.

Guo, Yingjie. 2008. "Class, Stratum and Group: The Politics of Description and Prescription." In *The New Rich in China*, edited by David S.G. Goodman, 38–52. Abingdon: Routledge.

Kharas, Homi, and Meagan Dooley. 2020. "China's influence on the global middle class." *Brookings Global China*. https://www.brookings.edu/research/chinas-influence-on-the-global-middle-class/.

Kirk, John. 2007. *Class, Culture and Social Change*. Basingstoke and New York: Palgrave Macmillan.

Lin, Thung-hong. 2008. *Social Classes in China: An Analysis of China's Transition to Capitalism*. PhD diss., Hong Kong University of Science and Technology.

Lu, Xueyi. 2002. *Dangdai Zhongguo shehui jieceng yanjiu baogao* [Research Report on the Social Stratification of Contemporary China]. Beijing: Shehui kexue wenxian chubanshe.

Mauger, Gérard. "Mode de Vie." *Universalis.fr, Encyclopaedia Universalis France Sas*. Accessed 15 April 2022. https://www.universalis.fr/encyclopedie/mode-de-vie/.

Moscovici, Serge. 1988. "Notes towards a description of social representations." *European Journal of Social Psychology* 18 (3): 211–250. doi:10.1002/ejsp.2420180303.

Rocca, Jean-Louis. 2017. *The Making of the Chinese Middle Class: Small Comfort and Great Expectations*. New York: Palgrave Macmillan US.

Schein, Louisa. 2001. "Urbanity, Cosmopolitanism, Consumption." In *China Urban: Ethnographies of Contemporary Culture*, edited by Nancy Chen, Constance Clerk, Suzanne Gottschang, and Lyn Jeffery, 225–241. Durham, NC: Duke University Press.

Skeggs, Beverly. 2004. *Class, Self, Culture*. London: Routledge.

Solé-Farràs, Jesús. 2014. *New Confucianism in Twenty-first Century China*. Abingdon: Routledge.

Thompson, Edward Palmer. 1966. *The Making of the English Working Class*. New York: Vintage Books.

Wang, Xiaolu, and Wing Thye Woo. 2011. "The Size and Distribution of Hidden Household Income in China." *Asian Economic Papers* 10 (1): 1–26. doi:10.1162/ASEP_a_00064.

Wright, Erik Olin. 1997. *Class Counts: Comparative Studies in Class Analysis.* Cambridge: Cambridge University Press.

Yasinskii, V. A., and M. Yu Kozhevnikov. 2022. "Double Circulation: A Growth Model for the Chinese Economy in the Next Fifteen Years." *Studies on Russian Economic Development* 33: 118–125. doi:10.1134/S1075700722010154.

Zavoretti, Roberta. 2017. *Rural Origins, City Lives. Class and Place in Contemporary China.* Seattle: University of Washington Press.

Zhang, Juwei, and Wen Zhao. 2019. "The unreported income and its impact on Gini coefficient in China." *Journal of Chinese Economic and Business Studies* 17 (3): 245–259. doi:10.1080/14765284.2019.1668656.

1

THE DISCURSIVE RECONFIGURATION

Class and discourse construction after reform

The Party-state has played a decisive role in the construction of a discourse on the middle class in contemporary urban China. Since the establishment of the PRC in 1949, the CCP has been the only ruling party and its institutions have been intimately intertwined with those of the state, including the armed forces. The CCP's attitude towards the function of ideology has been thus a determining factor in the role of politics in China everyday life. Whereas CCP's Marxist–Leninist ideology and Mao Zedong Thought dominated the early era, and class then mattered, after 1978 the Party-state completely embraced technocratic values, meritocratic efficiency, and pragmatism, and shifted its political agenda from class struggle to economic modernization. However, ideology has remained crucial in urban China today to the understanding of power relations and institutions, lifestyle and social distinctions, and thus the hegemonic system of social practices and the vocabulary that "shape the day-to-day existence" (Fields 1990, 110). Therefore, for the CCP elite, ideology is a significant tool, as is shown by the widespread existence of numerous mandated institutions within the Party apparatus and ideology dissemination channels (Brown 2018). It is generally accepted that the collusion of the Party-state with market forces has facilitated a system of digital media that serves the interests of the political and economic elite in the PRC (Zhao 2004). Since ideology provides symbolic references that assume "the role of cultural markers" in the construction of identity and class formation, the critical analysis of social paradigms, hegemonic classifications, and ideological discourses is central to a comprehensive understanding of the role of the Party-state in China's more recent construction of a middle-class lifestyle (Susen 2014). On that basis, this chapter aims to examine the historical, socio-political, and economic processes involved in the emergence of a Chinese middle-class lifestyle in the 1990s by elucidating class both as "a *well-founded historical artefact*" (Bourdieu 1987, 8–9, emphasis in original) and analysing the discursive construction of the concept of

DOI: 10.4324/9781003299301-2

"middle class" in *Renmin Wang*, the digital version of the newspaper *Renmin Ribao*, the mouthpiece of Central Committee of the CCP. Portions of this chapter have been published in the article "The Official Discourse of the Chinese Middle Class: Anxiety, Nationalism and Populism," of *Revista Española de Investigaciones Sociológicas* (REIS) 176, 141–156, reproduced by permission of Secretaría del Consejo Editorial, Centro de Investigaciones Sociológicas (CIS).

1.1 The Chinese middle class as a well-founded historical artefact (19th–21st century)

This section sketches the reconfiguration of the contemporary Chinese middle class in three phases: from the late Qing era to 1949, between 1949 and the middle of the 1990s, and from the middle of the 1990s until the COVID-19 pandemic. Starting in Britain in the 18th century, the Industrial Revolution transformed a largely rural, agrarian, and handicraft economy into an industrialized, urban one. These technological transformations spread to other parts of the world and introduced the modern capitalist economy and an urban lifestyle. The Industrial Revolution "pushed China to the periphery of the world system" while the unequal treaties established by foreign powers after the first Opium War (1839–1842) profoundly influenced the social structure of the late Qing society (Dong 2018, 436). In this historical and social context, this section positions the emergence of a small industrial middle class in response to industrialization in major Chinese cities in the second half of the 19th century.

The middle society: from the late Qing era to 1949

First, it must be admitted that it is not an easy task to evaluate the boundaries of the middle class in the Qing Dynasty (1636–1912). Social groups operated day to day within a complex network of relations, from the formal structure to the state and the informal structure of various non-administrative urban and rural systems to the clan and the nuclear family (Smith 2015, 149). Nobles were at the top in the Qing social order. Scholar-gentry groups, peasants, artisans, and merchants followed. In addition to these four major groups, members of the clergy, officials of the hereditary Army of the Green Standard, and "demeaned people" (*jianmin*) were also part of Qing society. This social structure was highly stratified until imperialism forcibly accelerated the integration of the domestic market into global capitalism, and introduced to China new forms of industrial consumerism and social distinctions in the late 19th century (Gerth 2020, 13–14). Moreover, as a result of industrial acceleration, new opportunity structures increased dramatically urbanization and social mobility, and began to blur old status differentiations in China.

There is considerable evidence to suggest the existence of an embryonic urban middle class composed of diverse social groups in late imperial times. Firstly, merchants and their children were marginalized because they relied on doing business or making money, an unacceptable behaviour for Confucian tradition. However, regarding economic and cultural capital, they can still be considered middle class. Secondly, while many members of the gentry such as landlords and degree holders lived in rural areas and engaged in local managerial services, others constituents of the gentry moved to the cities and benefited from commercial ventures with merchants and participated in some beginnings of democratic civil society in the 1900s; they were the so-called "new gentry" (*xin shishen*) (Hird 2009, 51; Rankin 2002, 319; Smith 2015, 136). However, these "Chinese national capitalists were never powerful, mainly because they lacked technology and solid support from a modern nation-state government" (Dong 2018, 436). Related to this group, there were "foreign enterprise white-collar workers" (*waiqi bailing*), that is, "the young bilingual intellectuals who worked for foreign merchants who appeared from as early as 1840," on the one hand, and "government officials in the expanding government sector" as well as "professors, lawyers, authors and artists in the developing liberal professions," on the other (Zhou 2005, 3; in Hird 2009, 51). Thirdly, migrant workers who worked at the national and Western companies established in China's treaty ports were also part of the middle class in the late Qing era. They learnt technical and managerial skills and were employed at the highest wage rates (Honig 1989, 250). In major cities such as Shanghai, all of them were able to acquire both economic and cultural capital, and gain access to urban resources such as department stores, museums, fashion magazines, etc. to enjoy a distinctive middle-class lifestyle. Such activities associated with cultural consumption and leisure became the paradigm of the modernity for both urban and rural areas.

Consequently, an incipient middle-class lifestyle in terms of occupational activity, education, activism, and cultural consumption emerged and self-expanded in Chinese cities (Zhao, Yu, and Li 2020; Rankin 2002). This middle-class lifestyle manifested in leisure and consumption of mass-produced products introduced after 1895 such as bicycles, umbrellas, toothbrushes, and fashionable articles of clothing, which became the precondition for urbanites. In early 20th century China, such growing middle-class consumer culture defined and spread modern Chinese nationalism by persuading people in China to see themselves as members of a modern nation-state in a similarly constituted world with nation-states (Gerth 2003, 3–4). The self-expanding nature of this middle-class lifestyle relied mainly on increasing industrial capitalism, Sino-Western contacts, and the socio-political articulations between the rural and the urban. Although in the first part of the 20th century over 80 per cent of the Chinese lived in the rural areas and less than 20 per cent lived in the cities, urban societies were extremely diversified and cosmopolitan, but also fragmented (Chen 2013, 45; Yeh 1997). After the revolutionary break of 1911, the incipient urban middle-class lifestyle that had emerged in the great port cities of the late Qing era developed further during the Republican era (1912–1949).

With the establishment of the Republic of China in 1912, and in order to maintain their privileges, the old Qing elites were forced to reconfigure their class location and cooperate with the new power holders and seekers such as warlords and bandit gang chiefs in agrarian areas, and with political party leaders in cities (Bergère 1997, 322). For instance, the nascent bourgeoisie were typically descendants of scholars' families and replaced the role of their families and gentry groups in late imperial times by rapidly gaining economic power and cultural capital in both rural and urban contexts. In general terms, the urban social structure in China's Republican era was characterized by the dominance of a small number of upper class or *shangdeng shehui* (official and urban gentry families which readily engaged in various commercial ventures, and rich merchants) over the large number of manual laborers, the so-called *xiadeng shehui*.

The centre of the republican social structure consisted of what Pejie Mao (2018) called the "middle society" (*zhongdent shehui* or *zhongdeng jieji*). It contained managers, office workers, civil servants, self-employed labourers, industrial technicians, schoolteachers, shopkeepers, and professionals in law, medicine, engineering, and architecture that constituted only 7 per cent of the Chinese population. However, since the Republican middle class was an inherently urban phenomenon, it has been estimated that in the mid-1930s about 40 per cent (1.5 million) of Shanghainese population were white-collar employees, including their family members (Lu 1999, 63–66). In contrast to the middle class in the late Qing era, the composition of the Republican middle society "expanded" to include a wider variety of "middle-income professionals," from new civil professionals that emerged after the abolition of state examinations in 1905 to graphic designers and "the emerging bourgeoisie." The most significant representatives of the latter were the "new types of educated literati and modern intellectuals" which emerged with the growth of capitalism and the national economy during World War I (Mao 2018, 622–624). The emergence of this urban middle society went hand in hand with a Western-influenced lifestyle that included the expansion of industrial consumerism, professional associationism, and, occasionally, social movements.

Beyond the recurring binary debates between free-market modernity (Western consumerism) versus China's nation-building priority (Confucian frugality), the Republican government developed a state consumerism attempted to shape and control material desires of the Chinese to manage domestic demand in every respect (Gerth 2020). Consequently, the state stimulated the embryonic middle-class lifestyle that emerged in the late Qing era by increasing wages and expanding mass production and a consumerist apparatus —from department stores and movie theatres to new forms of advertising, product distribution, and mail-order catalogues for rural areas (Zanasi 2015). Advertisements taught consumers "how to use the appropriate mass-produced products to portray a sophisticated and urbane identity," including both modest and expensive goods, from lipstick and toothpaste for whiter teeth, to luxurious wristwatches, bicycles, and sewing machines (Gerth 2020, 111). Whereas traditional Chinese culture emphasized the importance of moral qualities, *guanxi*, frugality, or local prestige, industrial consumerism expanded a new sense of modernization and status hierarchy based on income, consumption, individual autonomy, and urban cosmopolitism.

The lifestyle of Shanghai's middle society manifested this new paradigm and commercial wealth as a result of the interactions between domestic trade and international market, and between Chinese traditional culture and Western capitalist modernization. For example, a key feature of the Shanghainese lifestyle was the commodification of new ideas about work and a new image about women and the feminine. Whereas urban men were fashioned into office workers, business employees, and self-made businessmen, "urban women were transformed into household managers and keepers of domestic bliss" to reinforce the idealization of the *xiao jiating* (nuclear family) versus the traditional *da jiazu* (extended lineage) (Yeh 1997, 394). Simultaneously, an alternative stereotype of modern women as erotic constructs, and glamorous, fashionable, desirable, and available objects also emerged in urban contexts (Edwards 2000, 166). However, anti-imperialist intellectuals criticized these manifestations of modernity, self-indulgent consumerism, and leisured lifestyle. Such critical intellectuals came from nationalist groups that defended developing perspectives and state-sponsored campaigns —such as the New Life Movement campaign launched in 1934 as a part of the Nationalist Party of China (GMD) civilizing process—and were the ones who introduced new political and economic trends that were to culminate with the Communist regime.

The danwei *middle class: from 1949 to the 1990s*

After the Anti-Japanese War (1937–1945) and the Civil War (1927–1949), industrial production was resumed, and the social structure reconfigured considering political and cultural capital. When the CCP came to power in October 1949, and established the PRC, it changed the distribution of powers, conditions of existence, and conditioning factors according to its ideological programme in order to legitimize the new regime and privilege the new political elite. However, after 22 years of war, CCP leaders were compelled simultaneously to build its credentials as socialist revolutionaries by committing themselves to the creation of an egalitarian and classless society, and to revive the war-ravaged economy. In doing this, the communist leaders developed capitalists' industries for the nation to survive and prosper, thus revealing from the outset the constant "contradiction between the party's rhetoric of building socialism on its way toward communism and its capitalist policies" (Gerth 2020, 72). Simultaneously, the CCP founded three institutions, alongside the Party membership, for regulating privilege and redistributing power in urban areas, namely class categorization, the work unit (*danwei*), and the *hukou* registration.

In the early 1950s, the new government assigned hereditary family class categories to reconfigure the social structure inherited from the Qing feudalists and Republican capitalists. Policy was to promote not only the workers and peasants as the beneficiaries of the Communist project, but also the middle society and those industrialists who had supported the CCP. By contrast, landlords and entrepreneurs, those with foreign interests and those connected with the GMD were penalized harshly (Saich 2001, 29). Hence, a new state cadre class of 10 million

(3-4 per cent of the Chinese population) took place and became the new political elite, followed by 35 million state workers and employees, and 200 million peasants (more than 80 per cent of the overall population) at the bottom strata of the society (Dong 2018, 437). In this context, "cadres" were the managers and leaders in the state sector, most of whom were peasant revolutionaries with high political capital but little education.

Based on an elaborate system of over 60 class categories, every citizen was assigned a class category that was inherited patrilineally. The class categorization was a regulatory classification determined by a combination of person's socio-economic position —mainly based on the family's employment status, income sources and accumulated capital—and political loyalties as implied by behaviour of the male family head between 1946 and 1949 (Goodman 2014; Wu 2013). For married women, the main criteria for the class assignment were the social and political origin of the husband. Formally, class labels were divided into three broad categories: "red" (totalling some 82.3 per cent of the urban population), "ordinary" (some 14.3 per cent), and "black" (some 3.4 per cent) classes (Walder and Hu 2009). Despite intense local variations, these figures provide only the most approximate of guides and are associated with the official division of society into four classes: the workers and peasants, both with red labels; the urban petty bourgeoisie, that is, the Republican middle society; and the black class, the so-called national bourgeoisie or local entrepreneurs, which included the old urban gentry and rich merchants.

Unlike those from the "good" or "red" labels were highly favoured because they were people from "red proletarian" or "exploited" backgrounds —i.e., workers, poor and lower-middle peasants, soldiers and revolutionary activists—those from the "bad" or "black" class backgrounds faced discrimination and became the target of later campaigns (Kraus 1981). As Walder and Hu (2009) noted, the bad-class families were associated with the rich, the exploiting classes, or the so-called "resistance to the CCP," that is, those who had joined or fought on the Nationalist side. These "bad" class labels were removed from personal records in January 1979, and since then all class descriptors increasingly slipped from use. The rest of the population that was not directly involved in the exploitation of others, but neither was inherently loyal to the Party, was assigned politically ambiguous labels (1402). Although scholars have expressed divergent views on the net impacts of the class categorization in life chances due to policy variations and re-evaluations of labels after 1949, it is generally accepted that class labels had pervasively affected many individuals and their families in their application for admission to the CCP, access to education and careers, and search for marriage partners. In any case, once people had been categorized, the CCP implemented class struggle and land reform by confiscating violently land from landlords and then distributing it to poor and middle peasants.

In cities, though, the establishment of the new regime had major deficiencies. In fact, the communists had no experience in national government, and little in urban administration and leadership, while their relations with the urban working class were weak (Blecher 2009, 38). As victory returned them to many of the cities that they had been forced to abandon following repression by the Nationalists, CCP leaders also had to "build an industrial base and a working class whom they were supposed to represent" (Saich 2015, 32). In this frame of mind, to win the favour of the proletarian class and legitimize the Communist victory, cadres launched campaigns to mobilize workers against their employers, particularly the national bourgeoisie. They allegedly engaged in tax evasion, corruption, and counter-revolutionary activities, and finally the CCP took over their large enterprises and merged small ones into cooperatives.

However, as Andreas (2009) indicated, mass political campaigns were not as violent as in the countryside because the CCP needed the knowledge and managerial skills of the middle society and national bourgeoisie to complete the socialist transformation. Indeed, communist cadres compensated their lack of expertise and intellectual skills by offering "nominal compensation and management positions to entrepreneurs who cooperated, and the great majority of the managerial, professional, and technical staff in government offices, economic enterprises, schools, and other institutions remained in their posts" (19). This uncomfortable coexistence, and subsequent convergence, of the Republican educated bourgeoisie (cultural capital) and the communist elite (political capital) at the top of the post-revolutionary social order played a decisive role in the social structure of the PRC up to the present day. According to Andreas (2009), differences and tensions apart, these two groups agreed on the management of a series of regulations to legitimize, institutionalize, and transfer their privileges, and also on the foundation of a joint defence alliance against Mao's attacks, especially during the Cultural Revolution (1966–1976).

Although freedom of residence and movement accelerated economic recovery in the early 1950s, the resilience of tradition combined with the need for social control and the requirements of modernization soon facilitated the implementation of a strict migration policy in the PRC. As a result, the *hukou* system was soon established in some Chinese cities, to be extended to the rural areas in 1955 (Chan and Zhang 1999). By reassuming earlier systems of household registration and mutual surveillance —such as the millenarian *baojia*—the *hukou* system has bound almost every individual to the village or city of her or his mother's registration place and seriously restricted the opportunities for moving between urban centres and the countryside, to the detriment of rural population (Cheng and Selden 1994). The *hukou* system is very much a "birth-subscribed" system which has divided China socially into three status categories: rural residents, rural migrants residing in urban areas, and urban residents (Han and Whyte 2009, 198). In practice, although "some rural *hukou* holders could get work in the cities, "without official approval, they would lead a marginal existence, and their children could never enter the mainstream of urban society" (Davis 2000, 266). The main function of the *hukou* system was to facilitate urban–rural migration only when cheap labour was needed in urban factories, but this migration policy also caused class reproduction and increased the urban–rural gap (see also Chapter 3).

Meanwhile, all the state sector workers and employees (*zhigong*), totalling 90 per cent of the urban population, progressively benefited from the issuance of the

Labour Insurance Regulations of 1951. Since urban areas were essentially owned by the state and their employees were the state's direct responsibility, the national budget had to supply urban areas with employment, subsidized public housing, food, water, medical facilities, day care and schools for their children, police protection, lifetime pensions, disability pay, and other essential amenities of life (Banister 1987, 328; Davis 2000). In complete contrast, though, the state assumed direct responsibility for none of these services and welfare entitlements for the countryside (Cheng and Selden 1994, 644). Hence, since the Chinese state privileged the city (and the *zhigong* group) over the countryside (and peasants), *zhigong* and their offspring enjoyed better living and working conditions than peasants (Rocca 2017, 44–45). Despite the privileged status of the state sector workers and employees over the peasants, they possessed less political capital than the political elite and less cultural capital than the old educated elite. In any case, they were situated in the middle of the urban social hierarchy in terms of income.

Although the *hukou* system has been and remains central to the configuration of the Chinese state's administrative power and socio-economic eligibility, another device in urban areas to regulate social stratification was the Communist-style work units or *danwei* system. By the end of 1956, almost the entire urban workforce was reorganized into work units (*danwei*), which "were compounds, with half of the space used for work and the other half for residences" (Guo 2003, 110). The state provided housing, welfare, and security to urban dwellers in the workplace through this *danwei* system. Accordingly, *danwei* as the core unit of urban society became a community led by a unified leadership or party committee (Kwon 2017, 2). There was a detailed list of occupations or "workplace segmentation," each with different salaries, with which not only was the location of a *danwei* within the city, and each worker's hierarchical rank within the *danwei*, but the unit's status in the planned state-owned economy which also imposed inequality (Gold 2000; Bian 1994). For instance, "influential work-units had the connections and funding to construct more and better housing for their members and to secure privileged access to rationed goods" (Tang and Unger 2013, 93). Additionally, although domestic roles remained gendered, *danwei* socialized social reproduction and women's burden was somewhat alleviated by work-unit's facilities such as dining halls, laundries, and childcare and healthcare centres (Ji et al. 2017). In any case, workers and employees holding an urban *hukou* and working in a *danwei* can be considered part of what I call "*danwei* middle class," that is the middle class in the PRC until the dismantling of the *danwei* system in the late 1990s.

Gerth's (2020) *Uneding Capitalism* challenged the uniform treatment in China studies of the lifestyle in *danwei*. Mainstream scholars emphasized the power of these work-units to shape identity to its members, legitimacy to their activities, and instil a "correct" lifestyle consisting of "hard work and simple life" (*jianku pusu*) (Bray 2005, 157; Bin 1997, 46). However, Gerth (2020) found that social relations and individual identities in urban China were not simply tied to employers and absorbed within the collective (*danwei*) but that lifestyle had been created to market reforms around the desire for and acquisition of mass-produced goods such as bicycles, sewing machines, and wristwatches. On that basis, urbanites, especially in the eastern coastal cities, negotiated social identity through material possessions and consumption, in which money was rarely the biggest obstacle among the *danwei* middle class. Ration coupons or connections to illegal ration markets to acquire such coupons and cultural capital to consume "properly" were even more crucial for purchasing distinctive products such as bicycles (21). As a result, despite its anti-consumerism rhetoric, the Party-state developed a "socialist consumerism," which versioned all aspects of consumerism in market capitalist countries (consumer fashion, commerce, product branding, advertising, etc.), to dominate the accumulation and allocation of capital (4). Such evidence uncovers the proliferation of a middle-class lifestyle based not only on the production and distribution of mass-produced consumer goods intended to an urban group with enough economic and cultural capital to acquire them, but also on the presence of a social identity manifested through the acquisition or desirability of these goods.

To recapitulate, despite the socialist egalitarian rhetoric, and once the CCP implemented class labels, *hukou* and *danwei* system, confiscated productive property and introduced the hegemony of political and cultural capital, a new status hierarchy emerged in Chinese cities in the first half of the 1950s. Beyond the new political elite, the highly educated group, including doctors, university teachers, economists, engineers, artists and intellectuals, "was nationalized" (Yang 2008, 149). They were, in terms of social status and opportunities of "getting things through the backdoor" (*zou houmen*), at the same level as the political elite (Rocca 2017, 39). Further, as noted earlier, the *danwei* middle class was composed of the pre-revolutionary entrepreneurs who cooperated, and employees in Republican institutions who remained in their posts, as well as new urban social actors, including lower level "regular cadres" (*yiban ganbu*) —those who did not occupy managerial positions—and *zhigong* groups.

In addition, as the 1950s advanced, the shift to public-sector jobs occurred even more rapidly than the social transition to socialism, and the new regime still needed highly educated people to fill the many new technical and managerial positions created within the state sector (Davis 2000, 255–256). This time, though, the Party-state allocated new state jobs for graduates who completed their training after the establishment of the PRC to ensure their compatibility with socialist values. Therefore, these new state employees were also part of a *danwei* middle class that became a conglomerate composed of fragmented groups with different volume and composition of capitals, class backgrounds, and social trajectories.

Beyond the analysis of the PRC's social structure distribution, the discursive dimension of class struggle had also a direct impact on the lifestyle of the *danwei* middle class at certain moments due to Mao's efforts to strengthen his personal power and his concerns about social inequality. After the Great Leap (1958–1960) fiasco, Mao launched the Cultural Revolution (1966–1976) to purge the Party's "capitalist roaders" and call the proletariat to exercise "all-round dictatorship" over the "new elements of the bourgeoisie." As a result, Mao mobilized the students, mostly of middle-class origins, against "bourgeois intellectuals" and expanded to attack cadres and organization of the CCP, who were understood to act like bureaucrats and aspire to a "bourgeois life" (*zichan jieji shenghuo*), a concept connoting a wealthy and privileged, rather than a middle-class lifestyle (Lu 2018, 3). Even more fundamentally, however, is the fact that the Cultural Revolution "was rooted in both principled and personal disputes" (MacFarquhar 1974, 3). During the upheaval launched by Mao, many intellectuals and professionals who were criticized for having become "counter-revolutionaries," lost temporarily their positions and possessions, and "were sent to the countryside or the front-line-of-production for 're-education' —and some were even physically abused" (Goodman 2008, 26). In fact, Andreas (2009) noted, this campaign represented an attack aimed simultaneously at both the new political elite (and its technocratic vision) and the old educated elite (and its role of the remnant pre-revolutionary elites with high cultural capital) that unexpectedly forged "inter-elite unity."

Indeed, after Mao's death in 1976, and after sharp conflict between the two groups during the first decades of Communist rule, power struggles during the post-Mao interregnum (1976–1977) ultimately culminated in the convergence of "a technocratic project" ruled by a new "dominant class of Red experts" based largely on political and cultural capital, while the role of economic capital was still very limited (Andreas 2009, 5, 240). In December 1978, Deng Xiaoping assumed power and launched Four Modernizations and economic reforms at the Third Plenary Session of the 11th central Committee of the CCP. In contrast to Maoist rhetoric of class warfare and egalitarianism, Deng Xiaoping "prohibited debate about the direction of reform in terms of socialism versus capitalism" and declared that modernization and wealth redistribution in China could only be achieved through class differentiation by "letting some people get rich first" (Chun 2015). Both the new technocratic elite and the *danwei* middle class resumed the process of consolidation of their privileges, despite a temporary interruption due to the Cultural Revolution, by facilitating the founding of a stable social and political order (Walder and Hu 2009, 1421). In fact, the key task of the CCP had been shifted from ideological orthodoxy and "class struggle" in the Cultural Revolution to adoption of technocratic principles, pragmatic administration, scientific procedures, and political stability.

The transition to a stable new order can be understood through the amendments to the PRC Constitution. Whereas the first constitution of the PRC was adopted in 1954 and "was deeply influenced by the constitution of the Soviet Union and was regarded as a socialist-style constitution" (Mo 2009, 141), the version of this constitution promulgated in 1978 adapted new precepts to the change in the political situation in the PRC. In the 1978 constitutional version, the explicit mission of the proletariat, which was to exercise dictatorship over the bourgeoisie in the superstructure, was eliminated, while other structural changes were added. However, although the CCP adopted a more market-oriented development strategy, the value of political connections has continued to rule until the COVID-19 pandemic.

The end of the Cultural Revolution and the establishment of an increasingly technocratic and credentialing class order resulted in the resurfacing of pre-revolutionary social groups that had disappeared during the socialist era, such as individual businesspeople, and new occupations and professions oriented toward market reform and greater participation in the global economy. After the Cultural Revolution, urgent unemployment issues in urban areas compelled the Party-state to place most unemployed urban youth in both the state and collective sectors, launch economic measures to boost industrial production, quicken the pace of market growth, and permit private entrepreneurship in 1977 (Zang 2008, 61–63). Even though unemployment fell significantly as a result of these measures and the private sector was beginning to develop in the early 1980s, "there were still no explicit economic and political guarantees" that gave solidity to these "modernizing" changes (Toshiki and Zhao 2004, 8). To alleviate this lack of economic and political certainty, a constitutional amendment was passed in December 1982.

Although the 1982 amendment maintained the socialist public system as the economic foundation of the PRC, it also positioned "the individual economy" as a supplement to the socialist state-owned economy (Jones 1985, 707; Toshiki and Zhao 2004, 8–9). As this supplementary private economy was under the control of the administration, many businesspeople and their families became the prime beneficiaries of market reform and established an opaque link between their enrichment and the shares of power held by government officials and CCP cadres. Market reforms thus facilitated the transfer of the political and cultural capital accumulated during the Mao-dominated years to economic capital in post-reform China.

Considering the new legitimacy of the economic capital in the social space of the post-reform era, small and medium-sized entrepreneurs became the new constituents of the post-reform middle class. Whereas the small business sector was composed of family-run businesses with low-status people (*getihu*) (see also Chapter 2), the new enterprises that emerged during the first decades after reform were formed in one of four ways, differentiated by source of the initial capital and resource (Zang 2008, 28). The first way was through collective enterprises located in rural as well as urban China. These companies, the town and village enterprises (TVEs), were run by local leaders and *chengbao* cadres, and they looked for new ways to use the assets under their control. With the corporate reform of TVEs, the subsidiary companies began to operate in activities that were previously in the hands of the public sector. Thus, the second group of new enterprises emerged because of similar processes at work experienced by the state sector of economy.

In addition, the state provided some or all the equity financing to these start-ups, often using its facilities and the public budget. Hence, *chengdao* cadres used their political capital to become "de jure and de facto" entrepreneurs in charge of privatized state firms (first way) or spinoffs (second way) (Hsu 2006, 2). Thirdly, as Goodman (2008) has pointed out, although there certainly were private sector owner-operators who had developed their business from nothing, as their business grew and in order to scale-up access to factors of production, they were essentially required to surrender part of their equity to local governments and incorporate as collective enterprises (29).

Consequently, there was a high potential for confusion regarding ownership and control as with TVEs and companies developed within the state sector and state administration (30). Finally, the fourth way that new enterprises emerged in the PRC was through foreign investment in the form of joint ventures.

Although the 1982 constitutional revision supported the emergence of new middle-class constituents and entrepreneurs, such policy reforms would soon be deeply questioned within the Party due to the implication of some entrepreneurs, intellectuals, and business organizations in the Tiananmen Square protests during June 1989. As a result, businesspeople were officially banned from Party membership after the suppression of the demonstrations in Tiananmen Square. However, the leadership established that the Party would base its legitimacy on both economic growth and the development of what Dickson (2016) called a "strategy for survival." The Party's strategy involved a combination of repression, legitimation through a new social contract, and the co-optation of new elites, including temporarily banned entrepreneurs. The CCP in theory no longer described itself as a revolutionary party and instead characterized itself as China's ruling party. In practice it disempowered the state socialist working class by privileging the middle class and like-minded entrepreneurs with new regulations and techniques including modern political messaging.

After 1989, the middle class began to play an increasingly key role in the legitimization of the established order maintained by the Party-state since 1949 in three ways (Sánchez-Romera 2021a). Firstly, the government promoted the construction of a discourse on the middle class in the 1990s addressed both to intellectuals and to the whole population with the support of the media and modern methods of mass persuasion (Brady 2009). Concurrently, the Party-state adopted various measures to improve the living standard of intellectuals, accelerate the development of higher education, extend the job training industry, and encourage scientific research, including the sponsored sociological research on middle class, which is discussed in Chapter 2.

Secondly, in shifting its political agenda from class struggle to economic modernization, as Dickson (2016) suggested, the Party also changed its recruitment strategy by replacing the ideological zeal of the officials appointed in the Mao-dominate era with those who possessed professional skills. In this way, the Party made its objectives clear: to foster economic growth and thus ensure its legitimacy. Further, the CCP "recruited new members from the social group it relied on for support, that is college students, urban professionals, and private entrepreneurs" in order to create "institutional links between the Party and the beneficiaries of economic reform" (14). And finally, as a part of the second stage of reform starting in the 1990s, the Chinese government developed a process of social engineering through selective incentives to the *danwei* middle class and their children and promoted an official discourse on the middle class "prompted by a series of challenges facing society" (Rocca 2017, 13). The state sought to turn the middle class into its loyal political ally by raising their living standards and benefiting them through the sweeping market reforms, including privatization, education reform, and the liberalization of the housing market, that were underway.

The post-reform middle class: from the 1990s to the COVID-19 pandemic

Crucial to this analysis are the reforms in urban areas pertaining to the labour market and to wages implemented in the 1990s, which directly affected the formation of the middle class in the post-reform era. Deng's southern tour in 1992 boosted the second wave of reform and opening across the country. The 1993 constitutional amendment replaced the socialist notion of "planned economy" with Deng's doctrine of "socialist market economy" to promote speedy economic growth along capitalist lines (Sun 2019, 164). This involved the abolition of hiring quotas in state-owned enterprises, allowing firms to operate according to a profit-driven logic and the increased use of meritocratic hiring and promotion practices (Goodman and Zang 2008, 14). Therefore, enterprises were allowed to freely select and hire their employees according to the laws of market efficiency and productivity, which led to millions of layoffs —unemployment tripled between 1996 and 1998 (Yueh 2004, 150). Thus, many members of the *zhigong* group lost their jobs in *danwei* and even though many received subsidies, they lost their social status, which represented the end of the *danwei* middle class and a new reconfiguration of the social structure in the PRC, this time, though, due to privatization.

In addition to market reforms, the dismantling of the *danwei* system and the influx of foreign investment led to greater specialization and the rise of a new professionals and skilled employees. Cheng (2010) has grouped middle incomers into three major clusters: economic (including private sector entrepreneurs, *getihu*, stock and real-estate speculators, foreign joint-ventures employees, IT, and knowledge industry and services); political (government officials, office clerks, lawyers, and state sector managers); and cultural and education (including academic and educators, psychologists, scholars, media personalities, and intellectuals) (5). In this context, the 1999 constitutional amendment strengthened the key role of the private economy from a "supplement to the state-owned economy" to an "important component of the socialist market economy." Generally, considering economic and socio-geographical capital, the urban population of the early reform era progressively split into a dominant class (political and economic elite); a middle class composed of small entrepreneurs (*getihu*) employing fewer than ten workers, and stable or semi-permanent middle incomers; and a subordinate class composed mainly of temporary migrant workers and former workers of *zhigong* group who lost their jobs and were not reintegrated into the new *labour market*.

Moreover, education implementations, the extension of cultural consumption, and housing reforms were the pillars of the state's promotion of the new lifestyle of the Chinese middle class. Firstly, with the abolishment of state-controlled job assignment in the 1990s, training of workers was prescribed as the fundamental task of higher education, while both private and public sector demanded practical, flexible, openly specialized, and highly-skilled professionals. In order to supply this labour market demand, the Chinese government announced a sudden 47 per cent increase in university places in 1999 and subsequent double-digit growth year on year for the next decade to distribute cultural capital (Dai, Cai, and Zhu 2021). Further, the central government "extended major national festivities to week-long holidays" to stimulate the consumption of local tourism and the expansion of urbanization (Tomba 2014, 99). In addition, new national holidays popularized a mythologization of Chinese nation as a united entity with a common culture by managing, producing, and reproducing national and heteronormative practices, memories, and identities (Mpofu 2016, 28). Finally, the state linked the new middle-class lifestyle with home ownership by privileging the *danwei* middle class with subsided private housing, liberalizing the housing market in 1998 and extending mortgage loans to middle incomers.

The government certainly privatized urban properties that belonged to *danwei* through policies for the subsidization of homeownership aimed at former residents, the *danwei* middle class. In the process, the state sector employees were encouraged to buy their apartments from their work units at a discounted rate significantly below market value (Zhang 2008, 27). Concurrently, the government allowed banks to offer mortgages to Chinese citizens while increasing house rents to pressure urbanites to become homeowners (Rocca 2017; Tomba 2014). While many socialist workers became homeowners, *danwei* condominiums became gated communities. As a result, the *danwei* middle class became property owners at low cost through three channels: the privatization of existing *danwei* housing by selling their housing stocks to former residents/workers at very low price; the acquisition of new housing in many cases in the form of gated communities built by the *danwei* and sold to employees at subsidized prices; or by accessing subsidized loans to buy housing on the market (Nathan 2016, 10). Using Bourdieu's (1998) language, such "private appropriation" of public housing subsidized by the state would show the "conversion" of political capital into economic capital (homeownership) that benefited only the urban middle class. It is clear that the post-reform middle class is the result of "the intergenerational transfer of various types of capital within a family lineage [which] have reinforced the switchable potentials of the different capitals themselves" (Sun et al. 1998, in He 2000, 70) (see also Chapter 3). Thus, the publicly owned flats located in the *danwei* were sold to the workers who occupied them at a low price and, after the liberalization of the real-estate market at the end of the 1990s, housing quickly became an important discriminator of social status over income. This reflected, as Li and Sheng (2007) noted, a new difference in post-reform China between those "outside the system" (*tizhiwai*) working in the private sector and relying on their labour force, their properties and the market for a living, and those "inside the system" (*tizhinei*) being within the Party-system and depending upon power relations and connections.

The start of the 21st century saw the consolidation of these structural policies, along with the emergence of a new paradigm and social practices associated with the Chinese middle class. This social imaginary was predicated by media representations and symbolically reflected the establishment of a new social hierarchy in the post-reform era. Henceforward, the key players in the new lifestyle were the high-*suzhi* urbanites, or *high-quality*, citizens "who generate material wealth by producing, providing and consuming goods and services" (Guo 2008, 40). However, having a high-*suzhi*—that is, a "high human quality"—was not about spending a lot like the "new rich" who made their fortune on the back of their political capital in the 1980s but with becoming "competent consumers" and "to make themselves consumable" (Zavoretti 2017, 4, 112). This lifestyle and social differentiations harmed the peasants, migrant workers, and the new rich, as they were considered social groups with low-*suzhi* and little or too ostentatious capacity to consume.

Such a paradigm shift was made public when Jiang Zemin, president of the PRC between 1993 and 2002, gave a speech on 1 July 2001 at the CCP's 80th anniversary celebration. As businesspeople were officially banned from Party membership after the Tiananmen Square repression in 1989, President Jiang invited businessmen to become members of the CCP again on the grounds that, according to his ideological programme, the Three Represents Theory, the Party represented the advancement of China as a whole and the "advanced forces" of society, including businesspeople. As a result, political and economic elite forged a new "inter-elite unity" manifested in a new ideological programme and a paradigm and social practices more oriented towards consumption than production, what I call the lifestyle of the post-reform middle class in urban China.

Jiang's new theory portrayed capitalism as not being inherently contradictory to socialism. It set out a line focus on "a combination of economic achievement and socialist dogmas" to be followed by later Chinese leaders (Jia 2004, 266). The Three Represents Theory also aimed to maintain the Party's legitimate control of power and for it to remain unchallenged as a representative of the whole of Chinese society (Xin 2004, 5). At the same time, due to Beijing winning the competition to host the 2008 Olympic Games (July 2001) and China's accession to the World Trade Organization (WTO) agreed with the US (December 2001), the CCP increased its popular support and social influence (Xin 2004, 5) and saw thus its authority strongly legitimized.

Furthermore, given the objective of "common prosperity," President Jiang (2002) stated in a report presented in 2002 that necessary steps would be taken "to raise the proportion of the middle-income group and increase the income of the low-income group" (5). President Jiang's explicit support for the "middle-income group" and their economic interests manifests the state's willingness to promote a middle-class lifestyle in terms of income and consumption made up of "a group of middle incomers" rather than a "middle class" made up of politically class-conscious citizens. Jiang's statement not only officially inaugurated the state-sponsored discourse on the middle class as a lifestyle but also moved away from older state-sponsored discourses that proclaimed class as structured inequality and political consciousness.

Accordingly, in the post-reform era, social identity would be understood solely in terms of consumption, far from the dangerous space of politics and class consciousness. In practice, the constitutional amendments in 2004 implemented the property rights of average people, that is, housing and other valuable and identifying belongings of the middle class (Jia 2004, 263; Song 2004). As a result, the middle-class lifestyle based on housing ownership, urbanization, and capital accumulation became the new desired and desirable lifestyle in China's model of development while replacing the working class as the core of the Chinese society. Additionally, these middle-class aspirations went hand in hand with the achieving of poverty alleviation as the next stage after Deng's script to "let some people get rich first."

By using the Confucian concept of common prosperity or *xiaokang* society, President Jiang highlighted the ideological resemblances between Confucianism and communism to develop a new socialist culture that could fit the Party's permanence in power and create an alternative model of modernization as an international soft power strategy that could differ from the hegemonic Western paradigm (Solé-Farràs 2014, 61). Most important, though, was that Jiang's modernization model included the proposal to make the middle-income group (*zhongdeng shouru*) the dominant group in Chinese society which was taken up by subsequent PRC presidents. Therefore, even though the liberal approach to sociopolitical policies held a clear influence throughout Jiang Zemin's mandate, at the end of his term in office he showed greater concern about social inequality as a potential threat to the construction of the *xiaokang* society.

The emphasis that President Hu Jintao, Jiang's successor in 2003, and his Premier Wen Jiabao placed on harmonious society was reminiscent of the New Leftists' concern for peasants, social justice, and welfare issues. President Hu's (2006) notion of the harmonious society (*hexie shehui*), which was defined as the intrinsic nature of socialism with Chinese characteristics, highly important in ensuring the prosperity, rejuvenation, and happiness of the people of China, had a marked objective: to leave social polarization behind, integrate workers into the middle-income group and therefore create a "moderately prosperous" society, that is, a middle-class society. Within it there would be a very small number of rich and poor, and almost the entire population would be able to use their surplus income for purchasing goods or services and having a decent and modestly well-off life.

Theoretically, Hu's formulation involved a series of ideas related to social justice and equality mainly in response to the many non-harmonious phenomena—related to corruption, unemployment, safety, and the distribution of income, resources, and opportunities—that were associated with the PRC's rapid economic development (Ding and Xu 2015, 52). In practice, it confronted "rural–urban income disparities, to develop the state welfare net and to boost spending on education" (Li 2015, 130). Therefore, the creation of a harmonious society would integrate workers in the group that have an average salary by extending the constituents of the middle class to transform the polarized Chinese society into a *diamond-shaped social structure* with a minority of wealthy and poor.

However, this social harmonization would also amount to "a gradual standardization and sophistication of the ways and opinions of the population" (Rocca 2017, 120) within "an epistemic frame of power relations" and "explicit political campaigns and legislations" (Romero-Moreno 2018, 24–35). Many scholars saw

Hu's ideological programme as a populist attempt based on the combination of the neo-Confucianist values with a neo-Sinicization of Marxism to combat the moral vacuum in which China found itself because of the numerous cases of government corruption and commercial bribery (Saich 2015). President Hu's orthodox and conservative concept of the harmonious society cannot be dissociated from Elias's concept of "civilizing process" and indigenous Chinese notions such as civilization (*wenming*) and human quality (*suzhi*). Thus, it is through such concepts that the discourse on the middle class is composed and legitimizes urban middle incomers to reproduce social distinction and privileged positions, and reinforce class boundaries within social hierarchies in contemporary urban China.

With the Global Financial Crisis of 2007/2008, the official discourse on the middle class emphasized the economic role of urban middle incomers as the backbone of domestic consumption and major engine of growth to the economic development of the country. In addition, since the effects of the global recession were major cuts to social spending and "the narrative of moral failure" noted in the form of "greedy financial executives" of Western countries (Kling 2010), the state-sponsored discourse on the middle class added nationalistic elements. It promoted the perception of the civilized and self-discipline Chinese middle class as the vanguard in the struggle to build a "high-quality nation" as opposed to the economic and moral decadence of Western countries, as next the section in this chapter analyses. Although the Global Financial Crisis of 2007/2008 reinforced the urge to build a Harmonious Society, it was also a tough challenge for President Hu's economic policy and the feasibility of his social harmonization. The Chinese government, aware that its legitimacy derived from economic growth, implemented successful fiscal and monetary stimulus programmes which boosted the Chinese Dream of Xi Jinping, the new president of the PRC from 2013.

While his immediate predecessor, President Hu, had followed the reformist model of a gradual and peaceful transition for the country rather than rapid marketization and stress, President Xi signalled that "the time had arrived for China" and its middle class to assume their "rightful place in world affairs" (Benson 2016, 105). In his first speech as Party General Secretary, Xi Jinping mentioned the aspirations of the Chinese people to "have a beautiful life" and later as a president of the PRC detailed that the Chinese Dream was "the strength, prosperity and happiness of the people" (*Xinhua* 2012; Taylor 2015, 111) by exuding "a confidence that was lacking over the previous decade" (Saich 2015, 74). And confidence is indeed necessary to achieve the Chinese Dream and the great revival of the Middle Kingdom.

President Xi's concept alludes to the great dream of the Chinese nation in modern history to realize its "great rejuvenation." This ideological statement aims to restore optimism and enthusiasm for the future, especially among the young, through a national rejuvenation centred on urbanization, upward social mobility, and consumption (Ferdinand 2016; Taylor 2015). The Chinese Dream effectively conveys that both Xi and the Party are aware and care about the dreams of the average citizen, who longs for a new kind of middle-class urban life that can only be realized through unity and wealth sharing (Taylor 2015, 111). That is, Jing's goal of building a *xiaokang* society, or common prosperity, continued in Xi's hands in the form of a clear purpose achieved: China's poverty alleviation in 2021, the year that marks the 100th anniversary of the founding of the CCP. As a result, new discourses based on the self-granted legitimacy of the Party-state as an inter-class representative (Beltrán Antolín 2018) have emerged in the PRC since the Chinese government announced in February 2021 that nearly 100 million people had been lifted out of extreme poverty after a successful eight-year programme implemented by President Xi, totalling close to 800 million people out of poverty since 1980.

Far from following the model of the American Dream based on individualistic values, the emphasis was on making China a "strong and powerful" nation again (Xi 2013). In this respect, Xi Jinping's Chinese Dream plans to unite the country, the nation, and the people with a common past and a future that can only be built if the Chinese are united. Hence, by stressing the importance of the group over the individual, President Xi emphasized the nationalist and historical component as a simplified, normative, and single identity *vis-à-vis* the Other. However, the Chinese state is aiming at Western lifestyle "without being shaped by Western political standards" (Li 2015, 27). Xi's ideological formulation is linked to the concept of China's "great rejuvenation" after the "century of national humiliation" that the country suffered from the First Opium War (1839–1842) until the end of the Sino-Japanese War in 1945.

By doing this, as Zheng Wang (2014) noted, the discourse of the Chinese Dream challenges Chinese people for generating "a 'new national story' or a new narrative to replace the humiliation narrative" (3). Additionally, it should be borne in mind that the Chinese Dream has been globally defined in the 21st century in three ways: as a concept of Chinese tradition that re-emerged with new connotations in 2013; as an instrument to enhance the CCP's internal legitimacy; and as a method for the international dissemination of certain ideals (7). Under these conditions, the ruling elite, aware of the need to strengthen its legitimacy and to end the disparity between the incomes of rural and urban residents, aimed to continue the *middleization* reform of the socio-economic model launched during the previous period under Hu Jintao. Xi's concept of "two 100-years" was "a more concrete version of the abstract concept of national rejuvenation" that alluded to the programme of poverty alleviation for 2021 (the 100th anniversary of the CCP) and a fully developed middle-class nation by 2049 (the 100th anniversary of the PRC) (7). Thus, the expansion of the urban Chinese middle class through "stable domestic economic growth and consumption" (Taylor 2015, 116) has been and remains one of the cornerstones of President Xi's political programme.

Hence, through the theory of the Chinese Dream, Xi Jinping called for attention to the power of China at the national and individual level. According to Xi, the people of China must have better standards of living, that is, the standards of the middle class. Xi's initiative added to the tradition of the CCP a collective ideal of the future and attempted to convince the Chinese population "that the realization of the Chinese Dream leads to improved housing, education, public health, and social welfare" (Wang 2014, 7). This attitude of achieving a dream is not only a political promise but it also wants to establish motivational narratives as the value of all Chinese when it comes to posing challenges of individual self-improvement—again showing the Party's flexibility to establish itself as a political and ethical leader.

The new message seems to indicate an old logic of national and individual development based on "work hard and self-reliantly" and on the improvement of the "socialist rule of law" as reflected in the 2018 constitutional amendment. Presented as "the realization of four decades of efforts to create a specialized constitutional supervision organ" (Hand 2019, 138–139), this constitutional amendment was widely perceived outside the PRC as a proof of President Xi "is taking China back to personalistic leadership after decades of collective leadership" (Shirk 2018, 23). In the same line, the group's priority over the individual that implicitly transmits the Chinese Dream has been translated, in practice, into a combination of coercive neo-authoritarian measures to enforce economic development (Li 2015) and the implementation of policies to poverty eradication and common prosperity.

In conclusion, the Chinese Dream is sustained on a national scale in the official discourse on the middle class, not so much as the political ideal of a harmonious society but as an individual dream, which aspires to achieve a comfortable urban lifestyle typical of the post-industrial societies. It thus reflects the Party-state's purpose of stimulating domestic demand, accelerating the transformation of the economic growth model, and promoting sustained long-term development (Beltrán Antolín 2018, 140). In an article published in *People's Daily*, sociologist Cheng Li explains that the Chinese Dream created new economic opportunities and new sources of wealth, and it will be an opportunity for upward social mobility and achieving a middle-class lifestyle in the coming decades (Gao 2013). In this way, the significance of the imaginary created by the Chinese Dream is that it serves as a roadmap for not only the "middle-income group" but the entire Chinese population.

The Chinese media, along with the Party-state, has participated in the dissemination of this paradigm through the official discourse on the middle class. In fact, President Xi admonished his comrades in September 2013 "to work hard on 'consolidating and boosting mainstream public opinion, propagating the leitmotifs [of socialism with Chinese characteristics], and spreading positive energy'" (Lam 2015, 94). In this context, the next section analyses in detail the official discourse on the middle class in CCP's digital media by considering both the implicit and the explicit presentation of the news reported by assessing social change under the neo-authoritarian measures of the PRC's political regime and the role of discourse as a part of the everyday life in Chinese society.

1.2 A discourse construction on the middle class in *Renmin Wang*: Anxiety, populism, and paternalism

Since the start of the privatization of Chinese media in the 1990s, an increasing number of studies have investigated closely the transformation of this sector in the

PRC. During this period, Chinese journalists have been aware of the dual role that the newspaper industry "can be like an ordinary factory and generate a revenue (mainly through advertising), but it can also be part of the nation's ideological propaganda mechanism" (Scotton and Hachten 2010, 50–51). Since its foundation in 1946, the *Renmin Ribao* (*People's Daily* in its English edition) has been China's official "mouthpiece" due to its position as the "organ" of the Central Committee of the Party, and its direct link to the CCP's Propaganda Department (Wu 1994, 195). That is, the *Renmin Ribao*, and its digital version since 1997 *Renmin Wang* (*People's Daily Online* in its English version) have formed a crucial instrument of governmental power to establish the political reality of the country at each moment and, therefore, to analyse the official discourse on the middle class in China today.

Discourse can be understood as the result of an incessant process of collective (and, perhaps, involuntary) creation that intellectually structures a wide range of desires for living in an ideal way according to certain values, and the eventual unintentional actions benefiting this ideal (Solé-Farràs 2014, 1). Therefore, discourses not only produce knowledge, meaning, and its political intentions (that is, representations and paradigms), but also have a significant material effect by producing "practices that systematically form the objects of which they speak" (Foucault 1972, 49). Based on my previous research on the official discourse on the middle class in *Renmin Wang* (Sánchez-Romera 2021b), this section now completes the study on class and discourse construction in the PRC of this chapter by analysing how digital media reported the social phenomenon of the middle class in China before the COVID-19 pandemic.

Studies published on the treatment of information in different Chinese media confirm that "fusion of Party-state and market power has created a media system that serves the interests of the country's political and economic elite" (Zhao 2004, 179), and whose influence ensures that the press does not deviate too much from the government's position (Stockmann and Gallagher 2011, 442–443). With this premise in mind, a considerable number of investigations have examined what has been published in the *Renmin Ribao* on different social and political phenomena such as, for example, China's decision to join the WTO (Zhao 2003), the HIV/AIDS victims (Dong, Chang, and Chen 2008), Health Care Reform (Duckett and Langer 2013), homosexuality (Huang 2018), and climate change (Fan, Xue, and Xu 2018), among others.

This section quantitatively and qualitatively analyses the 427 articles in the Chinese-language digital version of the *Renmin Ribao* whose headlines contain the term "middle class," that is, *zhongchan jieji*—which is one of the most common ways used to refer to this social group (Goodman 2014, 4). These 427 articles have been identified through a systematic search of the database available digitally on the newspaper's website (http://www.people.com.cn/). Further, the selected journalistic texts were published between 1 January 2000, the year when the middle class was mentioned for the first time in connection with the Three Represents Theory of Jiang Zemin, whereupon the Party-state first promoted the middle class in the country, and 31 December 2015, the year in which Fifth Plenum of the Eighteenth Central Committee of the CCP was held. This meeting was a turning point away from the government policy decisions to that date, and towards the new policy measures to be implemented in the PRC until the COVID-19 pandemic began to spread in November 2019.

The number of articles published per year was first calculated to quantitatively analyse middle-class narratives. These were then coded according to the nationality of the middle class alluded to: Chinese or foreign, and within the foreign category, by country (US, UK, Japan, etc.). Following the methodological technique used in the studies conducted by Zhao (2003) and Duckett and Langer (2013), each article then was recoded for its predominant policy position, defined as: "pro-state" (in favour of a greater presence of the state and of distributive measures to favour the middle class); "pro-market" (meaning in favour of a greater role for the private sector and commercial values such as consumption, competitiveness, etc., in the conception of the Chinese middle class); "balanced" (showing both of these positions equally); "none" (without any reference to the pro-state or pro-market positions), and "unclassifiable."

Based on the historical-discursive method developed by Wodak (1996) as used by Sandby-Thomas (2014) in his analysis of how the CCP legitimizes its authority through the stability discourse, this section considers not only language and discourse, but also the political and ideological dimension of the messages in the press and the role of discourse in the social reproduction of power (van Dijk 2002, 2014). Hence, as Duckett and Langer (2013) also suggested, to probe these ideological underpinnings of *Renmin Wang*'s middle-class reporting, this study also examined the language they used—it focused on whether reporting reflected what have already been identified in the preceding sections as a state-sponsored discourse on the middle class. In this way, a phenomenon that is receiving increasing attention is analysed in a journalistic and conceptual way, not only by the media and academics, but also by the main international economic actors.

The pan-national narrative of dual mobility: the rise of the Chinese Dream and the decline of the American Dream

It is striking that more articles have been published in *Renmin Wang* (henceforth referred to as *RW*) on the middle class in other countries (261 articles) than on the Chinese middle class (149), especially at a time when the Chinese government is publicly expressing a clear political will to promote the middle class in China (see Table 1.1). This reflects the seemingly ambiguous and contradictory interplay of "the national" and "the global" in Chinese media since the beginning of the 21st century. Nonetheless, nationalism permeates the articles dealing with the foreign middle class, which addresses the need of the Party-State to compensate for the historical inequalities between China and Western states and is useful in defending the interests of the Chinese elites within their borders; this is the same dynamic described by Flint and Taylor (1985) in their analysis of 19th century European nationalism. This pro-Chinese discourse promoted by *RW* that is found in other articles on the middle class of other countries is based on three aspects.

First, there is an anti–American narrative present in almost all news items (94 per cent) related to the US middle class (117 articles), which represents a significant percentage (27 per cent) of the total sample. Anti-Americanism resurfaced in the Chinese press in the 1990s because both the end of the Cold War and the Tiananmen Square protests in 1989 placed the US and the PRC in irreconcilable positions of "mutual recrimination" (Lee 2003, 75). The US middle class is described in the articles published in *RW* as a group that is becoming precarious, both in terms of their decreasing income and population size. The quality of life of the American middle class is under threat not only because of the Global Financial Crisis of 2007/2008, but also because of the slow economic growth of the country before the global recession, the increase in inequality, and the crisis of legitimacy of US leaders *vis-à-vis* their constituents.

The articles noted that "America's infrastructure is in jeopardy" (*RW* 2008) and the values on which it is based, such as work, progress, equality, and optimism are "reeling" (*dongyao*) (*RW* 2012). This contrasts with the growth and enrichment experienced by the Chinese middle class, seen as being called to "take over from the American middle class," as repeatedly stated in the *RW*: "the 'Chinese Dream' is booming while the 'American Dream' is in decline" (2008); or similarly, "*dang Meiguo de taiyang luoshan shi, Zhongguo de baitian kaishile*" (when the sun sets on the US, the light will begin to shine on China) (2010d). This type of triumphalist rhetoric, regardless of the economic trends announced by empirical data, is in line with the Maoist tradition whereby a Marxist interpretation was made of the financial "crisis" associated with negative images of the US economy (Shambaugh 1988, 150). This interpretation was updated by Chinese propaganda to highlight the contradictory structural factors of American society today.

Secondly, the presence of a pan-national discourse that appeals to the shared identity of emerging economies *vis-à-vis* the minority world is verified. Despite the existence of ten articles that question the global growth of the middle class, the rest (251) utilized what will be called here the "dual mobility narrative." According to this, the middle classes of the liberal democracies—especially the US, UK, and

TABLE 1.1 Dominant nationalities of the middle class (MC) in news reporting, 2000–2015

	n	%
Chinese MC	149	35
Foreign MC (USA)	117	27
Foreign MC (other than US)	144	34
None	17	4
Total	427	100

Note. Percentages are rounded so may not add up to 100.
Source. Developed by the author from *RW*.

Taiwan—are getting poorer and shrinking in size, while the middle classes of the BRICS (Brazil, Russia, India, China, and South Africa) and other emerging markets are growing as if the two phenomena were interdependent, as a bi-directional merging of impoverishment and *middleclassization* of society.

Thirdly, the articles celebrate the role that the middle class will play in the majority world as an economic driver in the future of the global economy. Of all of them, the Chinese middle class best represents this phenomenon, even playing a redeeming role in the global economy by taking over the baton from the US middle class as by 2020 "Chinese consumers will lead global spending" (RW 2010c). However, according to these articles, the PRC's leadership will not interfere with the domestic policies of other countries and will not lead to the impoverishment of other regions. On the contrary, according to the sample of articles analysed, China's economic leadership will benefit everyone, both majority world and China's traditional competitors in the minority world: even "China's middle class will bring great opportunities to the US" (RW 2010d), for example, in terms of investment and tourism (RW 2014).

After analysing the nationalist discourse implicit in the articles on the foreign middle class, the question arises: why does the CCP use *RW* to promote a nationalist discourse in its articles on the middle class? One answer could be that nationalism has become the main instrument to secure public support for the regime, to legitimize it in the face of "the declining ideological efficacy of communism" and "the social changes brought about by the economic reform" that caused the social conflicts in both urban and rural areas in the late 1990s (Hyun

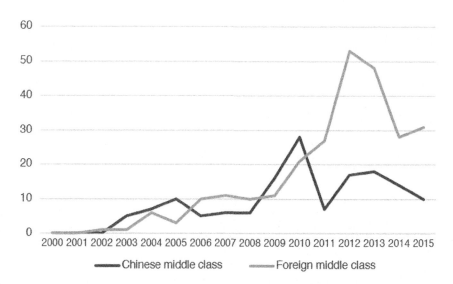

FIGURE 1.1 Distribution of articles on middle class (MC) in *RW,* 2000–2015. Source. Developed by the author from *RW.*

and Kim 2014, 766). Also revealing is the dates of publication of articles on the foreign middle classes (see Figure 1.1). Of these, 61 per cent were published in five years (2011–2015) compared to the remaining articles (39 per cent) which were published over a period of 11 years (2000–2010). The number of articles published increased significantly in 2012, the year in which the theory of the Chinese Dream was presented. A variable was then established between the beginning of the new ideological programme represented by the Chinese Dream, and a greater presence in *RW* of a nationalist and anti-American discourse that made Chinese economic development conditional on the impoverishment of the US middle class and its traditional allies in Asia and Europe. In this way, the concept of the middle class was bereft of its class-based identity and acquired a national-based identity.

Anxiety, indescribable pains, and populism

Pro-market articles (38 per cent) and pro-state articles (37 per cent) published in *RW* were represented almost equally. Only one article out of 149 articles specific to the Chinese middle class in the sample questioned whether the middle-class model of society proposed by the government was the best way to end inequality in the PRC. This absence of dissent from and criticism of the dominant official discourse is due, not so much to its lack of validity, as to the fact that it calls into question the authority of the CCP. Other than the oft-repeated, accepted precept that the middle class must be a majority in Chinese society because it is the back-bone of the country's economy (*Zhongguo caifu de zhongjian liliang*) and because it acts as a social stabilizer (*shehui wending qi*), there are different views on the most effective way to strengthen and expand this segment of the population. In addi-tion, a populist narrative is introduced that details the economic hardships in the form of loans and mortgages that the middle-class resorts to that affect their eco-nomic and emotional stability, but without providing structural solutions that would alleviate the effects of these adversities.

Pro-market news items advocated the consumerist role of the middle class and elevated it to a national necessity to ensure the PRC's full economic development in the not-too-distant future. This argument depoliticizes and naturalizes con-sumerist practices, normalizes the acceptance of the neoliberal logic implicit in such consumerist behaviour, and neutralizes the concept of social class inherent in the ideological essence of the PRC. These discursive incentives to consume, Zavoretti (2017) pointed out, "aim to appeal to all members of society while at the same time giving the illusion of granting the individual a distinctive identity that supposedly has nothing to do with the dangerous realm of politics" (112). Starting in 2009, and in the context of the Global Financial Crisis of 2007/2008, the number of articles inviting people to buy products associated with middle-class lifestyles—washing machines, SUVs, tourist destinations, European wine, etc.—increased considerably, with many of them starting with an allusion to the importance of this group's purchasing power for the Chinese economy and ending up with a direct incitement to consumption.

Therefore, achieving an established domestic consumption was presented as a national necessity and a patriotic act that would allow the country not only to move away from the export-led economic model but above all to overcome the Global Financial Crisis, as noted in the previous section. Thus, the pro-market consumerist message, on the one hand, promotes practices as a new distinctive symbol of China and its society and, on the other, empowers the economic elite and the domestic private sector, where these consumerist practices take place. However, these narratives are not only about the need to consume, but also about how to consume, that is, about high-*suzhi* consumption. One article explains that "those who are part of the economically more affluent middle class and embrace higher quality standards culturally and ideologically will become the essence of Chinese *xiaokang* society." As noted earlier, *suzhi* is the feature that distinguishes the middle class with quality from the new rich (*baofahu*), namely, "those who, despite being economically solvent, have a lower cultural and ideological quality" (RW 2003).

Nonetheless, not all articles published in *RW* on the Chinese middle class were optimistic about the growth of this group, as 37 per cent discussed the difficulties that people considered middle class face in the PRC. The pro-state articles alluded to the growing social inequality in China and the challenges that threaten the expansion of the middle class. An example of this are headlines such as: "Analysing the impoverishment of the middle class: why do they have high income and indescribable pain?" (RW 2005) or "The middle class is locked in: it is difficult to move up and easy to go down" (RW 2010b). Moreover, populist rhetoric pervades pro-state and pro-market articles as if it were a feature of the official middle-class discourse, regardless of political position. In line with Duckett and Langer's (2013), the rhetoric used by *RW* in the treatment of the middle class is populist and paternalistic because the main source of information about it is not the middle class itself, rather "elites and the media spoke *for* 'the people' and debated their needs and benefits, but gave them little opportunity to voice their own views and preferences" (659). Although members of the middle class were directly quoted 22 times and were the most quoted social actors (representing 31 per cent of the quotations), direct quotations are not widely used in the Chinese press, where there is a strong preference to quote actors indirectly and, in this case, the presence of the voice of the middle class was limited to 7 per cent of all testimonies.

The difficulties faced by the Chinese middle class were treated paternalistically by Chinese experts from public institutions, representatives of companies and multinationals, and even foreign journalists, who explained this vision of the Chinese middle class. Their opinions were the most frequently used in the articles, with few articles using the direct voice of the protagonists, i.e., individuals regarded to be part of the middle class. Considering the political nature of *RW*, the fact that the most mentioned and cited actors were representatives of the national and transnational business world suggests a clear pro-market orientation in the sample, indicating the CCP's willingness to strengthen and increase the power of the private sector compared with the public sector. In turn, the views of Chinese workers and farmers, those who will swell the ranks of the middle class soon, did not appear in any pieces of news, and their opinions on the main obstacles that prevented them from accessing the middle class (thus reaching the desired *xiaokang* society as soon as possible) were not portrayed in the articles.

In the article entitled "Top ten anxiety disorders suffered by the Chinese middle class" (RW 2010a), different experts, psychologists, artists, and estate agents assessed the lifestyle of the middle class. Middle-class anxiety was also linked to the lack of laws to protect private property in China and the concern about family expenses—health care, education, housing, care for the elderly—which makes middle incomers "slaves" (*nu*, a popular term) to mortgage payments, car payments, children's education, etc. and cause them to become "workaholics." This article has been coded as balanced because, although the text supports privatization and partly holds the middle class responsible for their situation (as workaholics), it also advocates an increase in public investment in education to relieve families of these expenses. While reporting on the problems of China's middle class, and on other non-elite groups, by proposing greater public investment, in the end the article legitimized the normative discourse of presenting the middle class as the backbone of China's economic growth and social stabilizer.

This is an example of populism that was very much present in pro-state and balanced articles. What could only be interpreted as a discourse advocating economic distribution to end the pressure on the weak middle class becomes one that justifies further privatization and the protection of the country's economic elite. These articles call for a change in government measures to increase the size of the middle class, whose main function is to strengthen domestic consumption and maintain economic growth, which is what most ensures the legitimacy of the CCP. The Party-state thus legitimizes its authority through specific interests that are presented as being in the general interest (Zhao 2003, 36). Additionally, it is the national economic elite who ultimately benefit as the recipients of the profits from consumption generated by the middle class, and who achieve a greater presence in an increasingly privatized and less protected social space.

What should be done? Problems, responsibilities, and solutions

While 79 per cent of pro-market articles took for granted the existence of a middle class in China and detailed the economic benefits that this group contributes to the national and even the international economy, a higher percentage of pro-state articles (83 per cent) also used economic arguments, but from a very different perspective. The latter questioned the growth (and even the existence) of China's emerging middle class because of their low economic capital, the anxiety they face in repaying the loans they have taken out, and other material problems such as the high costs of education and housing. While the pro-market articles posited the rise of the middle class in macroeconomic terms under the promise of a "superior" lifestyle and "good life," the majority position of the pro-state articles focused on the economic concerns of middle-class households and the emotional difficulties that this segment of the population faces in maintaining their lifestyle.

The main problems of the Chinese middle class mentioned in the pro-state and balanced articles included the values implicit in their lifestyle. Competitiveness at work and in education, the snobbery of the young urban middle class, consumerism—especially the fondness for foreign luxury brands—and a lack of social and political awareness were some values criticized and implicit in the middle-class lifestyle, according to *RW*. This type of discourse critical of capitalist values is what might be expected in a dominant way in the mouthpiece of the CCP, but it was very reduced and was found in only 37 per cent of all articles. The predominant image in *RW* was that an idealized citizen in China's urban society is being imposed based on the entrepreneurial subject "responsible for his/her own 'profits and losses' and the anxious manager of his or her embodied capital, whose success is measured in commodified expressions of social distinction" (Anagnost, 2008, 515). The *RW* thus presents the Chinese middle class as the middle class of a fully developed post-industrial society in which the basic needs of the entire population are covered, and social differences are mainly manifested through consumption.

The solutions presented in *RW* to the problems of the middle class were in line with this account of the entrepreneurial subject. The digital version of *Renmin Ribao* mainly called for alleviating the economic burden on the middle class through a greater state role (31 per cent), an improvement in existing services (17 per cent) and greater public investment (12 per cent). In this way, as several articles pointed out, the middle class would be able to devote a larger part of their budget to purchasing goods and services—again reinforcing the social construction of identity based on the "consumption-middle class" binomial. Although inequality appears as one of the most acute social problems, neither the working class, nor peasants, nor migrant workers, nor the economic elite were mentioned as specific groups in any significant way. As the mouthpiece of the CCP, it is striking that the only mention of the dominant class was through exemplary stories of self-improvement, or "success stories," charity work, and two interviews with the founders, both of them male, of large Chinese technology companies, where they defended the strengthening of the middle class and considered themselves to be knowledgeable about the social reality of their country.

In brief, this investigation confirms the presence of a normative discourse on the Chinese middle class in *RW* in the form of nationalist narratives based on anti-American, populist, normative, and paternalistic positions. Thus, when *RW* talks about the decline of the US middle class, it does not only report on a global trend in Western countries, but also promises the Chinese entrepreneur-subject a supposedly superior Chinese lifestyle. This is portrayed as a new hegemonic model that reflects the Chinese economic prominence and, consequently, legitimizes the CCP as the only ruling party in the PRC. In this discursive space, the Chinese Dream is postulated in the form of an individual and collective dream that aspires to achieve a comfortable middle-class lifestyle through sacrifice, material accumulation and self-discipline. Additionally, the dominant presence of national and transnational business and the almost total absence of political representatives in addressing the issue of the middle class in *RW* reveals a strong pro-market stance on social issues within the CCP.

This analysis of the official discourse on the middle class in *RW* has noted the depoliticization of consumerist practices, the absence of a form of class rhetoric that appeals to socialist values such as equality or solidarity, the invisibility of poverty by failing to give a voice to potential future constituents of the Chinese middle class, the incentive to create a distinct identity through consumption rather than the common good and politics, and the disengagement of the elite from their privileges by presenting economic enrichment as the sole result of individual effort. Through this discourse, the CCP has promoted narratives to persuade the readers of *RW* that supporting its authority is the most effective way of maintaining social stability, enhancing economic growth, and securing their class privileges.

After elucidating the middle class as a historical artefact before and after the establishment of the PRC in 1949, examining the construction of the discourse on the middle class in the 1990s and analysing the news articles published on *RW*, Chapter 1 has set out to contextualize and identify the most representative discursive spaces of the Party-state. Additionally, this chapter has considered the ideological programmes and speeches of Chinese leaders, the most significant constitutional amendments for the Chinese middle class since the mid-1990s, and the news about the middle class that appeared in the main CCP media, in order to verify the presence, in all of them, of a state-sponsored discourse on the middle class. The degree of this presence and the effective influence that this official discourse exercises on the intellectual debate on class and the manifestation in the lifestyle of the Chinese middle class are some of the elements which the following chapters will gauge from the intellectual narratives about the middle class generated in China studies (Chapter 2) and the narratives collected in Beijing (Chapters 3, 4, and 5) before the COVID-19 pandemic.

Bibliography

Anagnost, Ann. 2008. "From 'Class' to 'Social Strata': Grasping the Social Totality in Reform-era China." *Third World Quarterly* 29 (3): 497–519. doi:10.1080/01436590801931488.

Andreas, Joel. 2009. *Rise of the Red Engineers. The Cultural Revolution and the Origins of China's New Class*. Stanford, CA: Stanford University Press.

Banister, Judith. 1987. *China's Changing Population*. Stanford, CA: Stanford University Press.

Beltrán Antolín, Joaquín 2018. "El Partido ante la sociedad: La erradicación de la pobreza [The Party in the face of society: Eradicating poverty]." In *Viaje al Centro. El XIX Congreso del Partido Comunista Chino [Journey to the Centre. The 19th Congress of the CCP]*, edited by Joaquín Beltrán Antolín, 137–158. Barcelona: Edicions Bellaterra.

Benson, Linda. 2016. *China Since 1949*. Abingdon: Routledge.

Bergère, Marie-Claire. 1997. "Civil Society and Urban Change in Republican China." *The China Quarterly* 150: 309–328. doi:10.1017/S0305741000052498.

Bian, Yanjie. 1994. *Work and Inequality in Urban China*. Albany, NY: State University of New York Press.

Bin, Zhao. 1997. "Consumerism, Confucianism, Communism: Making Sense of China Today." *New Left Review* 222: 43–59.

Blecher, Marc. 2009. *China Against the Tides: Restructuring through Revolution, Radicalism and Reform*. London: Bloomsbury Publishing.

Bourdieu, Pierre. 1987. "What Makes a Social Class? On Theoretical and Practical Existence of Groups." *Berkeley Journal of Sociology* 32: 1–17.

Bourdieu, Pierre. 1998. *Practical Reason: On the Theory of Action*. Translated by Randall Johnson. Stanford, CA: Stanford University Press.

Brady, Anne-Marie. 2009. "Mass Persuasion as a Means of Legitimation and China's Popular Authoritarianism." *American Behavioral Scientist* 53 (3): 434–457. doi:10.1177/0002764209338802.

Bray, David. 2005. *Social Space and Governance in Urban China: the Danwei System from Origins to Reform*. Stanford, CA: Stanford University Press.

Brown, Kerry. 2018. "The Communist Party and Ideology." In *The SAGE Handbook of Contemporary China*, edited by Wiping Wu and Mark W. Fraizer, 287–301. London: Sage.

Chan, Kam Wing, and Li Zhang. 1999. "The *hukou* System and rural-urban migration in China: Processes and changes." *The China Quarterly* 160: 818–855. doi:10.1017/S0305741000001351.

Chen, Jie. 2013. *A Middle Class without Democracy: Economic Growth and the Prospects for Democratization in China*. New York: Oxford University Press.

Cheng, Li. 2010. "Introduction: The Rise of the Middle Class in the Middle Kingdom." In *China's Emerging Middle Class: Beyond Economic Transformation*, edited by Li Cheng, 3–31. Washington, DC: Brookings Institution Press.

Cheng, Tiejun, and Mark Selden. 1994. "The Origins and Social Consequences of China's Hukou System." *The China Quarterly* 139: 644–668. doi:10.1017/S0305741000043083.

Chun, Lin. 2015. "The Language of Class in China." *Socialist Register* 51: 24–53. http://eprints.lse.ac.uk/59694/1/__lse.ac.uk_storage_LIBRARY_Secondary_libfile_shared_repository_Content_Lin,%20C_Language%20of%20class_Lin_Language%20of%20class_2016.pdf.

Dai, Fengyan, Fang Cai and Yu Zhu. 2021. "Returns to higher education in China – evidence from the 1999 higher education expansion using a fuzzy regression discontinuity." *Applied Economics Letters* 29 (6): 1–6. doi:10.1080/13504851.2020.1871465.

Davis, Deborah S. 2000. "Social Class Transformation in Urban China." *Modern China* 26 (3): 251–275. doi:10.1177/009770040002600301.

Dickson, Bruce. 2016. *The Dictator's Dilemma: The Chinese Communist Party's Strategy for Survival*. Oxford: Oxford University Press.

Ding, Min, and Jie Xu. 2015. *The Chinese Way*. New York: Routledge.

Dong, Dong, Tsan-Kuo Chang, and Dan Chen. 2008. "Reporting AIDS and the Invisible Victims in China: Official Knowledge as News in the People's Daily, 1986–2002." *Journal of Health Communication* 13 (4): 357–374. doi:10.1080/10810730802063793.

Dong, Jie. 2018. "Taste, discourse and middle-class identity: An ethnography of Chinese Saabists." *Journal of Sociolinguistics* 22 (4): 432–453. doi:10.1111/josl.12309.

Duckett, Jane, and Ana Inés Langer. 2013. "Populism versus Neoliberalism: Diversity and Ideology in the Chinese Media's Narratives of Health Care Reform." *Modern China* 39 (6): 653–680. doi:10.1177/0097700413492602.

Edwards, Louise. 2000. "Policing the Modern Woman in Republican China." *Modern China* 26 (2): 115–147. doi:10.1177/009770040002600201.

Fan, Shiwei, Lan Xue, and Jianhua Xu. 2018. "What Drives Policy Attention to Climate Change in China?" *Sustainability* 10 (9): 1–20. doi:10.3390/su10092977.

Ferdinand, Peter. 2016. "Westward Ho-the China Dream and 'One Belt, One Road': Chinese Foreign Policy under Xi Jinping." *International Affairs* 92 (4): 941–957. doi:10.1111/1468-2346.12660.

Fields, Barbara Jeanne. 1990. "Slavery, Race and Ideology in the United States of America." *New Left Review* 181 (1): 95–118.

Flint, Colin, and Peter J.Taylor. 1985. *Political Geography. World-economy, Nation-state and Locality*. Harlow: Pearson Education Limited.

Foucault, Michel. 1972. *The Archaeology of Knowledge and the Discourse on Language*. Translated by A.M. Sheridan Smith. New York: Pantheon Books.

Gao, Pan. 2013. "Chinese Dream Depicts Blueprint for Middle Class: Expert." *People's Daily*, 16 November. http://en.people.cn/90785/8458425.html.

Gerth, Karl. 2003. *China Made. Consumer Culture and the Creation of the Nation*. Cambridge, MA: Harvard University Asia Center.

Gerth, Karl. 2020. *Unending Capitalism: How Consumerism Negated China's Communist Revolution*. Cambridge: Cambridge University Press.

Gold, Thomas B. 2000. "La Sociedad Urbana" [Urban Society]. In *China en Transición*, edited by Taciana Fisac and Steve Tsang, 47–76. Barcelona: Edicions Bellaterra.

Goodman, David S.G. 2008. "Why China has no new middle class: cadres, managers and entrepreneurs." In *The New Rich in China. Future Rulers, Present Lives*, edited by David S. G. Goodman, 23–37. Abingdon: Routledge.

Goodman, David S.G. 2014. *Class in Contemporary China*, Cambridge: Polity Press.

Goodman, David S.G., and Xiaowei Zang. 2008. "The new rich in China: the dimensions of social change." In *The New Rich in China. Future Rulers, Present Lives*, edited by David S.G. Goodman, 1–20. Abingdon: Routledge.

Guo, Xiaoqin. 2003. *State and Society in China's Democratic Transition: Confucianism, Leninism, and Economic Development*. New York: Routledge.

Guo, Yingjie. 2008. "Class, stratum and group: the politics of description and prescription." In *The New Rich in China. Future Rulers, Present Lives*, edited by David S.G. Goodman, 38–52. Abingdon: Routledge.

Han, Chunping, and Whyte, Martin King. 2009. "The social contours of distributive injustice feelings in contemporary China." In *Creating Wealth and Poverty in Postsocialist China*, edited by Deborah S. Davis and Wang Feng, 199–213. Stanford, CA: Stanford University Press.

Hand, Keith J. 2019. "Constitutional Supervision in China after the 2018 Amendment of the PRC Constitution: Refining the Narrative of Constitutional Supremacy in a Socialist Legal System." *Asian-Pacific Law & Policy Journal* 23 (2): 137–175. doi:10.2139/ssrn.3431293.

He Qinglian. 2000. "China Listing Social Structure." *New Left Review* (5): 68–99. https://newleftreview.org/issues/ii5/articles/qinglian-he-china-s-listing-social-structure.

Hird, Derek. 2009. *White-Collar Men and Masculinities in Contemporary Urban China*. PhD diss., University of Westminster.

Honig, Emily. 1989. "The Politics of Prejudice: Subei People in Republican-Era Shanghai." *Modern China* 15 (3): 243–274.

Hsu, Carolyn. 2006. "Cadres, Getihu, And Good Businesspeople: Making Sense OF Entrepreneurs in Early Post-Socialist China." *Urban Anthropology and Studies of Cultural Systems and World Economic Development* 35 (1): 1–38. https://www.jstor.org/stable/pdf/40553488.pdf.

Hu, Jintao. 2006. "Communiqué of the Sixth Plenum of the 16th CPC Central Committee." Accessed 18 October 2019. http://www.gov.cn/english/2006-10/11/content_410436.htm.

Huang, Yixiong. 2018. "Media Representation of *Tongxinglian* in China: A Case Study of the *People's Daily*." *Journal of Homosexuality* 65 (3): 338–360. doi:10.1080/00918369.2017.1317475.

Hyun, Ki Deuk, and Jinhee Kim. 2014. "The Role of New Media in Sustaining the Status Quo: Online Political Expression, Nationalism, and System Support in China." *Information, Communication & Society* 18 (7): 766–781. doi:10.1080/1369118x.2014.994543.

Ji, Yingchun, Xiaogang Wu, ShengweiSun, and Guangye He. 2017. "Unequal Care, Unequal Work: Toward a more Comprehensive Understanding of Gender Inequality in Post-Reform Urban China." *Sex Roles* 77: 765–778. doi:10.1007/s11199-017-0751-1.

Jia, Hepeng. 2004. "The Three Represents Campaign: Reform the Party or Indoctrinate the Capitalists?" *Cato Journal* 24 (3): 261–275.

Jiang, Zemin. 2002. "*Quanmin jianshe xiaokang shehui, kaichuang Zhongguo tese shehui zhuyi shiye xin jumian – zai Zhongguo gongchandang di shiliu ci quanguo daibiao dahui shang de baogao* [Build a Comprehensive Xiaokang Society and Create a New Order of Socialism with Chinese Characteristics: Report to the 16th Congress of the CCP]." *Renmin Ribao*. 18 November. http://data.people.com.cn/rmrb/20021118/1.

Jones, William C. 1985. "The Constitution of the People's Republic of China." *Washington University Law Review*, 63 (4). Accessed 18 January 2022. https://openscholarship.wustl.edu/cgi/viewcontent.cgi?article=2203&context=law_lawreview.

Kling, Arnold. 2010. "The financial crisis: Moral failure or cognitive failure." *Harvard Journal of Law & Public Policy* 33 (2): 507–518. https://annenberg.usc.edu/sites/default/files/The_Financial_Crisis.pdf.

Kraus, Richard Curt. 1981. *Class Conflict in Chinese Socialism*. New York: Columbia University Press.

Kwon, Soyoung. 2017. "Social Networks in the Workplace in Postreform Urban China." *SAGE Open*. doi:10.1177/2158244017712770.

Lam, Willy Wo-Lap. 2015. *Chinese Politics in the Era of Xi Jinping*. Abingdon: Routledge.

Lee, Chin-Chuan. 2003. "The Global and the National of the Chinese Media: Discourses, Market, Technology, and Ideology." In *Chinese Media, Global Contexts*, edited by Chin-Chuan Lee, 1–31. London: RoutledgeCurzon.

Li, He. 2015. *Political Thought and China's Transformation*. Basingstoke and New York: Palgrave Macmillan.

Li, Lulu, and Li Sheng. 2007. "*Shutu yilei—Dandai Zhongguo chengzhen chongchan jieji de leixing fengxi*" [Different Approaches and Different Types: A Typological Analysis of the Middle Class in Chinese Cities and Towns]. *Shehuixue Yanjiu* 22 (6): 15–37.

Lu, Hanchao. 1999. *Beyond the Neon Lights. Everyday Shanghai in the Early Twentieth Century*. Berkeley: University of California Press.

Lu, Hanchao. 2018. "Bourgeois Comfort under Proletarian Dictatorship: Home Life of Chinese Capitalists before the Cultural Revolution." *Journal of Social History* 52 (1): 74–100. doi:10.1093/jsh/shx145.

MacFarquhar, Roderick. 1974. *The Origins of the Cultural Revolution: Contradictions among the People 1956–1957*. Vol. 1. New York: Columbia University Press.

Mao, Peijie. 2018. "The Cultural Imaginary of "Middle Society" in Early Republican Shanghai." *Modern China* 44 (6): 620–651. doi:10.1177/0097700418766827.

Mo, Jihong. 2009. "The Constitutional Law of the People's Republic of China and Its Development." *Columbia Journal of Asian Law* 23: 137–185. doi:10.7916/cjal.v23i1.3287.

Mpofu, Shepherd. 2016. "Toxification of national holidays and national identity in Zimbabwe's post-2000 nationalism." *Journal of African Cultural Studies* 28 (1): 28–43.

Nathan, Andrew J. 2016. "The Puzzle of the Chinese Middle Class." *Journal of Democracy* 27: 5–19. doi:10.1353/jod.2016.0027.

Rankin, Mary. 2002. "Nationalistic Contestation and Mobilization Politics: Practice and Rhetoric of Railway-Rights Recovery at the End of the Qing." *Modern China* 28 (3): 315–361. doi:10.1177/00900402028003002.

Renmin Wang. 2003. "'Zhongchan jieji' jiang chengwei shehui zhuliu? (Redian jujiao) [Will the 'Middle Class' Become the Mainstream of Society?]." 17 February. http://www.people.com.cn/GB/paper2086/8483/796338.html.

Renmin Wang. 2005. "Jiexi pinqiong zhongchan jieji weishenme hui you gao shouru nan yan de tong? [Analyzing the Impoverishment of the Middle Class: Why Do They Have High Incomes and Indescribable pain?]." 31 March. http://finance.people.com.cn/money/GB/42887/3336228.html.

Renmin Wang. 2008. "Lutoushe: Zhongguo zhongchan jieji zai gan chao Meiguo zhongchan jieji? [Reuters: Is the Chinese Middle Class Catching up With the American Middle Class?]. 22 September. http://world.people.com.cn/GB/8212/8086688.html.

Renmin Wang. 2010a. "Zhongguo zhongchan jieji shi da 'jiaolu zheng' [Top Ten Anxiety Disorders suffered by China's Middle Class]." 14 July. http://auto.people.com.cn/GB/105315/105323/12146225.html.

Renmin Wang. 2010b. "'Zhongchan jieji' bei suoding: Xiangshang hen kunnan, xiang xia hen rongyi [The "Middle Class" Is Locked in: It Is Difficult to Move up, and Easy to Go Down]." 16 September. http://fj.people.com.cn/GB/181517/12742267.html.

Renmin Wang. 2010c. Baogao cheng 2020 nian zhongguo jin qi cheng zhongchan jieji laizi xiao chengshi [A Report Says that Nearly 70 percent of China's Middle Class Will Come from Small Cities in 2020]." 9 November. http://sx.people.com.cn/GB/189151/13169962.html.

Renmin Wang. 2010d. "Wai mei: Zhongguo zhongchan jieji gei Meiguo juda jihui [China's Middle Class Gives the U.S. a Huge Opportunity]." 11 November. http://ccnews.people.com.cn/GB/13190472.html.

Renmin Wang. 2012. "Meiguo zhongchan jieji chujing riyi elie jiating caifu chixu zou xia po [The U.S. Middle Class Is in A Worsening Situation, Family Wealth Continues to Decline]." 25 July. http://world.people.com.cn/GB/n/2012/0725/c157278-18597994.html.

Renmin Wang. 2014. "Baogao cheng: Zhongguo zhongchan jieji jueqi gaibian meiguo huaren qu jingji [The Report Says: The Rise of the Chinese Middle Class Changes the Economy of the American Chinese Area]." 7 June. http://chinese.people.com.cn/n/2014/0607/c42309-25117125.html.

Rocca, Jean-Louis. 2017. *The Making of the Chinese Middle Class: Small Comfort and Great Expectations.* New York: Palgrave Macmillan US.

Romero-Moreno, Aran. 2018. "From Process of Civilization to Policy of Civilization: A Holistic Review of the Chinese Concept *wenming.*" *(con) textos: Revista d'Antropologia i Investigació Social* 8: 23–36. https://revistes.ub.edu/index.php/contextos/article/view/31308/31344.

Saich, Tony. 2001. *Governance and Politics of China.* New York: Palgrave Macmillan.

Saich, Tony. 2015. *Governance and Politics of China.* Basingstoke: Palgrave Macmillan.

Sánchez-Romera, Alfonso. 2021a. "La clase media urbana de la República Popular China. Nuevas prácticas y representaciones sociales." [The urban middle class of the People's Republic of China. New social practices and representations]. In *Asia Oriental. Transnacionalismo, Sociedad y Cultura [East Asia. Transnationalism, Society and Culture]*, edited by Joaquín Beltrán Antolín, 115–137. Barcelona: Edicions Bellaterra.

Sánchez-Romera, Alfonso. 2021b. "The Official Discourse of the Chinese Middle Class: Anxiety, Nationalism and Populism." *Revista Española de Investigaciones Sociológicas* 176: 141–156. doi:10.5477/cis/reis.176.141. https://reis.cis.es/REIS/PDF/REIS_176_08_ENG1632244116667.pdf.

Sandby-Thomas, Peter. 2014. "Stability Overwhelms Everything." In *Discourse, Politics and Media in Contemporary China*, edited by Qing Cao, Hailong Tian and Paul Chilton, 26–47. Amsterdam: John Benjamins Publishing Company.

Scotton, James, and William Hachten. 2010. *New Media for a New China*. Oxford: Wiley-Blackwell.

Shambaugh, David L. 1988. "Anti-Americanism in China." *The Annals of the American Academy of Political and Social Science* 497 (1): 142–156. doi:10.1177/0002716288497001012.

Shirk, Susan L. 2018. "The Return to Personalistic Rule." *Journal of Democracy* 29 (2): 22–36. doi:10.1353/jod.2018.0022.

Smith, Richard J. 2015. *The Qing Dynasty and traditional Chinese culture*. Lanham, MD: Rowman & Littlefield Publishers.

Solé-Farràs, Jesús. 2014. *New Confucianism in Twenty-first Century China*. Abingdon and New York: Routledge.

Song, M. 2004. "Baohu hefa siyou caihan zhongru xianfa jinshi furen dingxinwan? [Does Constitutional Protection of Legal Private Property Only Benefit the Wealthy?]." *Zhongguo Jjingi Zhoukan* 10.

Stockmann, Daniela, Mary E.Gallagher. 2011. "Remote Control: How the Media Sustain Authoritarian Rule in China." *Comparative Political Studies* 44 (4): 436–467. doi:10.1177/0010414010394773.

Sun, Li. 2019. *Rural Urban Migration and Policy Intervention in China*. Singapore: Palgrave Macmillan.

Sun, Liping *et al.* 1998. "Trends and Risks of Changes in China's Social Structure in the Near Future." *Strategy and Management* 5.

Susen, Simon. 2014. "Reflections on ideology: Lessons from Pierre Bourdieu and Luc Boltanski." *Thesis Eleven* 124 (1): 90–113. doi:10.1177/0725513614552444.

Tang, Beibei, and Jonathan Unger. 2013. "The Socioeconomic Status, Co-optation and Political Conservatism of the Educated Middle Class: A Case Study of University Teachers." In *Middle Class China. Identity and Behaviour*, edited by Minglu Chen and David S.G. Goodman, 90–109. Cheltenham: Edward Elgar.

Taylor, Jon. 2015. "The China Dream is an Urban Dream: Assessing the CPC's National New-Type Urbanization Plan." *Journal of Chinese Political Science* 20 (2): 107–120. doi:10.1007/s11366-015-9341-7.

Tomba, Luigi. 2014. *The Government Next Door: Neighborhood Politics in Urban China*. Ithaca, NY: Cornell University Press.

Toshiki, Kanamori, and Zhao, Zhijun. 2004. "Private Sector Development in the People's Republic of China." *Asian Development Bank, Working Paper Series* 27: 1–84. Accessed 18 January 2022. https://www.adb.org/sites/default/files/publication/159390/adbi-private-sector-development-people-republic-china.pdf.

Van Dijk, Teun A. 2002. "The interdisciplinary study of news as discourse." In *A Handbook of Qualitative Methodologies for Mass Communication Research*, edited by Klaus Bruhn Jensen and Nicholas W. Jankowski, 108–120. London: Routledge.

Van Dijk, Teun A. 2014. *Discourse and Knowledge*. Cambridge: Cambridge University Press.

Walder, Andrew G., and Songhua Hu. 2009. "Revolution, Reform, and Status Inheritance: Urban China, 1949–1996." *American Journal of Sociology* 114 (5): 1395–1427. doi:10.1086/595949.

Wang, Zheng. 2014. "The Chinese Dream: Concept and Context." *Journal of Chinese Political Science* 19: 1–13. doi:10.1007/s11366-013-9272-0.

Wodak, Ruth. 1996. *Disorders of Discourse*. London: Longman.

Wu, Guoguang, 1994. "Command Communication: The Politics of Editorial Formulation in the People's Daily." *The China Quarterly* 137: 194–211. doi:10.1017/S0305741000034111.

Wu, Yiching. 2013. "How State Enumeration Spoiled Mao's Last Revolution." *Journal of Modern Chinese History* 7 (2): 200–217. doi:10.1080/17535654.2013.850867.

Xi, Jinping. 2013. *Zai di shier jie quanguo renmin daibiao dahui di yi ci huiyi shang de jianghua* [Speech at the first Plenary Session of the 12th National People's Assembly]. Accessed January 18, 2022. http://www.jxaevc.com/dang/ShowArticle.asp?ArticleID= 3260.

Xin, Chen. 2004. "Social changes and the revival of liberal education in China since the 1990s." *Asia Pacific Education Review* 5 (1): 1–13. doi:10.1007/BF03026274.

Xinhua. 2012. "Xi Pledges 'Great Renewal of Chinese Nation." *Xinhua*, 11 December. https://www.mfa.gov.cn/ce/cefj//eng/gdxw/t993967.htm.

Yang, Jingqing. 2008. "Professors, doctors, and lawyers. The variable wealth of the professional classes." In *The New Rich in China*, edited by David S.G. Goodman, 148–167. Abingdon and New York: Routledge, pp. 171–186.

Yeh, Wen-hsin. 1997. "Shanghai Modernity: Commerce and Culture in a Republican City." *The China Quarterly* 150: 375–394. doi:10.1017/S0305741000052528.

Yueh, Linda Y. 2004. "Wage Reforms in China during the 1990s." *Asian Economic Journal* 18 (2): 149–164. doi:10.1111/j.1467-8381.2004.00187.x.

Zanasi, Margherita. 2015. "Frugal Modernity: Livelihood and Consumption in Republican China." *The Journal of Asian Studies* 74 (2): 391–409. doi:10.1017/S0021911815000029.

Zang, Xiaowei. 2008. "Market Transition, Wealth, and Status Claims." In *The New Rich in China. Future Rulers, Present Lives*, edited by David S.G. Goodman, 53–70. Abingdon: Routledge.

Zavoretti, Roberta. 2017. *Rural Origins, City Lives. Class and Place in Contemporary China.* Seattle: University of Washington Press.

Zhang, Li. 2008. "Private Homes, Distinct Lifestyles: Performing a New Middle Class." In *Privatizing China: Socialism from Afar*, edited by Li Zhang and Aihwa Ong, 23–40. Ithaca, NY: Cornell University Press.

Zhao, Liang, Yu Dahua, and Li Hongna. 2020. "Psychological Preference of Consumer Behaviour in Late Qing Dynasty." *Revista Argentina de Clínica Psicológica* 29 (1): 1169. doi:10.24205/03276716.2020.167.

Zhao, Yuezhi. 2003. "Neo-liberal Globalization, the Dream for a Strong Nation, and Chinese Press Discourses on the WTO." In *Chinese Media, Global Contexts*, edited by Chin-Chuan Lee, 32–55. London: Routledge Curzon.

Zhao, Yuezhi. 2004. "The State, the Market, and Media Control in China." In *Who Owns the Media? Global Trends and Local Resistances*, edited by Pradip N. Thomas and Naharom Zaharom, 179–212. London: Southbound Sdn. Bhd.

Zhou, Xiaohong. 2005. "Zhongguo zhongchan jieceng de lishi yu xianzhuang" [The history and current situation of the Chinese middle class]. In *Zhongguo zhongchan jieceng diaocha* [*Survey of the Chinese middle class*], edited by Xiaohong Zhou. Beijing: Shehui kexue wenxian chubanshe.

2

THE INTELLECTUAL RECONFIGURATION

Definitions, ideology, and the hidden agenda

For over three decades, China's middle class has been the subject of much debate but little agreement. Class as structured inequality (related to capital possession), class as lifestyle (practices and representations of social identity), and class as political potential (*class for itself*) are all involved in the intellectual debate on the Chinese middle class that has emerged after reform in the PRC. However, in order to shed light on the middle class's formative process, it can be noted that for the most part intellectual debate has centred on two important issues. The first is definitional, and the second issue involves sociological articulations from an ontological approach over class in China today (Li 2010). Therefore, this chapter distinguishes the various criteria for defining "middle class" as a social construct created by discourse from two analytical approaches: the consideration of the Chinese middle class more as a dominant interpretation sponsored by political and economic elites through the articulation of identity and meaning in accordance with the new social imaginary that Chinese society is drawing; and the conceptualization of class as intellectual expressions in accordance with the diversity of thought and ideological commitments in China studies. Thus, the Chinese middle class becomes an underlying force of theoretical support for a profound reconfiguration of social relations in the post-reform era. As scholars both outside and inside China estimate the size of the middle class differently based on different criteria, and due to the dual perspective, that this study uses—class as a state-sponsored discourse and class as intellectual commitments—this chapter aims to identify the underlying forces in intellectual debates on class in China studies and estimate their legitimation in bringing about new imaginaries and representations in contemporary urban China.

Since there is scholarly controversy over which criteria should be used to determine who belongs to the Chinese middle class, it is "hard to estimate the size" of this group "in a definitive way and to clearly describe its characteristics"

DOI: 10.4324/9781003299301-3

(Li 2010, 152). It must be admitted, indeed, that is not an easy task to provide a definition of a concept "borrowed from Western research" that has for decades accumulated polysemies from many diverse theoretical perspectives and socio-political contexts. In the case of the Chinese middle class, moreover, one major obstacle to understanding the considerable variety of different perspectives is ter-minology. The terms that scholars use to refer to "class" and "classes" are rendered in several different ways in Chinese, of which two are most commonly used: *jieji*, a politically sensitive word that comes from the CCP's Marxist–Leninist ideology and is often translated as "class," and *jieceng*, which linguistically denotes "stratum" or "strata" (Goodman 2014, 4). Whereas class is generally "a major organizing concept" associated with the structures of production, distribution, and exchange in the transition to industrialism, status classifications are described as "when occupations are ranked according to their perceived levels of prestige or social standing" (Crompton 1998, 4, 11). It has also been noted that the Chinese terms for middle property stratum (*zhongchan jieceng*) and middle property class (*zhongchan jieji*) also include the concept of ownership (*chan*), which is consistent with a Marxist connotation on ownership of the means of production.

Further, China's authorities have long disliked the term "middle class" (*zhong-chan jieji*); they prefer the term "middle-income stratum" (*zhongdeng shouru jieceng*) for political reasons. This was because the term "middle class" had acquired ideo-logical connotations when it was referenced by liberal scholars during the 1980s, who thought the growth of the Chinese middle class would bring about political changes, in particular political democratization (Li 2010, 141). For this reason, some scholars speak of "classes," others of "strata," and still other of "groups." Consequently, as Guo (2008, 39) noted, the understanding of these categories, accompanied by contestation and conflation, is not simply a matter of academic concern but also one with implications related to the historical context and com-peting values, economic interests, theories, and ideological positions in China studies, as this chapter attempts further to illustrate.

In *The Making of the Chinese Middle Class*, Jean-Louis Rocca (2017) explained that although scholars, journalists, communist leaders, and the average Chinese middle incomer approach from different views the topic of the Chinese middle class, they all agree on several premises. Firstly, the middle class is the key to driving economic growth and investment; it is a force of modernization and sta-bility that limits the power of the rich and stimulates upward social mobility of the poor. It "acts as a buffer" between the political and economic elites and the sub-ordinate classes, "reducing the chances of conflict between the two and limiting social inequalities." Secondly, social imaginary of the Chinese middle class is characterized by the idea that "there is an embryonic middle class" and although it is still "too small" it is only a matter of time before it becomes "a 'real' middle class." Third, "there is an absolute need to build a real middle class" that will assume the role of an ideal class by promoting efficient and stable delivery of government provided by the Party-state, which should, in turn, extend its size and benefit all of society (3). However, it is here that the agreement ends.

Despite such consensus on the importance of the social, economic, and political role of the middle class in China today, differences in scholarly discussion revolve around the very definition of the Chinese middle class. Depending on the defining criteria used, the size and consumption capacity of the China middle class can vary significantly. Therefore, classificatory schemes produced by China studies provide a very accurate reflection of the diversity of thought of the intellectual world rather than a precise picture of the Chinese middle class. This involves that behind every definition of the Chinese middle class lies political, ideological, and/or economic interests. Particularly, the controversial questions in China's studies are: Who makes up the Chinese middle class? Which social groups should be included in the Chinese middle class? And from a methodological perspective, how can the Chinese middle class be identified?

First, Western-centred standards dominate scholarly inquiry on the identification of the Chinese middle class. In the case of the existence of the Chinese middle class, despite a few notable exceptions, Western scholars have been hesitant to acknowledge its existence, let alone explore its political implications (Cheng 2010a, 7). In response to this, Dickson (2016) argued that Cheng presumed that Chinese scholars offered more credible insights on Chinese politics and economy because they shared the same perspective on the "distinct socio-political" nature of the middle class, while foreign scholars held another, more "slow" or sceptical. In addition, the second problem with the assertion is that Cheng suggested that China could "only be understood in terms of its own history, and that the experience of other countries provides no insight into a country's political trajectory." However, "no country is totally unique," and comparative analysis of two countries "can still provide insight into why one option was adopted in one country and a different one in another country" (23). The above discussion indicates, as Mobo Gao (2018) suggested, not only the significance of how conceptual frameworks orientate one's selection of research agendas and empirical data, but also certain hegemonic positions in the process of narrativizing China.

Indeed, beyond the debate about the "fast ascendance amid slow acceptance" of the emergence of China's middle class, Cheng's criticism seems to express a sense of frustration and powerlessness among some Chinese intellectuals about the evidence that the West not only produces systems of classificatory schemes on the Chinese society but also is entitled to classify such a society. The West, Gao (2018) remarked, "has the right to knowledge and has the power and resources to produce knowledge about China-to construct China" nowadays (1). Other aspects, as Ming Dong Gu (2013) noticed, are the inadequate critical models used to explore Chinese realities and the need to raise some questions both about the location of the discourse and, therefore, its implications of power.

In the case of the topic of this book, the Chinese middle class, the point is to determine what phenomenon scholars both Western and Chinese seek to express by using the concept of the middle class, and why (Rocca 2017, 11), and through what social practices and representations this phenomenon manifests itself in Chinese urban society. Observational work and case study material on this phenomenon indicate that a post-industrial middle-class lifestyle emerged in the post-reform era (Goodman and Robinson 1996; Cartier 2008; Fan 2002; Sun 2008). In this context, the analysis of the intellectual debate in China studies presented here aims to give a signification or theoretical context to the formation of the Chinese middle class by evaluating conceptual frameworks, research agendas, and national and transnational interests after the second wave of reforms of the 1990s.

Having now set forth these brief considerations on the scope of the middle-class definitional debate, this chapter attempts further on to define the space in which the cluster of intellectual narratives about the paradigm of the Chinese middle class are generated in China studies, to review pertinent work on the debate concerning the standard criteria for defining the middle-class subject, and to comment upon its relevance to this research. Additionally, it necessarily implies discussing the framework of the sociological debate about social identity in China by taking into consideration its components and characteristics, surveying the discursive spaces that this debate has found to express itself, and identifying its hidden agenda and scope of influence. Such primary objectives should be coupled with the argument of research design for the study, in this case that the current academic categorization of the "Chinese middle class" reflects the diversity of thought in China studies; ideology and intellectual discourse have been considered essential to political life and policymaking since Deng launched the reform program in 1978; and "the socio-political context and contestation have added a complex ideological dimension to the description of social groupings and structures" in the PRC (Guo 2008, 39). Therefore, an understanding of these related issues is essential to contextualize the lifestyle of the post-reform middle class and how a new social construction of identity emerged in the PRC after the reforms of the 1990s.

2.1 The reconfiguration concept: the significance of the middle class's emergence in China studies

After the post-Mao interregnum (1976–1977), Deng Xiaoping assumed power and was determined to adopt a more market-oriented development strategy to legitimize the CCP's aspirations to continue exerting an ideological and moral guidance over the Chinese population. The radical egalitarianism and class struggle rhetoric carried out during the Mao-dominated era were progressively removed. The new ruling class aimed to rebuild the PRC's economy and society after the devastating Cultural Revolution (1966–1976) and install a stable class order. To do this, party officials embraced a technocratic agenda by recognizing the legitimacy of cultural capital, making intellectuals the prime target of party recruitment, and facilitating the convergence of political and intellectual elites (Andreas 2009, 234). After the market reforms launched in 1978 by Deng Xiaoping, other factors also played a key role in the emergence of new social relations and lifestyles such as the convergence of capital conversion, the implementation of structural policies, the Party's strategy for survival, and the first manifestations of openness and globalization, in particular after China's accession to the WTO.

In the process, economic and socio-political consequences of the reform and open-door policy led not only to economic growth, the active introduction of foreign capital and technology, management knowhow, and rising national incomes, but also to severe changes and greater social differentiation between urban and rural China. In this respect, while the socialist elite resumed the consolidation of their privileges under reform, despite "a temporary interruption" due to the Cultural Revolution (Walder and Hu 2009), new social practices and discourses emerged by producing and reproducing social inequalities and class distinctions. In fact, middle-class groups differed profoundly from one another in terms of the construction of social identity—such as occupation, spatial trajectories, and consumption patterns.

Under these conditions, the Chinese middle class became a mobile socio-economic construct that consisted of culturally fragmented and heterogeneous groups that, simultaneously, manifested a "semantic unity" and "coherent lifestyles" with a similar volume and composition of capital (Weininger 2005, 95). While bearing this complexity in mind, and in order to better review and evaluate the context of the narratives of middle class and the intellectual debate in China Studies surrounding this topic, this study distinguishes three waves, or phases, from the literature:

- The initial wave: from the mid-1980s to the mid-1990s
- The construction wave: from the mid-1990s to the mid-2000s
- The reconfigurational wave: from the mid-2000s to the COVID-19 pandemic

This chronological schema is based on the analysis conducted in 2009 by Li (2009b) using a database of major PRC academic journal and periodical articles with "middle class" in their titles from 1979 to 2007. The initial small wave of academic interest in the mid-1980s reflects discussion of the introduction of the household responsibility system, which basically decollectivized agriculture and allowed the emergence of town and village enterprises (TVEs), the reappearance of the notion of human quality (*suzhi*), and the emergence of the "Market transition theory." The second wave, in the mid-1990s, manifests the construction period of the paradigm of the Chinese middle class, "the age of the middle class" (Xu 2002). Sociological research went beyond the classical Marxist approach on class analysis and started focusing on the historical experience of Western societies to formulate a normative discourse on the Chinese middle class. This construction wave ended by the mid-2000s with both the publication of Zhou's characterization of China middle class as the consumer avant-garde but political rear guard (*xiaofei qianwei, zhengzhi houwei*) and with the starting point of an increasing number of scholarly publications focused on various subjective aspects of the post-reform middle class. Finally, the third wave, the most recent and largest, is indicative of this "surge in multifaceted research" in the mid-2000s, attempting to approach the subject in an epochal change of worldviews in the midst of global crises, climate emergences, and reconfigurations of old certainties and new aspirations, which culminated with the COVID-19 pandemic. Then, this three-phase schema is further developed to illustrate chronologically the intellectual debate about the PRC's middle class and to understand structural uniformities of the formation of social identity in contemporary urban China.

The initial wave: from the mid-1980s to the mid-1990s

According to the content analysis on journal articles with "middle class" in their titles conducted by Li (2009b), the Chinese academia started the discussion of this social group in the mid-1980s. At that time there was no mention of a proper Chinese middle class or of a class narrative of social change in sociology journals. This initial small wave of scholarly interest was focused on the first socioeconomic manifestations of market economy, that is, the emergence of rural industrialists in TVEs. Cheng (2010a) noted that "the term middle class was rarely used during the first four decades of the PRC," it "remained foreign to the Chinese" (7). It was only later when the CCP changed its policy to permit private entrepreneurship in 1977 that the term "middle class" began to appear in Chinese academic journals and periodicals. At the time, Zang (2008) argued, "the state economy was greatly weakened during the Cultural Revolution of 1966–1976 and this problem was compounded with the return to the cities of nearly 18 million 'educated youth' whom the CCP had sent to rural areas during the Cultural Revolution." The Chinese government "modified its policy toward private business to create a new labour market for urban unemployed youth" (62), and thus maintain social stability and legitimize the CCP as the sole ruling party in the PRC.

In the early 1980s, underprivileged and uneducated people such as rural peasants, ex-criminals, and workers with a non-skilled and low-paid jobs "took advantage of this policy change since they could not otherwise find a better job elsewhere in the cities" (Gold 1990, 157–178) and, unexpectedly, "became the backbone of a small or 'individual business' sector (*getihu*)." However, they were "marginalized because of their humble origins, poor educational attainment," and "because they often relied on trade speculation in making profits" (Zang 2008, 62). Many of the emergent rural industrialists—owners of TVEs in rural areas—and the private entrepreneurs—newcomers to the Chinese cities—came from this social group. According to the PRC's sociologists, these rural industrialists and urban entrepreneurs were not a proper "middle class" in large part because these "individual businesses" "came from an uneducated group, the so-called 'new rich', both *baofahu* or *tuhao* in Chinese" (Cheng 2010a, 8). During the 1980s, though, less than 1 per cent of the national population and 11 per cent of the urban population of 18-year-olds were higher education graduates (Li 2010, 139). Therefore, some Chinese scholars considered such individual businesses with humble origins and little cultural capital in a derogatory way, as if they lacked the disposition and "human quality" necessary to become competent middle-class individuals.

However, the emergence of private entrepreneurs and the implementation of market reforms in the PRC was compared by a substantial body of research to the

Eastern European experience, especially the post-communist transition of Poland and Hungary that also had taken place during the 1980s. In particular, the "Market transition theory" (Nee 1989, 1991, 1996) contended that the post-socialist transition in the PRC was a simultaneous process of "transfer of power favouring direct producers," on the one hand, and "the decline in the value of political capital," on the other (Nee 1989, 666, 671). As a result of this transition from state socialist redistribution to markets, "the value of education" would increase and ultimately cultural capital would have "a positive effect on household income in a marketlike economy" and facilitate the emergence of a Chinese bourgeoisie as a factor of "changes in power" (Nee 1989, 674, 667). Although the Market transition theory focused on the interactions between the political and economic elites, it has largely influenced research on the impacts of market reforms on political economy and social change. Such studies are often in line with some approaches proposed by Modernization theorists (see Section 2.2).

Significantly, a further indication of the nature of initiation over this period is the reappearance of the notion of "human quality" (*suzhi*). While Goodman (2014) set the origin of *suzhi* with state campaigns to introduce birth control (in the 1970s) and then education reform (1980s), Anagnost (2004) highlighted that "the discourse of population quality (*renkou suzhi*) may have first appeared in the 1980s, in state documents investigating rural poverty that attributed China's failure to modernize to the 'low quality' (*suzhi dī*) of its population, especially in rural areas" (190). As noted earlier, as economic reforms stimulated privatization and dismantled the institutions of state socialism, what is clear is that the idea of *suzhi* was added to the paradigm of the Chinese middle class as hegemonic model of excellence.

In the earlier socialist state, the official discourse of the CCP reconfigured and appealed to traditional concepts such as *suzhi* and *harmony* to "ground essential elements of its political line" (Solé-Farràs 2014, 221). Similarly, Anagnost (2004) highlighted, as a concept taken from Chinese cultural tradition and integrated into CCP's ideology, *suzhi* re-emerged in the post-reform era as a representation of the "in state policy focus from regulating births to raising the quality of the population as a whole; in other words, a shift from quantity to quality." The intellectual context of the initial wave of scholarly debate of middle class "has been extended from a discourse of backwardness and development," that is, the quality of the masses and, in particular the migrant workers, "to encompass the minute social distinctions defining a 'person of quality' in practices of consumption and the incitement of a middle-class desire for social mobility" (190). As manifestations of "abject bodies" in urban contexts, as Judith Butler (1993) would name it, migrant workers embodied the social imaginary of low-*suzhi* entities (Jacka 2009). As a result, mainstream perspectives in China studies considered that practices of high *suzhi* not only reflected the ideal of middle-class living but also legitimized the privileged position of the middle class as "people of quality" and their social distinctions in urban contexts. However, the validity of the rhetoric of *suzhi* to explain social inequality is only effective if it goes hand in hand with other categorizations such as gender, ethnicity, sexuality, or the aforementioned class background of migrant workers.

With "reform and openness" during the 1980s, the notion of *suzhi* introduced "a sense and sensibility of the self's value in the market economy" by compelling "a conception of the human subject as lacking, in need of constant readjustment, supplementation, and continual retraining" (*zhongsheng xuexi*)" (Yan 2003, 511). It reduced the heterogeneity of human beings and the ephemeralness of rhetorical narratives such as harmony, civility, and modernity by coding their value and capitalization for "'progress." In this regard, *suzhi* is closely akin to the concept of coloniality as a constitutive and specific element of the world pattern of capitalist power (Quijano 2014). On that basis, the paradigm of *suzhi* enables persons of superior human quality—that is, privileged citizens—to distance themselves from those whom they deem inferior through practices of distinction, and thus place individuals "in a specific position in the civilization ladder of Chinese society" (Tomba 2014, 85).

Consequently, *suzhi* soon became the hegemonic pattern of excellence with a central role in contemporary processes of citizenship, simultaneously contributing to justification and understandings of the responsibilities, obligations, privileges, disadvantages, and rights that connect members of Chinese society to the state (Jacka 2009, 524). The attainment of the middle-class/high-*suzhi* ideal is presented as a natural desire to excel in competition and consumption (Zavoretti 2017, 44), becoming a part of contemporary public culture. In the end, this conceptualization forces the ethics of market through the acquisition of various middle-class goods, leisure activities, and services, and the emergence of social representations in a variety of popular, as well as official, discourses in urban China today.

To return to our analysis on the initial small wave of scholarly focused on the Chinese middle class, it was after the Tiananmen Incident of 1989 and the resumption of the open-door policy that the interest in the middle class emerged in China studies. Two factors, Cheng (2010a) noted, had been particularly instrumental in increasing both public awareness of and scholarly interest in the middle class: "the Chinese business community's drive to promote the image of Chinese consumers as potentially the 'world's largest middle-class market'," and the Chinese government's decision to "enlarge the size of the middle-income group" (8) as part of the Party-state's legitimization strategy. Certainly, in the wake of the events of 1989 "the days of the CCP seemed numbered, many China watchers predicted the imminent downfall of the Party" (Dickson 2016, 1). But they were wrong. The CCP's strategy for survival included "a combination of repression, legitimation and co-optation of new elites into the Party" (Dickson 2016, 7). As noted in Chapter 1, the Party-state shifted its political agenda from class struggle—based on the empowerment of the state socialist working class—to economic modernization—with the middle class as the ideal actor on the social stage.

Overall, the re-emergence of rhetorical tools like the concept of *suzhi* shows how intellectual discourse matters, and how deeply the Party-state's agenda as well as the role of the Chinese academia and intellectuals, and the internalizing everyday practices of Chinese society are interrelated in the post-reform era. In the case of the Chinese middle class, only since the mid-1990s has research on this topic started its way into China's intellectual mainstream, while it has featured widely in public debate. Furthermore, to the extent that Chinese sociologists might also be seen as a part of the middle class, it is argued that the relationship to and identification with the subject of the research by its researchers is problematic when considered in any post-repression context such as the Tiananmen Incident of 1989. However, the initial concern of the construction wave was to gauge and document the shifting stratification order that involved China's accession to the World Trade Organization (WTO) in 2001—described by former President Hu Jintao as a "milestone in China's reform and opening-up and socialist modernization drive" (WTO 2011).

The construction wave: from the mid-1990s to the mid-2000s

Starting in the mid-1990s, the construction wave represents the construction period of a state-sponsored discourse on the middle class in the PRC. The discourse construction commenced with "an uptick of interest in the middle classes of foreign countries" and "the surge of multifaceted research" on this emerging class (Cheng 2010b, 58–59). Although such a surge of research began in this second wave, it was not until the beginning of the third wave in the mid-2000s that a growing number of scholarly studies began to focus on subjective criteria without completely abandoning objective approaches—including size, composition, rate of expansion, and characteristics such as income, consumption patterns, cultural norms, and political attitudes (Li 2009b). The publication in 2005 of Zhou Xiaohong's characterization of China's middle class as "the consumer avant-garde but political rear guard" (*xiaofei qianwei, zhengzhi houwei*) marked also the end of the construction wave as this section attempts further to illustrate.

After the Tiananmen incident, the Party "shifted its recruitment strategy" as a consequence of its need to survival by replacing "the officials appointed in the Maoist era who had more ideological zeal than practical skills" (Dickson 2016, 13–14). To recruit the right members according to the new ideological and economic goal, the CCP leaders were aware that they first had to know the candidates in depth and the type of social stratification they would have to face in the future. That is why, in the mid-1990s, most of sociological research was directly sponsored by official organizations. This showed how Deng and his successors, like the 19th century self-strengtheners, regarded intellectuals as essential to achieve their project of modernization invested in the nation as a whole (Li 2015, 4). In particular, the CCP leaders encouraged scholars to do research on the issue of middle class, starting with the Western middle class.

In the process, a strategic plan to build up a breakthrough in quality higher education began to be implemented in the mid-1990s by adopting the policy of decentralization—massification of higher education—and marketization—development of world-class universities (Ngok 2008). The interest in making education better served the CCP's strategy for survival and, of course, China's economic development and modernization. However, university teachers were dissatisfied. Compared to others with similar social and educational backgrounds, Goodman (2014) noted, their total remuneration was lower because of the much larger bonuses given to employees in other sectors, and many were forced to take second jobs. In the wake of the events of the Tiananmen incident in 1989, due to the involvement of both students and academic staff in leadership roles, "the government moved to improve salaries and conditions for university teachers" and, as a result, "a new relationship with the Party-state was established, particularly during the late 1990s when university staff, as members of the state sector, were privileged through the processes of housing reform" (157). Of course, one could easily point to the importance of Party-state in "social engineering," a concept defined by Tomba (2014, 89) as the specific policies and practices through which the state selectively promoted the creation of a middle class such as housing, neighbourhoods, and, in this case, research sponsorship. However, in view of the new dynamics in the process of social engineering, the question here is: who was the social engineer? In other words, who made the Chinese middle class?

In the 1950s, social sciences were prohibited for the sake of the historical materialism as the only legitimate discipline in the PRC. Nevertheless, as Cheng (2010b) argued, most of the Chinese scholars who conducted research on the middle class in the 1990s were sociologists who were raised in the 1950s and 1960s—namely Li Chunling, Li Lulu, Li Peilin, Li Qiang, Li Youmei, Liu Xin, Lu Hanlong, Lu Xueyi, Sun Liping, Zhou Xiaohong, and Zhu Guanglei. At the end of the last century, sociological research may have reflected the fact that political controls remained in place over certain academic disciplines (59). Most of the influential Chinese scholars working on this subject were "sent-down youths" who were forced to spend many years in the countryside during the Cultural Revolution. When they returned to the cities, all the scholars belonging to the first generation of Chinese sociologists spent time abroad—mainly in Western countries and Japan—as visiting scholars or degree candidates. The time they spent studying at academic institutions abroad "served to familiarize them with Western social science's cutting-edge theories" and methodologies and introduced them accurately to the Chinese audience (62). Further, after the reform and opening, Chinese society provided a sociological field study for Chinese scholars for both discussing the dynamic changes of social stratification and creating opportunities for proving their work value to society. This involved that, from the end of the 1980s, the PRC's sociologists searched for prestige and political influence—that is, symbolic and economic capital.

Consequently, the increasing number of studies on the emergence of a middle class and social change in China went hand in hand with the growing influence of Chinese sociologists on the intellectual and official discourse. Clearly, Cheng (2010b) also noted, their academic pursuits became indispensable as a source of information for both the Chinese government and the public (59). And in the end, their influence on the decision-making process and public debate was real. In addition, Rocca (2017) pointed out that this "generational phenomenon" explains the technocratic ideology, the influence of the Anglo-Saxon academic community and the modernizing vision behind the concept and the scholarly studies of Chinese middle class conducted from the second wave on. Thus, as early as the end of the 1990s and the beginning of the 2000s, the debate about the middle class, its composition, and its role in social, politic, and economic change in the PRC was then a matter of scientific knowledge.

Simultaneously, many scholars focusing on the "Western experience" and the role of middle class in the emergence of democratization processes referred to Modernization theorists, in particular Moore, Huntington, and Lipset. From the postcolonial perspective, the Western experience and Modernization theory approach to analyse social change in the PRC can be considered as an example of Eurocentrism and "coloniality of power." However, among PRC scholars, the "Lipset thesis," named for social scientist Seymour Martin Lipset (1922–2006), which holds that democracy is more likely in well-off countries than in poorer ones, was stood on its head (Reilly 2013). As Cheng (2010a) highlighted, Lipset (and also Huntington) recognized the importance of the middle class in democratic stability, which they attribute to moderate and institutionalized class conflict rather than more radical and potentially violent conflicts (19–20).

For Lipset, Nathan (2016) pointed out, economic growth and democracy are directly related, and argued that economic development would enlarge the middle class who, eventually, would support political change and democratization (5). Based on this theory, a long-standing Western maxim stressing the vital role of the middle class in democracy has postulated that there was a dynamic correlation, or even a causal relationship, between the expansion of the middle class and political democratization (19) and the mirage of "progress" in the social imaginary. As a result, many Western and Chinese second-wave scholars and some Market transition theorists predicted that the Chinese middle class, as it grew, would exert more pressure for liberalization and political change (8). Concurrently, the discourse on modernization, together with the introduction of the capitalist paradigms of competition, confrontation, exclusion, and monetary hierarchization during the second wave of market reforms in the 1990s framed not only the wider changes in Chinese society as a movement to more equality, democracy, and self-fulfilment, but also the new social asymmetries and gendered aspects of everyday relationships (Hird 2009). In any case, at the beginning of the 21st century, the common question in China studies was: is democratization a prerequisite for China's economic growth?

Answering this question would thus require an analysis of the idea of the Chinese middle-class subject as the harbinger of democracy and political participation. For this reason, Chinese scholars, including those who have close ties to the political establishment, have also paid close attention to the political attitudes of China's middle-class individuals. However, Li (2015) noted that since the 1990s witnessed the increasing differentiation of the Chinese intelligentsia into two major schools of thought, namely, New Leftism and liberalism, migrant peasants and laid-off workers have become natural allies in the New Left's struggle against prevalent neoliberal practice in the name of market efficiency and globalization. Meanwhile, the liberals have maintained that the free market would in the long run support the growth and the rise of the Chinese middle class and its access to political power (116–126) and, in the end, such a growing middle class would help the spread of liberalism (28). Overall, from the mid-1990s, the dominant view within the PRC's scholarly circles, both liberals and the New Left camps, was that because the middle class had often been considered a privileged ally of the regime, it was an unlikely agent of democratic change.

As time went by, an increasing number of Chinese scholars began to rethink the political role of the middle class and wonder if "yesterday's political target could be today's political ally, so too could today's political ally become tomorrow's political rabble-rouser" (Cheng 2010b, 72). At the same time, outside China, the large number of foreign scholars who supported modernization theories emphasized, from various analytical angles, the statement that a new class of highly educated, civilized, urban-based citizens was a precondition for an eventual transition to democracy in the PRC. What is clear, nevertheless, is that democracy building was the most important debate in the field of China's studies in the first decade of the 21st century.

In summary, as early as the end of the 1990s and the beginning of the 2000s, both democratization and the establishment of capitalism—the two key commandments of the Modernization theory—were identified with the emergence of an urban middle class by those attempting to understand the transformation of the PRC's political economy. Although at the beginning of the 2000s, democratization theorists contended that the middle class was potentially able to bring democracy to China, a few years later it was clear that their optimism did not last long (Rocca 2017, 173, 78). Such disappointment among many Chinese and foreign scholars, in conjunction with the publication of Zhou Xiaohong's two books in 2005 and the surge of research on the Chinese middle class from a variety of defining aspects, marked the end of the second wave.

Indeed, in *Zhongguo zhongchan jieceng diaocha* [Survey of the Chinese Middle Strata], Zhou (2005) underscored the notion that the PRC's middle class lacked shared core values. In this approach, the Chinese middle class was not about politics or democratization change, and so not a social structure in the way that classes had previously been understood (class as a social group with a shared class consciousness). Zhou's characterization of China's middle class as the consumer avant-garde but political rear guard (*xiaofei qianwei, zhengzhi houwei*) indicated the loss of confidence in the ability of the "emerged middle incomers" to act politically as a "real" middle class. In parallel to this, both Western and Chinese sociologists categorized middle-class subjects by employing an increasing variety of objective and subjective criteria, and the differences in scholarly discussion centred on how these criteria principles lead to identification of the constituents of this social group.

The reconfigurational wave: from the mid-2000s to the COVID-19 pandemic

The third wave is indicative of the development in multifaceted research on various aspects of the middle class that had already emerged in the construction wave.

It reflects both the complexity that the middle class is gaining in the process of social formation in China, and the need to understand the transformations of modern society in which the old certainties are falling away and something new is trying to emerge in a world that is metamorphosing (Beck 2016). Since market reforms, the PRC has experienced a radical transformative path that the Global Financial Crisis of 2007/08 and the COVID-19 pandemic have accelerated. Such dominant perception appeals to grasp this metamorphosis of the world as a necessary approach to understand the turmoil of the present. Therefore, in this new social space, class is not a homogenous concept anymore. Rather, in global societies with transnational relations and mobile lifestyles, class is a constantly reconfigurational phenomenon with practitioners and representations but without a neutral and "static" definition. However, class needs to be reconfigured and made visible precisely to understand the multiple dimensions of the new social relations.

In the case of the PRC, class analysis evidence heterogeneity rather than homogeneity in the lifestyles emerged in the post-reform era. However, capital possession is still a decisive factor in identifying class grouping. Indeed, as Guo (2008) explained, the "middle class" is not so much a uniform, homogeneous, and unproblematic concept, rather it is "a hodgepodge of intermediate groups, an embodiment of desirable values," and a shorthand for "the mainstream of a harmonious well-off society, or new master of the country in place of the working class" (39). From this perspective, in order to understand the complex reconfiguration of the old certainties in a metamorphosing world, an increasing number of studies use objective approaches (income, educational attainment, newspapers articles, level of consumption, constitutional amendments, occupation, official statements, etc.) combined with subjective sources of information (interviews, observations of individual practices).

In any case, the political attitudes of the Chinese middle class in the public sphere were still an important topic of concern in China studies at the start of the reconfigurational wave. For instance, Zhou and Chen (2010) noted that the organizational actions of this group target issues of group interest concerning specific actors rather than the fundamental problems in politics and social life such as corruption, political representation, censorship, and authoritarianism (102). In fact, a common example of the middle classes acting in defence of their own group interest is housing quality through the homeowners' movements (Zou 2005; Cai 2005; Chen 2009; Rocca 2013; Zhang Lei 2005). In line with Zhou's (2005) assumption that the Chinese middle class is a consumption avant-garde but a political rear guard, Jie Chen's (2013) *A Middle Class without Democracy* analysed the attitudinal and behavioural orientation of the PRC's middle class to democracy and democratization and indicated that this social grouping was keen to protect their individual rights but reluctant to exercise collective action to challenge the state. However, Chen is not alone in having no hope for the appearance of a "real" middle class in the near future; a significant number of sociologists continue to deny any class consciousness to China's middle class (Shen 2010; Cheng 2010b; Zhou 2008, 110–126; Lu 2010).

Simultaneously, an increasing number of scholars believe that the growing number of NGOs and social organizations in the country would also foster greater middle-class consciousness (Chen 2013; Zhang Wei 2004; Zhang Lei 2005; Zhang Wei 2005; Pan and Ma 2008). For instance, many social scientists believe that the emerging homeowners' movement could give birth to a unified collective agency for democratization in the PRC. However, there is considerable evidence to suggest that despite the increase in associationism in urban China, it tends to create consensual arenas of interaction with the state that avoid confrontation. Postcolonial approaches of civil society in China, such as Salmenkari's (2012), have questioned the definition of civil society "through its alleged autonomy from the state" and have paid attention to the "horizontal linkages among various social actors to constitute a civil society in China."

In this book, civil society is understood as "the set of activities carried out by society outside of the initiatives proposed by the political parties and the state" by mediating "between established powers and citizens, being a kind a regulatory mechanism that corrects the drift of political life in democratic countries and defends citizens' political interests in those which are not" (Sáiz 2015, 8). As the phenomenon of homeowners' movement has unfolded, many scholars have become less optimistic about the capacity of the current middle class to change (politically) China. The fact that fewer papers have been published on the middle class's political attitudes since the end of the 2000s signals a decline of the intellectual debate about this issue.

Consequently, social scientists and intellectuals started to engage in serious academic and private research on micro and macrostructural relationships and the topic of the "real class," e.g., the interrelationships with the division of labour, social stratification, and social mobility. Those studies have contributed to the public and intellectual debate in two ways. On the one hand, Rocca (2017) pointed out that many Western and Chinese scholars shifted their emphasis away from the role of the "anesthetized" middle class in politics and they started using more objective criteria "easily presented in nice graphs and scientific discourse" to try to identify this grouping (4). Chinese state agencies produced income-based studies to identify the middle class as part of their objective to "stimulate domestic demand" (55). Additionally, experts working for international organizations such as the Asian Development Bank or the World Bank, and for multinational corporations and consulting firms and investment banks such as McKinsey or BPN Paribas Peregrine also tried to measure the Chinese middle-class phenomenon and published comprehensive objective and quantitative data-rich studies.

On the other hand, multifaceted research on various aspects of the middle class based on qualitative data, or a compound of qualitative and quantitative data, started in the second wave and proliferated in the reconfigurational wave. It denoted an attempt to gauge, on the one hand, "the inner experience of the Chinese people" and how they have interiorized rapid social changes considering micro-level results of the macro-level changes, "while providing on the other hand a natural and unique window to contemporary Chinese social changes"

(Zhou 2017). Many notable examples include Amy Hanser's (2008) empirical work on the new construction of "structures of entitlement"—which make middle class and elite groups feel more entitled to public forms of respect and social esteem in settings like luxury department stores; the essays assembled by Zhang and Ong (2008) in *Privatizing China* whose ethnographic fieldwork comprised practices in China everyday life as a novel mix of neoliberal and socialist elements, of individual choices and state objectives; and Chen and Fan's (2015) study on the divergence between subjective and objective status using regression analyses from 10 waves of nationally representative surveys from 2003 to 2012.

Additionally, authoritative work that reviewed the many competing claims in scholarship has also been completed by several works: Tang's (2018) *China's Housing Middle Class*, Tomba's (2014) *The Government Next Door*, and Rocca (2017) with his inspiring book *The Making of the Chinese Middle Class*. Interestingly, Deborah Davis's (1992, 2000, 2014) works on social stratification and state interventionism, Gerth's (2020) *Unending Capitalism*, and Andreas's (2009) *Rise of the Red Engineers* have challenged the conventional mainstream perspective concerning the PRC's political history, which often continues to be exclusively associated with the masculine construal of power of one person, Mao Zedong. Without doubt, He's (2000) assessment of class reproduction in the 1990s shed light on the understanding of class as a process of intergenerational transfer of capital in the post-reform era.

Remarkably, Lu's (2010) proposal to replace the notion of "middle class" with the pragmatic notion of "small prosperity" (*xiaokang*) or "moderately prosperous society" (*xiaokang shehui*) represents a substantial and reflexive study because this concept falls within the traditional notion of "moderation" (*zhongyong*), a core value for the middle-class conceptualization. As Cheng (2010a) highlighted, the notion of *xiaokang* helps us to understand "the cultural and ideological foundation for China's transition to a market economy in the reform era" and "also because it has been used to justify the state's major policy drive to expand the middle class" (23). After Deng Xiaoping launched a reform program in the 1980s, Lu (2010) argued, China began to transform from the communist goal of establishing a utopian *datong* (commonwealth) society, where everything belongs to the public and everyone shares social resources and wealth, to the pragmatic approach of building a *xiaokong* (moderate prosperous) society—where all members and their families own their private resources and live a life based on law and governed by elites. *Datong* in its classic traditional sense is an ideal society and *xiaokang*, on the other hand, is a realistic and competitive society (108, 111). Consequently, it is essential that ancient and cultural factors such as *xiaokang* be considered in order to study China's social structure and middle class.

Furthermore, Ann Anagnost's (2004, 2008) analyses on China's middle-class values, and David S. G. Goodman's seminal book *Class in Contemporary China* (2014) and edited book *The New Rich in China* (2008) are outstanding contributions to knowledge about class formation in the PRC. Goodman considered that the idea of middle class promoted by the Party-state "is more a discourse than a social structure" (93). Such conceptualization agreed with Anagnost (2008), who stated the task of the middle class was "inciting aspiring individuals no matter their social status to adhere to new social norms of middle-class identity often defined around consumer practices" (498). To solve these issues, many investigations added education, income, and consumption as the decisive criteria to distinguish the middle class from other classes. Such approaches showed that a multifaceted perspective is the most efficient sociological tool to approach class analysis in China today. Therefore, to understand the fragmentation approaches and heterogeneity criteria within the intellectual debate about the Chinese middle class, the different definitions used must be analysed considering historical context and the controversial question about this issue, that is, what is the operational definition of middle class?

2.2 Definitions and compositions

The individuals and groups in present-day China who belong to the middle class are often just situated literally in the middle in terms of income, education, and occupation. Yet, this numerical definition may be too narrow and not sociologically rigorous (Hsiao 2010, 256). In fact, as noted earlier, the understanding of class in China varies with the observer, and this too is a marker of the social and political change that has emerged with reform since 1978 (Goodman 2014, 5; Li 2010, 55). Western and Chinese scholars have employed a wide variety of objective and subjective criteria for defining the Chinese middle class which reflect not only divergent and conflicting approaches to assessing those criteria, but also their political preferences and the key propositions of different schools of thought in China studies. Usually, as Li Chunling (2010), from the Chinese Academy of Social Sciences (CASS) Institute of Sociology pointed out, four criteria were used to define the middle class in China: income, occupation, education, and consumption. A member of the middle class thus should be a person holding a professional or managerial job with relatively high and stable income, have received a higher education and be able to afford a comfortable lifestyle with a relatively high standard of living.

These four criteria are inherently linked to cumulative factors that situate historically the emergence of a post-industrial lifestyle related to consumption rather than production in the PRC. Therefore, these cumulative factors have been associated with the middle-income group in contemporary urban China. They include the socio-political, economic, cultural, and historic events that converged in a very short period, from the middle of the 1990s to the end of the 2000s, in the PRC. In particular, the factors identified in the process of the "middlization" of the urban society in China are: globalization, after the integration with the world economy and China's accession to the WTO; income growth; the rapid socio-economic development and the advancement of communication technologies; urban deindustrialization; the production and reproduction of a state-sponsored discourse on the middle class; the capitalist paradigms of competition, confrontation, exclusion, and monetary hierarchization introduced by market forces; the desire to civilize China; new "classification struggles" over the new social distinctions in the post-reform era; new institutional arrangements and policy interventions in different national and urban contexts; labour migration; the expectations placed on the Chinese middle class to change the political system; the CCP's strategy for survival; and the reconfiguration and subsequent collusion of socialist legacies and cultural Chinese traditions. It may be convenient to analyse China's middle-class definitions and compositions in this way, by linking Li's (2010) four criteria and these cumulative factors.

Concerning urbanization, and economic and income growth, many scholars consider that stable-and-fast economic growth and the increase in income from the middle of the 1990s to the end of the 2000s were intrinsically associated with the emergence of China's middle class. However, it should be remembered that the so-called "objective criteria" based on income and capital accumulation is difficult to measure in China as grey income and black income—both at home and abroad—are difficult to define and consider; they are not observed by official statistics in the PRC. Despite the fast income growth over the last four decades in Chinese households (per capita income grew more than eightfold in the last 40 years), income inequality between urban and rural per capita family income is still determinant (Li 2010; NBSC 2001, 2018). The vast income disparity between urban and rural households in 1978 has been confirmed for over four decades.

According to *China Statistical Yearbook 2018*, an annual national household survey prepared and provided by the Ministry of Civil Affairs, the difference between the family income in urban households (343.4 yuan) and rural areas (134 yuan) was 209.4 yuan in 1978; nearly 40 years after, in 2017, the difference between the family income in urban households (36,396 yuan) and rural areas (13,432 yuan) was 22,964 yuan (NBSC 2018). In other words, in 1978 the difference between per capita family income for urban and rural areas was more than twice (64 per cent), and by 2017 it had increased to 67.5 per cent (NBSC 2018). The difference between urban and rural per capita family income has only increased 3.5 per cent, but urban income is still more than double the average of the rural income.

Although GDP is not an objective parameter, rather it is "a completely arbitrary measure" (Castells 2017, 69), most of the investigations based on "objective criteria" have been using GDP for identifying the middle class in China studies. Therefore, this section does not adopt GDP as an objective parameter, but it uses GDP as an additional statistical variable, along with urban and rural income, for identifying some variables that affected the narrative of the PRC's economic growth to a greater or lesser extent. On that basis, in 1978 China's GDP was only 364.5 billion Chinese yuan, but it reached 82,712.1 billion yuan by 2017, nearly 230 times the 1978 figure. Although the Chinese economy growth rate in 2019 was the weakest since the first quarter of 1992, the average annual economic growth over 40 years (1978–2018) was 9.5 per cent and overtook the US to become the world's largest economy according to the purchasing power parity measure in 2014 (Fan, Ma, and Wang 2019, 8).

China's rapid GDP growth lifted hundreds of millions of Chinese from poverty, but "the improvement of people's living standards owed more to increased nonagricultural employment than to higher wages" (Garnaut, Song, and Fang 2018, 17). In any case, strong employment growth in urban areas, due to rapid economic growth and urbanization, has been a characteristic feature in the consolidation of the PRC's 40 years of marketization.

Also, by the 1990s, as mentioned earlier, recruitment quotas for state enterprises were abolished and firms were largely allowed to choose their employees, which was a drastic change from the official policy of full employment (Yueh 2004, 150). In this way, the increased income inequality between urban and rural families since 1978 can mainly be explained by coding the precarization of urban farmers' wages in the urban contexts as rural income. However, precarization is not a phenomenon exclusive to the rural context. According to Guy Standing (2017), the emergence of the post-reform middle class goes hand in hand with the emerging precariat consisting of largely urbanized youth, who have neither a rural economy background and trajectory into the precariat nor the proletarian background (167). Certainly, many "young educated urban dwellers scurry between short-term income-earning activities and rely on friends and relatives to survive" (169). Hence, the growth of the PRC's middle class is also part of this dual process of an increasing urban–rural income gap, on the one hand, and an increasing urban population composed of rural *hukou* holders, new urban *hukou* holders, and urban precariat, on the other.

Furthermore, by 1978 there were only 193 cities in China; in 2019 the number had increased to 66,258. Considering the urbanization of China during the reform era, the urban population increased steadily between 1978 and 2017. It rose from 173 million in 1978 to 813 million in 2017. As a result of the socio-economic changes since the 1990s, the Chinese population is not rural anymore. The size of the middle class boomed with the increasing urbanization, especially since 2011 through reforms by the government in China, whereas the middle class was barely visible (4 per cent of urban households) about 15 years ago (Davison 2014; Miles 2014; Kardes 2016, 708). Today, about 42 per cent of the PRC's population lives in rural areas with disadvantageous living conditions, and low incomes and educational levels.

In addition, the analysis of the IMF Working Paper on Inequality in China (Jain-Chandra et al. 2018) found that China has seen a sharp reduction of poverty since 2010—the current rural poverty standard is 2,300 yuan (in 2010's constant prices) per person, according to NBSC—but also a substantial increase of inequality—"income inequality increased since the early 1980s but recently experienced a levelling-off and modest decline" (Jain-Chandra et al. 2018, 3, 5). In considering the Gini coefficient, the PRC has moved from relative equality (20 in 1978) and moderate inequality (32.2 in 1990) to become "one of the most unequal countries" (46.8 in 2018) (Goodman 2014, 45; Jain-Chandra et al. 2018, 4). The fact that "China has seen a sharp reduction of poverty" but has become "one of the most unequal countries" might be directly related to the argument mentioned above on income inequality between urban and rural families.

Remarkably, despite earlier disagreements, social scientists both outside and inside China appeared to have generally agreed on the understanding of the social phenomenon of the Chinese middle class as a process of urbanization and income inequalities rather than solely in terms of occupation and stratification drawn from Modernization theories and the historical experience elsewhere. As shown by Hart-Landsberg and Burkett (2004), the Chinese case is witness to the polarization model—growth leads inevitably to stark social inequality—in Marx's *Capital* which postulates that the antagonism between capital and labour in production is basic to understanding the historical development of capitalism and its simplification of class antagonism with two great classes directly facing each other.

Hence, social scientists in the reconfigurational wave believed that "the concept of a middle-class stratum defined by income alone differs essentially from the concept of a middle class" because "that such an income group includes diverse people," for whom it is impossible to develop a shared social identity and lifestyle (Li 2010, 142). Indeed, more and more researchers have evaluated social relations among new elites and new social groupings (including a small but comfortable salaried middle class, small-scale private entrepreneurs, migrant workers, and the emerging Chinese precariat) to understand how cultural distinctions and social inequalities are produced, reproduced, and legitimated in the daily life of Chinese society (Hanser 2008; Zavoretti 2017). That is why consumption practices, indigenous concepts, placement in the occupational structure, and educational attainment and family educational patterns were usual criteria to define this diverse group of people in the reconfigurational wave (Hong and Zhao 2015; Sun and Zhang 2014; Zhang 2020). However, the differences in scholarly discussion centre now on which professional groups should be included as elements of the middle class and, in particular private entrepreneurs.

The rationale for the most used occupational coding among sociologists has been derived from the traditional model developed by neo-Marxist and neo-Weberian theorists based on the divisions between manual labour/employees and mental labour/employers (Li 2009a, 54–58), as well as those between white-collar workers and blue-collar workers (Zhou 2005). For example, *Research Report on Social Strata in Contemporary China*, edited by Lu (2002) and his colleagues at the CASS Institute of Sociology, is the most influential study of the social strata of the post-reform era based on a series of surveys that have been undertaken since 2000 to the present day. Lu and his colleagues used three resources—education, economic capital, and social capital—in order to build up ten socio-professional strata or classes. The formal antecedents of the ten-group typology proposed by Lu Xueyi in 2002 were drawn from the work of Anthony Giddens (1973) and Erik Olin Wright (1997).

Although this new approach initiated by Lu relies entirely on Western typologies, Cheng (2010a) noted, it "owed more to theories of social stratification than conventional Marxist class analysis" (58). Further, this typology "highlights class in contemporary society as being derived not only from the means of production, but also from the position in the authority structure and the possession of skills and expertise" (Goodman 2014, 58). Yet, as an explanatory tool focused on occupation, the CASS categorization has certain limitations. To solve these problems, subsequent studies conducted in the PRC by Western and Chinese scholars decided to add other criteria such as consumption, homeownership, subjective social status, education attainment, lifestyle, or social origin to the definition of China's middle class.

Nevertheless, different subjective and objective criteria adopted by different scholars lead to huge disparities when the attempt is made to assess the size of the middle class. As Wynne noted in his 1998 study on the emergence of the new middle class in British society, such analyses on contemporary middle class are "problematic on a number of counts but especially so because of their implicit failure to operationalize adequately the concept of class in relational terms" (Wynne 1998, 19). In other investigations on China's middle class, scholars refocused their attention from social change in China to examine not just other social criteria such as gender (Chen 2008) and ethnicity (Mackerras 2005; Schein 2000, 2008) but to problematize the very concept of inequality itself.

Particularly, the income inequality between urban and rural households and development between different regions are key factors to the examination of privilege and disadvantage in China today. Since the "income gap between regions in China widened with economic reform," emerging middle incomers can be understood as an urban phenomenon from eastern coastal cities as well as from the metropolitan areas of Beijing, Tianjin and Shanghai (Cai Wang, and Yang 2002, 197). However, it is heterogeneity that characterizes the Chinese middle class. To assume that the middle class comprises a homogeneous grouping simply because income inequality has been increasing in the eastern regions and decreasing in the central and western regions is to ignore three important features: first, the distribution of wealth across the country is quite diverse; second, the actual inequality (more or less pronounced) between rural and urban areas within each province and each region (Li, Luo and Sicular 2012); and third, the degree of cultural fragmentation and heterogeneity rather than homogeneity in the everyday social practices of middle-class subjects.

Failure to recognize the above points involves a failure to recognize the differing social differentiation to class categorization and class definition in contemporary urban China. In order to avoid these deficiencies, more and more sociologists have gone beyond the inherent flaws in subjective and objective criteria by linking, on the one hand, subjectivism and objectivism and social structure and practices (Bourdieu 1984) and addressing, on the other, class as a power structure co-constructed with gender, sexuality, ethnicity, and so on, where the situation determines which form of oppression (or intersection of oppressions) gains the upper hand (Crenshaw 1989; Holgersson 2017). The analysis on the middle-class criteria and composition supports the thesis that different definitions of middle class can denote quite diverse social groupings as well as their size. Therefore, now it may be convenient to analyse the hidden agenda concealed in major definitions of China's middle class.

2.3 A hidden agenda

In order to ensure a critical and coherent inquiry into the intellectual debate about class in China, this chapter also surveys the ultimate hidden agendas highlighted by both Western and Chinese scholars of the concept of middle class in the PRC. Therefore, this section suggests an additional dimension of analysis based, on the one hand, on the evidence of discrepancies in the "normative approach" between theory and empirical knowledge—"because every definition of the middle class conceals a hidden agenda" (Rocca 2017, 4)—and the fact that the identification of social groupings "have become entangled in webs of theories, paradigms and ideological positions, as well as prescriptions for idealised social configurations" due to the socio-political context in the PRC and the complex political dimension to the definition of the post-reform middle class (Guo 2008, 39). Hence, the political, cultural. and economic orientations behind the foundation and conceptualizations of the Chinese middle class, together with its capacity for social change, are of crucial significance for understanding this social group and its role in public debate. Therefore, two questions primarily arise about the ideological space of the intellectual debates and their implications for power: What are the main narratives of the middle class in China's studies? And what is the size of China's middle class used for?

There are, of course, a variety of answers to these questions. In a sense, the spectrum of possible answers corresponds to some of the most important scholarly debates about the Chinese middle class: the first concerns its definition; the second, its potential political roles; the third, its economic and business expectations; the fourth, its ideological values; and the fifth, vested interests (Cheng 2010a, 12; Rocca 2017, 4). Three considerations, however, are particularly instrumental in increasing both public debate and scholarly interest in this topic. First is the "Chinese government's decision to 'enlarge the size of the middle-income group'"; second, and equally important, is "the Chinese business community's drive" to disseminate the image of Chinese middle class as "potentially the 'world's largest middleclass market'" (Cheng 2010a, 8); third is the political agenda of most scholars addressing the issue of the middle class by supporting Modernization theories and market liberalization, on the one hand, or distrusting the reform and advocating a strong state role in defending the vulnerable groups (*ruoshi qunti*), on the other. Let us look in detail at each of these three aspects that make up the hidden agendas on the Chinese middle class in public debate.

Firstly, in relation to the academic discussions, it is argued that behind the Chinese government's definitions of the size and estimated growth of the middle class, there are two reasons that lay the foundation for the PRC to develop a growing middle-class grouping. That is, ensuring social stability coupled with the legitimization of the present regime characterize the key concepts for the Chinese government's decision to inflate the size of the middle class. Hence, the official perspective on the middle class's definition is "as inclusive as possible" (Goodman 2013, 55) to promote the idea that "the middle class will be grown in order to reduce the potential for social instability at the same time as increasing people's standard of living, so the emphasis is on the size of the middle class" (Li 2010, 140). However, the prominent presence of the Chinese middle class in public debate in recent decades has served, to a large extent, to shift the focus of attention away from the emergence of an increasingly richer dominant class and a poorer subordinate class.

Similarly, while talking about the middle class is talking about comfort and harmony, talking about rich and poor is talking about discomfort and inequality. Indeed, whereas income inequity grows, one uncomfortable piece of evidence comes up: according to the Forbes' World Billionaires List 2021, Beijing overtook New York City to become in 2020 the city with the greatest number of billionaires in the world. Under these conditions, scholars agree that the middle class has a "buffer function" (*huanchong gongneng*) in facilitating upward social mobility and reducing frictions between the dominant class and the subordinate classes (Zhang Lei 2005). By presenting Chinese society as an emerging diamond-shaped social structure (literally named in official documents "olive-shaped society") with the middle class as the most populous grouping, the CCP underline its legitimization as the only political party in the PRC by presenting itself as the guarantor of the Chinese population, "wholeheartedly serving the people" and "defending the interests of the country and the people" (Constitution of the Communist Party of China, 24 October 2017). Therefore, the achievement of a middle-class society with a common prosperity needs a stable political order, a harmonious social structure. And both the goal of "middlization" of society and the endurance of the Party-state compose an indispensable binary to achieve that promise of prosperity, comfort, and harmony that represents the paradigm of the Chinese middle class and challenges all citizens.

Secondly, scholars and experts working for foreign companies, such as multinational corporations (Johnson&Johnson, Coach, L'Oréal, Kimberly-Clark), consulting firms (McKinsey, Merrill Lynch), investment banks/brokerage (BPN Paribas Peregrine) or CEO-led organizations of global private sectors (World Travel & Tourism Council), regularly publish studies promoting the idea that there is a very high proportion of middle class in Chinese society. However, as Cheng (2010a) noted, most of these studies, especially those commissioned by large multinational banks and consulting firms, "were conducted by groups of economists consisting of local Chinese researchers, foreign-educated PRC nationals, and expatriates based in China" who used methodologies "quite opaque" away from "meeting the standards of rigorous academic research." Such surveys correspond to two related reasons: the widely noted idea that "an extant middle class in China has often been the primary driver of foreign investment" and "business activities in the country," and the assumption that the foreign business community in China and big companies (such as those mentioned above) benefit to paint an optimistic picture of business prospects. Hence, "the possibility of stimulating domestic consumption in the world's most populous country … has understandably captured the imagination" of both the business community in China and the experts who work for them (8–10). However, such an imaginary has not only reinforced the idea that the Chinese middle class is a sizeable market segment with homogeneous consumption patterns, but also has spread consumerism values by reducing the needs of the Chinese middle class in terms of market parameters.

Thirdly, today China studies are still informed by the "modernizing" understanding of the Chinese society. Research is conducted to identify any challenge or resistance to the Party-state as a maker of political change to the establishment of capitalism and liberal democracy. According to them, all social movements, business organizations, homeowners' associations, environmental mobilizations, and religious groupings that have organized protests against the regime are eligible to be part of the middle-class political attitudes to democratize China. They apply a western-embedded political framework to the Chinese society by supporting market liberalization, democratization, and social resistance to the CCP rule.

As noted earlier, Modernization theories state that civil society and the formation of a "real middle class" are structural conditions for democratic transition, a "modernizing" and developmental path from which the PRC could not escape. According to this consideration, if the Chinese middle class cannot transform China from the current neo-authoritarian political system to a liberal democracy, it is because Chinese society is a victim of "political alienation" (Zhang Wei 2005). Such prevalent capitalist principles, Zhang and Ong (2008) noted, are articulated in the name of private accumulation and self-interest "the heavy hand" of state control (1–3). The Chinese state thus regulates "from a distance the fullest expression of self-interest" (16). It is a technology of governing that undermines any contribution to the advancement of the nation's historical path to modernity. On that basis, the aim of the Chinese state would be to possess a real middle class who would embrace economic liberalism with political liberalism and support market individuation with political individualism.

Similarly, to the question, "What is the actual size of China middle class?" has come the response: the estimated size varies depending on the criteria employed. One issue of contention, for example, is whether private entrepreneurs should be included in the definition of the middle class. While Zhou (2008) did not include managers of large and medium-sized enterprises, private entrepreneurs, professional and technical staff or joint ventured enterprises in his definition of the middle class, Li (2005) did include all these categories.

Meanwhile, Lu (2002) and his colleagues at CASS treated class separately as an economic base and as an ideological superstructure. They identified in a 2002 report "a 'modern' social structure comprising three gradational but otherwise unrelated strata (upper, middle and lower), which were further divided into ten sub-strata" or *jieceng* (including Party-state cadres, middle- and high-ranking managers of large and medium-sized enterprises, private entrepreneurs, etc.) (Guo 2008, 48). Although, from 2010 the broader categories had become less specific, this categorization schema has been the basis for a series of official reports that had sized the Chinese middle class since that date. According to these reports, while the middle class was already 21 per cent of the population in 2001 and constituted

23 per cent of China's total in 2009, there was a certain impact on China's sociologists when Lu Xueyi predicted that this class would constitute 40 per cent of the population—on par with Western economies—by 2025.

Also, in October 2015, *China Daily* indicated that "the Global Wealth Report by the Credit Suisse Research Institute in Switzerland, said China had the largest middle class, 109 million people, compared with the United States' 92 million" (of course, as a proportion of the population, the middle class of the US, accounting for about 30 per cent and China about 8 per cent). However, the report defined middle-class people as those with assets of between 50,000 euros and 500,000 euros (between 350,000 and 3,520,000 yuan), while the PRC's statistics agency put the figure at nearly 25 per cent in 2015, less than a third of the population by defining middle-class households as those making 25,000 yuan to 250,000 yuan. Such differences in sizing the Chinese middle class may indicate, on the one hand, that multiple orientations coexist among this class today, and that it still "has a long way to go before it forms a homogeneous middle-class identity and culture" (Li 2010, 155). On the other, disparities in sizing this group reflected the degree to which we may be witnessing the emergence not of a new Chinese middle class per se but rather the emergence of a new middle-class lifestyle, and the increasing fragmentation of an anachronistic concept of middle class understood solely in terms of economic indicators.

Although mainstream researchers have been conducting the same studies again and again in different cities with different empirical data and using scientific discourse and objective criteria such as income to identify and quantify the significance of the Chinese middle class, their findings have varied considerably. The problem with these approaches, thus, is not about the quality of the empirical work, but the lack of a deep contextualization of this social phenomenon. Class background, geographic origin, gender, lifestyle (with high- or low-*suzhi* practices) are also key factors to determine class location and social distinctions in the PRC. However, the consideration of the Chinese middle class as a state-sponsored discourse and "*a well-founded historical artefact*" also showed that the framework used in China studies is misleading and explains the phenomenon of the Chinese middle class poorly. Although social science studies are carried out in an historical context and their approaches and problems are an expression of that frame, today China studies are still informed by a Western and *modernizing* vision of the middle class, which is considered a "new class" that supports democratization, market liberalization, and the developmental and the natural path described by the Modernization theorists.

However, the Chinese middle class appears to contradict this path to democratization. Indeed, *modernizing* expectations have frequently replaced analyses of the complexities of the actual middle class and civil societies in the PRC, reducing their explanatory value and practical utility, and allowing researchers to disregard relevant factors that do not match their homogenizing presumptions (Salmenkari 2012). Consequently, often the term is used politically by different actors involved at regional, national, and international level to mask their interests—e.g., projects for privatization, reducing the state's role in social service provision, deploying a nationalistic rhetoric, legitimizing the CCP's rule or, by contrast, promoting social contestation to the established order and political change. At worst, the "middle class theory" is not only used for ideological grounds by both Chinese and non-Chinese scholars and players in the financial markets, but also for social engineering as a "process of civilization" (Elias 1969), a national plan for poverty eradication, a modernizing path, and/or as a key component of Xi Jinping's Chinese Dream and China's "great rejuvenation" project.

After having framed the intellectual debate about the Chinese middle class in the general intellectual socio-political framework of China studies, and having completed this contextualization by illustrating the perspectives on class and the streams that make up the current criteria of its definition and discursive spaces—that is, the hidden agenda concealed and the methodological approaches planned—in the next chapter the methodological plan of this book about the lifestyle of the post-reform middle class begins by exploring the third focal point from which this book has planned to approach it; that is to say, by assessing the semi-structured interviews conducted in Beijing in 2017 and 2018. In doing this, the next chapter examines the social and spatial trajectories and cultural consumption practices of the sample as a process of the construction of social identity and manifestations of class differences in contemporary urban China.

Bibliography

Anagnost, Ann. 2004. "The Corporeal Politics of Quality (*suzhi*)." *Public Culture* 16: 189–208. doi:10.1215/08992363-16-2-189.

Anagnost, Ann. 2008. "From 'Class' to 'Social Strata': Grasping the Social Totality in Reform-era China." *Third World Quarterly* 29 (3): 497–519. doi:10.1080/01436590801931488.

Andreas, Joel. 2009. *Rise of the Red Engineers. The Cultural Revolution and the Origins of China's New Class*. Stanford, CA: Stanford University Press. Beck, Ulrich. 2016. *The Metamorphosis of the World*. Cambridge and Malden: Polity Press.

Bourdieu, Pierre. 1984. *Distinction. A Social Critique of the Judgement of Taste*. Translated by Richard Nice. Cambridge, MA: Harvard University Press.

Butler, Judith. 1993. *Bodies That Matter: O the Discursive Limits of "Sex."* New York: Routledge.

Cai, Fang, Dewen Wang, and Du Yang. 2002. "Regional Disparity and Economic Growth in China." *China Economic Review* 13 (2–3):197–212. doi:10.1016/s1043-951x(02)00072-x.

Cai, Yongshun. 2005. "China's Moderate Middle Class: The Case of Homeowners' Resistance." *Asian Survey* 45 (5): 777–799. doi:10.1525/as.2005.45.5.777.

Cartier, Carolyn. 2008. "The Shanghai-Hong Kong Connection: Fine Jewellery Consumption and the Demand for Diamonds." In *The New Rich in China*, edited by David S. G. Goodman, 187–200. Abingdon: Routledge.

Castells, Manuel. 2017. "Rethinking Development in the Global Information Age." In *Castells in Africa. Universities & Development*, edited by Johan Muller, Nico Cloete and François van Schalkwyk, 67–91. Cape Town: African Minds.

Chen, Jie. 2013. *A Middle Class without Democracy: Economic Growth and the Prospects for Democratization in China*. New York: Oxford University Press.

Chen, Minglu. 2008. "Entrepreneurial Women: Personal Wealth, Local Politics and Tradition." In In *The New Rich in China*, edited by David S.G. Goodman, 112–125. Abingdon: Routledge.

Chen, Peng. 2009. "Cong 'chanquan' zouxiang 'gongminquan'. Dangqian zhongguo chengshi yezhu weiquan yanjiu [From Property Rights to Citizens' Rights. A Study on Homeowners' Rights Defence in Contemporary Urban China]." *Kaifang Shidai*, 4: 126–139.

Chen, Yunsong, and Xiaoguang Fan. 2015. "Discordance between Subjective and Objective Social Status in Contemporary China." *The Journal of Chinese Sociology* 2 (14): 1–20. doi:10.1186/s40711-015-0017-7.

Cheng, Li. 2010a. "Introduction: The Rise of the Middle Class in the Middle Kingdom." In *China's Emerging Middle Class: Beyond Economic Transformation*, edited by Li Cheng, 3–31. Washington, DC: Brookings Institution Press.

Cheng, Li. 2010b. "Chinese Scholarship on the Middle Class: From Social Stratification to Political Potential." In *China's Emerging Middle Class: Beyond Economic Transformation*, edited by Li Cheng, 55–83. Washington, DC: Brookings Institution Press.

Crenshaw, Kimberle. 1989. "Demarginalizing the Intersection of Race and Sex: A Black Feminist Critique of Antidiscrimination Doctrine, Feminist Theory and Antiracist Politics." *University of Chicago Legal Forum*1989 (1): 8. https://chicagounbound.uchicago.edu/uclf/vol1989/iss1/8/?utm_source=chicagounbound.uchicago.edu%2Fuclf%2Fvol1989%2Fiss1%2F8&utm_medium=PDF&utm_campaign=PDFCoverPages.

Crompton, Rosemary. 1998. *Class and Stratification*. Cambridge: Polity Press.

Davis, Deborah S. 1992. "Skidding." *Modern China* 8 (4): 410–437. doi:10.1177/009770049201800402.

Davis, Deborah S. 2000. "Social Class Transformation in Urban China." *Modern China* 26 (3): 251–275. doi:10.1177/009770040002600301.

Davis, Deborah S. 2014. "Privatization of Marriage in Post-socialist China." *Modern China* 40 (6): 551–577. doi:10.1177/0097700414536528.

Davison, Nicola. 2014. "China Enjoys Design Renaissance Thanks to Rise of Middle Class." *Financial Times*, 11 March. Accessed 18 October 2021. https://www.ft.com/content/74f09d76-a9f2-11e3-adab-00144feab7de.

Dickson, Bruce. 2016. *The Dictator's Dilemma: The Chinese Communist Party's Strategy for Survival*. Oxford: Oxford University Press.

Miles, James. 2014. "Building the Dream." *The Economist*, 16 April. https://www.economist.com/special-report/2014/04/16/building-the-dream.

Elias, Norbert. 1969. *The Civilizing Process*. Oxford: Blackwell.

Fan, Chengze Simon. 2002. "Economic Development and the Changing Patterns of Consumption in Urban China". In *Consumption in Asia: Lifestyle and identities*, edited by Beng-Huat Chua, 82–97. London: Routledge.

Fan, Gang; Guangrong Ma, and Xiaolu Wang. 2019. "Institutional Reform and Economic Growth of China: 40-year Progress toward Marketization." *Acta Oeconomica* 69 (1): 7–20. doi:10.1556/032.2019.69.S1.2.

Gao, Mobo. 2018. *Constructing China. Clashing Views of the People's Republic*. London: Pluto Press.

Garnaut, Ross, Ligang Song, and Cai Fang. 2018. "40 Years of China's Reform and Development: How Reform Captured China's Demographic Dividend." In *China's 40 Years of Reform and Development: 1978–2018*, edited by Ross Garnaut, Ligang Song and Cai Fang, 5–25. Acton: ANU Press.

Gerth, Karl. 2020. *Unending Capitalism: How Consumerism Negated China's Communist Revolution*. Cambridge: Cambridge University Press.

Giddens, Anthony. 1973. *The Class Structure of Advanced Societies*. London: Hutchinson.

Gold, Thomas B. 1990. "Urban Private Business and Social Change." In *Chinese Society on the Eve of Tiananmen*, edited by Deborah Davis and Ezra F. Vogel, 157–178. Cambridge, MA: Harvard University Press.

Goodman, David S.G., ed. 2008. *The New Rich in China*. Abingdon: Routledge.

Goodman, David S.G. 2013. "Middle Class China: Dreams and Aspirations." *Journal of Chinese Political Science* 19 (1): 49–67.

Goodman, David S.G. 2014. *Class in Contemporary China*. Cambridge: Polity Press.

Goodman, David S.G., and Richard Robinson, eds. 1996. *The New Rich in Asia*. Abingdon: Routledge.

Gu, Ming Dong. 2013. *Sinologism. An Alternative to Orientalism and Postcolonialism*. Abingdon: Routledge.

Guo, Yingjie. 2008. "Class, Stratum and Group: The Politics of Description and Prescription." In *The New Rich in China*, edited by David S.G. Goodman, 38–52. Abingdon: Routledge.

Gustafsson, Bjorn, Terry Sicular, and Yang Xiuna. 2017. "2017–14 China's Emerging Global Middle Class." Working Paper, Centre for Human Capital and Productivity. Accessed October 18, 2021. https://ir.lib.uwo.ca/cgi/viewcontent.cgi?article=1126&context=economicscibc.

Hanser, Amy. 2008. *Service Encounters: Class, Gender, and the Market for Social Distinction in Urban China*. Stanford, CA: Stanford University Press.

Hart-Landsberg, Martin, and Paul Burkett. 2004. *China and Socialism: Market Reforms and Class Struggle*. New York: Monthly Review Press.

He, Qinglian. 2000. "China Listing Social Structure." *New Left Review* (5): 68–99. https://newleftreview.org/issues/ii5/articles/qinglian-he-china-s-listing-social-structure.

Hird, Derek. 2009. *White-collar Men and Masculinities in Contemporary Urban China*. PhD diss., University of Westminster.

Holgersson, Ulrika. 2017. *Class*. Abingdon: Routledge.

Hong, Yanbi, and Yandong Zhao. 2015. "From Capital to Habitus: Class Differentiation of Family Educational Patterns in Urban China." *The Journal of Chinese Sociology* 2: 18. doi:10.1186/s40711-015-0021-y.

Hsiao, Hsin-Huang Michael. 2010. "Placing China's Middle Class in the Asia-Pacific Context." In *China's Emerging Middle Class: Beyond Economic Transformation*, edited by Li Cheng, 245–263. Washington, DC: Brookings Institution Press. Jacka, Tamara. 2009. "Cultivating Citizens: Suzhi (Quality) Discourse in the PRC." *Positions: East Asia Cultures Critique* 17 (3): 523–535. doi:10.1215/10679847-2009-013.

Jain-Chandra, Sonali, Niny Khor, Rui Mano, Johanna Schauer, Philippe Wingender, and Juzhong Zhuang. 2018. "Inequality in China – Trends, Drivers and Policy Remedies." Working Paper, International Monetary Fund. Accessed 18 October 2021. https://www.imf.org/en/Publications/WP/Issues/2018/06/05/Inequality-in-China-Trends-Drivers-and-Policy-Remedies-45878.

Kardes, Ilke. 2016. "Reaching Middle Class Consumers in Emerging Markets: Unlocking Market Potential through Urban-based Analysis." *International Business Review* 25 (3): 703–710. doi:10.1016/j.ibusrev.2016.03.005.

Li, Chunling. 2005. *Duanlie yu suipian: dangdai Zhongguo shehui jieceng fenhua shili fenxi [Cleavage and Fragmentation: An Empirical Analysis of Social Stratification in Contemporary China]*. Beijing: Shehui Kexue Chubanshe. Li, Chunling. 2009a. *Duanlie yu suipina: Dangdai Zhongguo shehui jieceng fenhua shizheng fenxi [Clavage and Fragment: An Empirical Analysis on the Social Stratification of Contemporary China]*. Beijing: Social Sciences Academic Press.

Li, Chunling. 2009b. "Zhongguo zhongchan jieji yanjiu de lilun quxiang ji guanzhudian de bianhua [Theoretical Orientation and the Change of Focus in the Study of the Middle Class in China]." In *Bijiao shiyexia de zhongchan jieji xingcheng: guocheng, yingxiang yiji shehui jingji houguo [Formation of the Middle Class in Comparative Perspective: Process,*

Influence, and Socioeconomic Consequences], edited by Li Chunling. Beijing: Social Sciences Academic Press.

Li, Chunling. 2010. "Characterizing China's Middle Class: Heterogeneous Composition and Multiple Identities." In *China's Emerging Middle Class*, edited by Li Cheng, 135–156. Washington, DC: Brookings Institution Press. Li, He. 2015. *Political Thought and China's Transformation*. Basingstoke: Palgrave Macmillan.

Li, Shi, Chuliang Luo, and Terry Sicular. 2012. "Overview: Income Inequality and Poverty in China, 2002–2007." Working Paper, University of Western Ontario. Accessed 18 October 2021. https://www.econstor.eu/bitstream/10419/70341/1/670727598.pdf.

Liu, Jingming. 2006. "Expansion of Higher Education in China and Inequality in Entrance Opportunities: 1978–2003." *Shehui* 3.

Lu, Hanlong. 2010. *The Chinese Middle Class and China's Emerging Middle Class: Beyond Economic Transformation*, edited by Cheng Li, 104–131. Washington, DC: Brookings Institution Press.

Lu, Xueyi, ed. 2002. *Dangdai Zhongguo shehui jieceng yanjiu baogao* [*Research Report on the Social Stratification of Contemporary China*]. Beijing: Shehui kexue wenxian chubanshe.

Mackerras, Colin. 2005. "China's Ethnic Minorities and the Middle Classes: An Overview." *International Journal of Social Economics* 32 (9): 814–826. doi:10.1108/03068290510612593.

Maurer-Fazio, Margaret. 1999. "Earnings and Education in China's Transition to a Market Economy." *China Economic Review* 1. doi:10.1016/S1043-951X(99)00003-6.

Nathan, Andrew J. 2016. "The Puzzle of the Chinese Middle Class." *Journal of Democracy* 27: 5–19. doi:10.1353/jod.2016.0027.

NBSC (National Bureau of Statistics of China). 2001. *China Statistical Yearbook*. Beijing: China Statistics Press. http://www.stats.gov.cn/english/statisticaldata/yearlydata/YB2001e/ml/indexE.htm.

NBSC (National Bureau of Statistics of China). 2018. *China Statistical Yearbook*. Beijing: China Statistics Press. http://www.stats.gov.cn/tjsj/ndsj/2018/indexeh.htm.

Nee, Victor. 1989. "A Theory of Market Transition: From Redistribution to Markets in State Socialism." *American Sociological Review* 54: 663–681.

Nee, Victor. 1991. "Social Inequalities in Reforming State Socialis: Between Redistribution and Markets in China." *American Sociological Re`view* 56: 267–282.

Nee, Victor. 1996. "The Emergence of a Market Society: Changing Mechanisms of Stratification in China." *American Journal of Sociology* 101: 908–949.

Ngok, Kinglun. 2008. "Massification, bureaucratization and questing for "world-class" status." *International Journal of Educational Management* 22 (6): 547–564. doi:10.1108/09513540810895453.

Pan, Wei, and Ma Yan. 2008. *Jujiao dangdai zhongguo jiazhiguan* [Focus on contemporary Chinese values]. Beijing: Shenghuo dushu xinzhi sanlian shudian.

Quijano, Aníbal. 2014. *Cuestiones y Horizontes. De la Dependencia Histórico-Estructural a la Colonialidad/Descolonialidad del Poder* [Issues and Horizons. From Historical-Structural Dependence to the Coloniality/Decoloniality of Power]. Buenos Aires: CLACSO.

Reilly, Benjamin. 2013. "Southeast Asia: In the Shadow of China." *Journal of Democracy* 24 (1): 156–164. doi:10.1353/jod.2013.0013.

Rocca, Jean-Louis. 2013. "Homeowners' Movements: Narratives on the Political Behaviours of the Middle Class." In *Middle Class China: Identity and Behaviour*, edited by Minglu Chen and David S.G. Goodman, 110–134. Cheltenham: Edward Elgar.

Rocca, Jean-Louis. 2017. *The Making of the Chinese Middle Class: Small Comfort and Great Expectations*. New York: Palgrave Macmillan US.

Sáiz, Amelia. 2015. "Mujeres y Sociedad Civil en la Diáspora China: el Caso Español [Women and Civil Society in the Chinese Diaspora: The Case of Spain]." *Inter Asia Paper* 47: 1–35.

Salmenkari, Taru. 2012. "Theoretical Poverty in the Research on Chinese Civil Society." *Modern Asian Studies* 47 (2): 682–711. doi:10.1017/s0026749x12000273.

Schein, Louisa. 2000. *Minority Rules: the Miao and the Feminine in China's Cultural Politics.* Durham, NC: Duke University Press.

Schein, Louisa. 2008. "Neoliberalism and Hmong/Miao Transnational Media Ventures." In *Privatizing China*, edited by Li Zhang and Aihwa Ong, 103–119. Ithaca, NY: Cornell University Press.

Shen, Ruiying. 2010. "'Zizai' huo 'ziwei': zhongchan jieji yu jieji yishi ['In Itself' or 'for itself': Middle Class and Class Consciousness]." *Shanghai daxue xuebao* 1: 18–27.

Solé-Farràs, Jesús. 2014. *New Confucianism in Twenty-first Century China.* Abingdon: Routledge.

Standing, Guy. 2017. "The Precariat in China: A Comment on Conceptual Confusion." *Rural China* 14: 165–170. doi:10.1163/22136746-01401009.

Sun, Wanning. 2008. "Men, Women and the Maid: at Home with the New Rich." In *The New Rich in China*, edited by David S.G.Goodman, 213–228. Abingdon: Routledge.

Sun, Xiulin, and Can Zhang. 2014. "Shaghai qingnian zhongchan jieceng de shechi pin xiaofei yanjiu [A Study of Young Middle Class' Luxury Consumption in Shanghai]." *Qingnian yanjiu* 2014–2015.

Tang, Beibei. 2018. *China's Housing Middle Class. Changing Urban Life in Gated Communities.* Abingdon: Routledge.

Tomba, Luigi. 2004. "Creating an Urban Middle Class. Social Engineering in Beijing." *The China Journal* 51: 1–32. doi:10.2307/3182144.

Tomba, Luigi. 2014. *The Government Next Door: Neighborhood Politics in Urban China.* Ithaca, NY: Cornell University Press.

Walder, Andrew G., and Songhua Hu. 2009. "Revolution, Reform, and Status Inheritance: Urban China, 1949–1996." *American Journal of Sociology* 114 (5): 1395–1427. doi:10.1086/595949.

Weininger, Elliot B. 2005. "Foundations of Pierre Bourdieu's Class Analysis." In *Approaches to Class Analysis*, edited by Erik Olin Wright, 82–118. Cambridge: Cambridge University Press.

Wright, Erik Olin. 1997. *Class Counts: Comparative Studies in Class Analysis.* Cambridge: Cambridge University Press.

WTO. 2011. "China in the WTO: Past, Present and Future. Permanent Mission of China to the WTO." Accessed 18 October 2021. https://www.wto.org/english/thewto_e/a cc_e/s7lu_e.pdf.

Wynne, Derek. 1998. *Leisure, Lifestyle and the New Middle Class. A Case Study.* London: Routledge.

Xu, Jiang. 2002. "Xin zhongchan jieji jueqi: Zhongguo fuyu shidai dekaishi [The Rise of a New Middle Class: The Beginning of China's Prosperity]." *Jingmao Shijie* 8: 43–47.

Yan, Hairong. 2003. "Neoliberal Governmentality and Neohumanism: Organizing Suzhi/ Value Flow through Labor Recruitment Networks." *Cultural Anthropology* 18: 494–523. doi:10.1525/can.2003.18.4.493.

Yueh, Linda Y. 2004. "Wage Reforms in China during the 1990s." *Asian Economic Journal* 18 (2): 149–164. doi:10.1111/j.1467-8381.2004.00187.x.

Zang, Xiaowei. 2008. "Market Transition, Wealth, and Status Claims." In *The New Rich in China*, edited by David S.G. Goodman, 53–70. Abingdon: Routledge.

Zavoretti, Roberta. 2017. *Rural Origins, City Lives. Class and Place in Contemporary China.* Seattle: University of Washington Press.

Zhang, Lei. 2005. "Yezhu weiquan yundong: Chansheng yuanyin ji dongyuan jizhi, dui Beijing shi ji ge xiaoqu ge'an de kaocha[Beijing House Owners' Right Protection

Movement: Reason of Breakout and Mobilization Mechanism]." *Shehuixue Yanjiu* 2005–2006.

Zhang, Li. 2010. *In Search of Paradise: Middle-class Living in a Chinese Metropolis*. Ithaca, NY: Cornell University Press.

Zhang, Li, and Aihwa Ong. 2008. *Privatizing China*. Ithaca, NY: Cornell University Press.

Zhang, Wei. 2004." Zhongchan jieji yu zhengzhi zhixu [The Middle Class and the Political Order]." *Jianghan luntan* 1: 59.

Zhang, Wei. 2005. *Chongtu yu bianshu: zhongguo shehui zhongjian jieceng zhengzhi fenxi* [*Conflicts and Variables: Political Analysis of Chinese Middle Strata*]. Beijing: Shehui kexue wenxian chubanshe.

Zhang, Weiwei. 2020. "Consumption, taste, and the economic transition in modern China." *Consumption Markets & Culture* 23 (1): 1–20. doi:10.1080/10253866.2018.1467316.

Zhou, Xiaohong. 2005. "Zhongguo zhongchan jieceng de lishi yu xianzhuang" [The history and current situation of the Chinese middle class]. In *Zhongguo zhongchan jieceng diaocha* [*Survey of the Chinese middle class*], edited by Zhou Xiaohong. Beijing: Shehui kexue wenxian chubanshe.

Zhou, Xiaohong. 2008. "Chinese Middle Class: Reality or Illusion?" In *Patterns of Middle Class Consumption in China and India*, edited by Christopher Jaffrelot and Peter van der Veer, 110–126. London: Sage.

Zhou, Xiaohong. 2017. "The Inner Experience of the Chinese People: Window on an Evolution of Mentality." In *Inner Experience of the Chinese People*, edited by Zhou Xiaohong, 1–14. Singapore: Springer.

Zhou, Xiaohong, and Chen Qin. 2010. "Globalization, Social Transformation, and the Construction of China's Middle Class." In *China's Emerging Class*, edited by Cheng Li, 84–103. Washington, DC: Brookings Institution Press.

Zou, Shubin. 2005. "Chengshi yezhu weiquan yundong: tedian ji qi yingxiang [The Rights Movement of Urban Property Owners]." *Shenzhen daxue xuebao (renwen shehui kexue ban)* 2005–2006.

3

CLASS REPRODUCTION AND CULTURAL CONSUMPTION

The reconfiguration of the distinctive trajectories from the centre

Market reforms have emphasized experiences related to cultural consumption, leisure, and non-material concerns over experiences associated with productive activity in the PRC. The lifestyle paradigm is a crucial lens for theoretical and empirical investigations in contemporary urban China. It provides insights into contemporary social changes that may otherwise be missed. In the post-reform era, unequal distribution of material, cultural, social, and symbolic rewards are manifested through lifestyle. The "new state/market-based social stratification" implemented in the 1990s, and traditional Confucian culture have substantially influenced a "lifestyle shift," especially in urban areas (Xu and Wu 2016). Therefore, the urban middle class embodies a distinctive lifestyle that reflects its class position in social hierarchy in terms of economic, cultural, and social capital possession. Informal conversations and semi-structured interviews conducted in Beijing with middle class individuals in 2017 and 2018 revealed the routes taken to their current class location and the construction of their social identity in terms of cultural consumption patterns and educational attainment since the reforms of the 1990s.

Firstly, the questions of social distinctions and boundaries between classes included in this chapter consider the three main dimensions of class formation, namely the amount of capital, the proportion of capital formation, and the evolution of the historical track of status position (Weininger 2005, 84; Hong and Zhao 2015, 4). Secondly, by using the social space as a framework and the lifestyle paradigm, this chapter also evaluates the forms of capital and the manifestations of cultural consumption and class hierarchies in contemporary urban China. Certainly, the assessment of "trajectories of social mobility" and consumption habits of the urban middle class allows us to understand the link between the rationalizing project of modernity involved in the lifestyle of the post-reform middle class and the social phenomena of "intergenerational transfer" of inequality and privilege in

DOI: 10.4324/9781003299301-4

the PRC (Sun et al. 1998, in He 2000, 70; Goodman 2014). Such trajectories can be seen to relate not only to the consumption practices and taste of the Chinese middle class, but also to the unique conditions of structuring and perpetuation of privilege and inequality in urban contexts immediately before the COVID-19 pandemic.

3.1 Social and spatial trajectories from the centre

In the contemporary Chinese society, social and spatial mobility share an intricate relationship. In large cities, mobility trajectories have been highly consistent with the socio-economic changes of the reform era and have reflected the new inequalities and social hierarchies created in the PRC after the second stage of market reforms of the 1990s. Whereas corporeal mobilities are increasingly manifested in everyday practices and contribute to continual processes of de-differentiation, social fluidity following market transition has declined, as the status hierarchy and the link between origin and destination in vertical social status have significantly strengthened (Zhou and Xie 2019). In this context, the aim here is to explore the life trajectories of our informants to understand the expectations, decision-making processes, and changes in mobility patterns of the post-reform middle class.

To the extent that the informants of this case study can be identified as members of the Chinese middle class regarding their residence in Beijing, age, occupation, and educational attainment, it can also be seen as a case study that attempts to say something about a set of wider social processes associated with political, social, and cultural transformations in contemporary urban China. Additionally, considering social subjective status, our sample showed that nearly 80 per cent of the informants considered themselves as middle class; the rest, little more than 20 per cent, did not know where they were situated or they did so without referring to any middle stratum, or they placed themselves around it without being precise. On that basis, this section intends to establish two significant arguments in the nature of the social and spatial trajectories of the Chinese middle class based on the assertion that class in the PRC is best understood in terms of the "intergenerational transfers of various types of capital within a family lineage [which] have reinforced the switchable potentials of the different capitals themselves" (Sun et al. 1998, in He 2000, 70), on the one hand; and the shift from production-led migration to consumption-led mobility in contemporary China observed by Xu and Wu (2016), on the other.

Firstly, in order to understand the process of class reproduction within the Chinese middle class, the indication of the social origins of our informants has been obtained by considering the occupations of their mothers and fathers (see Table 3.1). The findings indicate that 82.5 per cent of them come from the *danwei* middle-class backgrounds, thus upward social mobility is a minority in the sample. Although the results indicate that most respondents' parents were industrial workers in a *danwei* (30 per cent), the proportion of members of professional and technical staff is also particularly significant among respondents' parents (27.5 per cent). In any case, both categories belong to the *danwei* middle class, composed of urban workers and employees (*zhigong*). Additionally, the figures indicate that a sizable minority (10 per cent) of those with origins in the farm workers or peasants have achieved considerable mobility.

To a large extent, therefore, the results confirm that the post-reform middle class is the result of "the intergenerational transfer of various types of capital" (Sun et al. 1998, in He 2000, 70), "privileges and disadvantages" (Goodman 2014, 33) or, in other words, a social phenomenon of class reproduction (Rocca 2017, 43–48). Additionally, since entry into professional occupations over the last decades is primarily guarded by educational qualifications, these results suggest that this minority from peasantry origins have achieved this mobility through educational attainment which, in the case of my informants, took place during the 1980s and 1990s. Among mothers' occupational categories, the least common categorizations are those of housewife and private entrepreneur, which were indicated by solely 5 per cent of respondents; and, among fathers' occupational categories, are those of manager and private entrepreneur, which were indicated by also 5 per cent of our sample.

TABLE 3.1 Social origin and occupational activity

Parents' occupational categories	Father (n = 20) %	Mother (n = 20) %	Father and mother (n = 40) %
Political/economic elite	–	–	–
Managers of state/private sector	5	–	2.5
Medium-sized entrepreneurs	5	5	5
Small-sized entrepreneurs	–	–	–
Professional and technical staff in state/private sector	35	20	27.5
Administrative staff in state/private sector	15	20	17.5
Customer service and trade employees	–	–	–
Industrial workers in state/private sector	30	30	30
Farm workers	10	10	10
Urban and rural unemployed and semi-employed	–	–	–
Reproductive labourers	–	5	2.5
Refused/don't know/no answer	–	10	5

Source: Data compiled by the author.

As noted in Chapter 1, this intergenerational class transmission was essentially sponsored by the Party-state in the 1990s. As a part of the CCP's "strategy for survival" and the second wave of market reforms implemented by the state to enhance the regime legitimacy after the Tiananmen Square protests of 1989, the privileged position of the *danwei* middle class had to be maintained and enhanced. This phenomenon of class transmission facilitated by the Party-state can also be understood as a result of a "new social contract" established between the Party and the urban middle class after the Tiananmen Incident. Thus, "[i]n exchange for remaining the sole ruling force, the Party must keep the promises of the 1950s in terms of improving living conditions" (Rocca 2017, 23). In any case, the Party-state needed a political ally and an efficient consumer capable of boosting China's domestic consumption. The mechanisms used in the 1990s by the Party-state to ensure the intergenerational transfer of capital in urban areas and thus secure the connivance of the middle class were to subsidize urban dwellers for the purchase of private housing while giving priority to their children for access to higher education and the labour market.

On the other hand, although the Chinese government almost doubled the number of university places in 1999 and over the next ten years it continued to grow considerably, the existing extent of inequality and social mobility has been maintained (Hu and Hibel 2014). Hence, higher education was clearly positively correlated with income level and the market reforms of the 1990s raised the value of academic credentials hugely, but new imbalances were quickly introduced through new market forces, change in employment policies, skills mismatch in the labour market, and increase in the size of the informal sector (Andreas 2009, 255–256; Mok and Qian 2018). Not only have the expanded opportunities not been equally distributed across different social groups, but new Chinese university students have led to the "massification" of higher education and intensified "positional competition" (Mok and Qian 2018). In China's precarious labour market, a higher education degree is no longer a guarantee of employment unless it has been completed abroad or at one of China's top universities (located in cities such as Beijing, Shanghai, Zhejiang, Hangzhou, Nanjing, Hefei, and Wuhan).

Additionally, social inequality has intensified between those who have access to China's premier universities, that is, the children of the urban middle classes which can invest in private supplementary tutoring to do well on the *gaokao* exam, thus ensuring access to their chosen university, and those who have no access. Moreover, Chinese premier universities have prioritized local dwellers by keeping places for them through their affiliated high schools. Local governments in cities exerted pressure on universities and on the education administration to preserve and even increase the number of positions reserved for locals to reduce employment rate and guarantee social peace as graduates from local top-ranked universities get prestigious and well-paid jobs (Rocca 2017, 47). Thus, access to higher education was not so much a matter of academic record as it was a matter of class and *hukou*.

Further, as the Chinese government either provided scholarships to send students abroad or allowed families to send their children to attend university overseas, even for the urbanites who were unable to obtain admission in China's premier universities, their parents were still able to use their economic and/or social capital (*guanxi*) to send them to study abroad and secure class reproduction (Tsang 2013). Therefore, as Sun Liping and his colleagues suggested, there is no room for a "new" middle class as "the resources necessary for one have already been cornered" by the *danwei* middle class following the "transferability between political, economic and cultural capitals in China" (Sun et al. 1998, in He 2000, 70). In fact, almost all the participants (95 per cent) were aware of the importance of education attainment not only in the construction of social identity and the underlying of social positions but also as a powerful resource, the possession of which endows them with the capacity to act in the social world from a better position (Wynne 1998, 24). Not surprisingly, 85 per cent of respondents had a postgraduate qualification. As a result, beyond the influence of non-education-related factors, the frameworks established by education governance in China have promoted class transferability through educational attainment.

Secondly, rather than a mere massive rural–urban migration due to rapid indus-trialization after the reforms of the 1990s, migration has increasingly been shown to be a class-based consumption in the PRC. The interurban phenomena of "spatia-lization of class" and elective belonging are relevant to understanding the structure of both economic and symbolic hierarchies in the Chinese society. Furthermore, this intersection of mobility and lifestyle reflects class differences through new middle-class practices associated, for example, with tourism, retired "snowbirds," and occupational status (business trips). In addition, new discourses have also emerged as a combination of new mobile lifestyles with old techniques of social control, notably the *hukou* system and the *Chunyun* travel. Based on different state interventions over time, rural–urban migration in the history of the PRC has gone from being prohibited between 1949 and 1983 through the *hukou* system to being liberalized and even facilitated from 2002 onwards by the state due to cheap labour that was needed by the factories and companies in the cities (Sun 2019, 164). Consequently, these changes in mobility patterns also reveal a shift from production-led peasant worker migration to a middle-class consumption-led mobility.

Of particular importance was that although Beijing's middle class is mainly com-posed by migrants from other Chinese regions, they have not been socially mobile, rather they have reproduced their class origins. Two of the twenty informants (10 per cent) were locals—i.e. born and raised in Beijing—the rest were born and raised in other provinces, except for one who was born in a southern province of China and grew up in the capital. Moreover, it should be remembered that most of the middle class in Beijing are people without long-standing local attachments. These non-economic migrants have deliberately moved to Beijing to enrol at university and stayed there to live as a means of maintaining their own perceived social position in the relative isolation of a small urban or rural community.

Hence, the emergence of the post-reform lifestyle of the Chinese middle class is associated with the Chinese Dream as a commitment to "assure equal rights between urban and rural residents and freedom of human migration," so that farmers can voluntarily leave the countryside and agricultural work to pursue work in cities, enjoy the benefits of modern urban life, contribute to social harmony, and thus achieve the dream of becoming a registered city resident, a long-held aspiration of Chinese farmers and migrant workers (Wei 2019, *vii–viii*). The paradigm of the Chinese middle class is thus a significant part of the large-scale rapid urbanization implemented by the government for sustained high economic growth and poverty reduction. As a result, the spatial trajectories of informants, that is, moving to Beijing to enjoy a modern and urban life, has long been the dream of the large group of unprivileged.

The social trajectory of most of informants began when they moved to study at a university in Beijing. They met their future partners among their fellow students and then settled in Beijing, since capital is concentrated in big cities, as well as the best job opportunities for young recent graduates, the service sector, centres of consumption, entertainment facilities, and the largest housing markets. Cities also offer prestigious schools for their children to secure class perpetuation through the accumulation of new capital. The narratives of informants who are originally from other provinces manifested, as de Oliveira (2002) noted in her study at the Spanish/Portuguese border, "self-identification strategies" relative to "the theoretical paradigms of the centre-periphery, regionalist, essentialist" (rural, traditional, Chinese, socialist) and "non-essentialist" (urban, modern, global, capitalist). Beijing presents the economic and administrative capital of China with abundant professional opportunity, while their hometowns are viewed as affordable and quiet places at the periphery, but far behind Beijing both quantitatively (richer, bigger, with more chances) and qualitatively (modern, high-*suzhi*, civilized city).

Experiences of mobility challenge traditional relationships between individuals, families, and communities, and between rural and urban contexts. As a result of these interactions, the self-identification strategies of respondents were affirmed through daily behaviour (practices) and discourses and paradigms (representations). For instance, evidence suggested certain distinctive dispositions among the informants with respect to the community they left behind in their hometowns which can be found in Mr. Lai and Mrs. Yin's words. Whereas Mr. Lai, who hailed from Guizhou, lamented that his friends in his hometown did not understand the busy rhythm of Beijing's urban life (see also Chapter 5), Mrs. Yin, originally from a small town in Shanxi province, considered herself a harder-working person and with higher social status than the fellow citizens in her hometown because of her urban lifestyle. She argued,

> People in my hometown don't want to come to Beijing because they believe there are many difficulties, there's more adversity. You have to wake up very early, take the subway to go to work and work harder. In my city, you can get a job and not have to work so hard. It's more relaxed. Bosses aren't as demanding, but they don't earn a lot … They don't make a lot of money, their salaries are lower, but living costs are also much lower. That's why they

don't have any stress … Some prefer to live in small cities, but the younger ones might think there are more opportunities in Beijing. They can earn more money and grow there, become more successful, that's why it all depends.

Beyond the fact that her assessment seemed to subtly associate poverty with the lack of effort, Mrs. Yin identified herself by spatial mobility based on practices that moneyed urban groups, and especially those with a better education, adopted in order to attain social status (Liu-Farrer 2016, 506). She considered herself a harder-working person, more successful in terms of cultural and economic capital, better-educated, more industrious and braver than the inhabitants of her hometown. In other words, she has a higher *suzhi* than them, and the only reason, she argued, was her personal effort; she did not allude to her middle-class background:

When I came, I was not a local to Beijing. I grew up in a small city in north-eastern China, passed the *gaokao* and the university's entrance exam. I attended university and got diplomas in advanced studies. In the end, I obtained a Beijing *hukou* along with a job at the university, but my friends or former classmates my age, the ones who did not succeed in the *gaokao*, would prob-ably have become migrant workers in Beijing. They didn't want to come to Beijing, but they would've become migrant workers; maybe not involved in cleaning work, but they'd work in some supermarket.

As noted earlier, and without putting into question Mrs. Yin's personal effort, it is still evident that access to certain opportunities such as higher education is not so much a matter of knowledge, effort, and skills as it is a matter of class since our informants' responses showed that only 10 per cent of them experienced any upward movement in the social ladder with regards to their class origins; only two of the participants had parents who were farmers. Her narrative of personal effort and self-improvement was in line with the paradigm of the Chinese middle class and the Chinese Dream's promise of social and spatial mobility as a result of mer-itocracy and individual disposition. Additionally, spatial mobility within the PRC is also perceived to fashion oneself as a modern subject (Chu 2010). Younger single informants also argued that they chose to study at a university in Beijing rather than a university near their hometown not only because graduating from a Beijing university ensures a job with a higher salary but also because it was a way to move away from the family sphere to acquire greater individual freedom.

Urbanization and the rise of the heteronormative nuclear family in the PRC has greatly encouraged increased consumption since the second wave of reforms of the 1990s. As a cycle of cause and effect, China's fast urbanization has been based upon high consumption of energy and resources as the demands of the urban population increased for housing, water, electricity, transportation, food, and education (Wei 2019). Additionally, the collective *danwei* system was dismantled and the extended traditional Chinese family was divided into small nuclear families to increase consumption of goods and services. As was the case with all married informants originating from outside Beijing, young married couples living independently began to spend independently on housing, home appliances, furniture, electricity, water, paid reproductive labour (in some cases), vehicles, etc. As noted earlier, young couples prefer to stay and set up their own households in big cities to enjoy the production and consumption benefits of modern urban life. On that basis, housing consumption has become the most common and distinctive consumption pattern among the post-reform middle class (Tang 2022, 68). In particular, the urban gated communities that emerged in the late 1990s exemplify not only the complex intersection between urbanization, migration, and consumption in contemporary China but also the social space most associated with the lifestyle of the urban middle class.

Indeed, these residential areas were characterized by their "closed" space with landscaping inside the complex, fences, and security guards that would not only protect residents from "the dangers" of urban life but also act as an exclusive social island (Sun 2008, 220). Gated communities, as Tomba (2014) pointed out, were the result of "specific measures facilitated and regulated by the state" in three different ways: as a social engineering process through public planning (171); as a normative tool to establish the technologies of the self by combining self-government and self-discipline techniques; and as a discursive rationalization of such structural segregation by disseminating the ideology of *suzhi*, civilization, and heteronormativity to protect the vested interests and privileges of all involved players, that is, from real-estate developers to individual homeowners, and from local cadres to urban governments with governance and speculative interests (172). A fourth way would be as an urban governing strategy of large-scale relocation, segregation and "spatialization of class in the city" (Zhang 2010). In practice, these modern residential neighbourhoods were advertised to potential buyers in terms of comfortable lifestyle, high-*suzhi* neighbourhood, and a new middle-class identity (Anagnost 2008). The expansion of these residential areas in the suburbs coincided with the Community Building campaign (*shequ jianshe*), which aimed to reorganize urban residential communities through a new paradigm of representativity between urban dwellers and the state (see also Chapter 5). The gated communities thus have radically changed the landscape of Chinese cities as a new social and architectural space for self-discipline, privacy, and class segregation through consumption practices.

After having contextualized the shift from production-led migration to consumption-led mobility in contemporary China and framing the process of class reproduction within the Chinese middle class, the next section plans to examine the consumption practices of the sample as a process of the construction of social identity and class distinctions before the COVID-19 pandemic in Beijing.

3.2 Cultural consumption

With the rise in standards of living in the PRC since the second stage of reforms of the 1990s, "it is argued that issues related to *consumption*, rather than production," have been playing an increasingly important part in shaping lifestyles in urban areas (Crompton 1998, 166, emphasis in original). Although exports continue to drive China's economy, the Chinese government aims to rebalance China's main source of growth by moving away from exports and towards domestic consumption by investing in infrastructure, adopting key digital technologies, and encouraging a middle-class consumption. In drawing the outlines of this section on a class-based consumption, we must be aware that the concept of cultural consumption can be understood as a consumption of goods and services with two prevailing functions, "primarily aesthetic functions and only secondarily instrumental." Cultural consumption is linked not only with "the sphere of arts, culture and leisure, encompassing consumption behaviours as visited cultural events" and reading books, but also with watching TV, clothing, furnishing, or eating out in restaurants (Rössel, Schenk, and Weingartner 2017, 1). In fact, as noted earlier, "classification struggles" over social hierarchy over individuals and classes take place in the arena of cultural consumption.

In this context, since the publication of Zhou's (2005) characterization of China's middle class as the consumer avant-garde but political rear guard (*xiaofei qianwei, zhengzhi houwei*), it has been a constant increase in the level of academic attention directed at the "conspicuous consumption" of the Chinese middle class. In fact, the Western theoretical paradigm of the conspicuous consumerism derived from Veblen's *The Theory of the Leisure Class* (1899) describes and explains "a behaviour in which an individual displays wealth through a high degree of luxury expenditures on consumption and services" (Podoshen, Li, and Zhang 2010, 17). Materialist, individualist, and hedonist values have been linked to the post-reform lifestyle that has emerged in recent decades. However, as Weiwei Zhang (2020) highlighted, China's consumer society not only includes these Western values, but also habits from traditional Chinese culture, in particular frugality, humility, and thrift, a Confucian-centred orientation, and a collective and family-based definition of identity based on indigenous concepts such as face (*mianzi*), social obligations in personal relationships (*renqing*), and *guanxi*.

Indeed, an elaboration of socio-historical circumstances and cultural backgrounds is vital to analyse how cultural consumption practices are used by distinct social groups in the PRC. Such an approach is considered particularly important in any attempt to explore not only whether post-reform middle class is more a cultural than an economic construct, but also to evaluate the degree of homogeneity associated with cultural consumption and identity construction within the urban middle class. Drawing on reviews of published literature, and semi-structured interviews with key cultural consumption markers, this section attempts to evaluate the manifestations of cultural consumption practices associated with a post-industrial lifestyle by analysing social hierarchy (online and offline shopping), legitimate culture (middlebrow consumption of cultural products), and cultural capital acquisition (education as class-based consumption) in contemporary urban China.

Shopping: social hierarchy, uniqueness, and frugality

The COVID-19 pandemic has accelerated the expansion of online shopping as a global phenomenon. The leading platforms firms in the PRC such as Alibaba (Taobao, Tmall), JD.com (Jingdong, Yihaodian), and Suning (*suningyigou*) have continued growing and their impact on lifestyle has accelerated. However, before the onset of COVID-19, the PRC was already the largest e-commerce market in the world, accounting for 45 per cent of global e-commerce transaction value in 2018 (McKinsey & Company 2021). As online shopping has continued to have a large growth potential among Chinese urban consumers, an increasing number of scholars have shown an interest in investing in the online shopping decision process in recent years. Whereas quantitative studies have claimed that the rise in online shopping is due to functional factors such as lower prices, comfort, and greater choices, qualitative researchers have focused on China's socio-historical events and cultural background to decipher online consumer behaviours. However, here the questions are: what are the reasons behind this massive increase in online shopping? And how do they impact on the social construction of identity of middle incomers in Beijing?

Firstly, one of the strongest factors influencing our informants' decision to shop online was price—especially the search for deals, coupon codes, and discounts. They also preferred to shop online for greater variety and because they could compare items by price, reviews, and features, and find rare items and new brands. For instance, Mr. Wen admitted that he had been searching for information and comparing prices on different online platforms during the last few days before the interview about a vacuum cleaner manufactured in the US with "a high price." He confessed, "I don't need such a powerful vacuum cleaner for my small apartment, but I like it ... The brand is very good, but it is still expensive, and I don't know whether to buy it or not." He seemed to be negotiating between his individualistic and hedonistic feelings ("I like it") and the material aspects ("it is still very expensive") for the purchase of a household appliance.

In explaining the interactional process of online shopping, Mr. Wen and the other informants behaved like conscientious consumers by discerning in the product selection process, seeking discounted prices, and crowdsourcing opinions before making a purchase decision. Therefore, these findings contradict the common perception that Chinese middle incomers are the "consumer avant-garde" or conspicuous consumers. In any case, although the narratives of our informants about their social consumption practices did not manifest lavish spending on luxury goods purely for showing off their apparent affluence, they may purchase certain products in an attempt to be seen in a better light in the greater social hierarchy.

Furthermore, crowds, sales pressure, and status competition involved in the interpersonal interaction of physical stores were also other reasons why our informants opted to shop online. According to Mr. Yang, online shopping was also a way to "avoid wasting time at the centrally located shopping malls" because they were usually crowded "with teenagers and people from all over." Indeed, as our Beijing-born informant indicated, online shopping was less stressful; there was no point in queuing up and no need to tolerate crowds and people with low-*suzhi* like customers "from all over" and the salespeople, who were usually migrant workers. Similarly, Mr. Qiao pointed out that lack of education was a characteristic of the migrant workers. He remembered working as a doctor in a hospital in Beijing and how migrant workers behaved, "It's that interaction that makes people uncomfortable … It's their behaviour, like pointing at you [*gestured pointing with his finger*], you know?" According to Mr. Qiao, "they are not educated enough," in other words, they did not have enough *suzhi*.

Beyond the actual consumption of goods, middle-class consumers were also faced with various interactional and performative tasks in shopping experiences in physical stores. Hence, contemporary social identities were constructed in *the arena of consumption* through "a complex system of mutually overlapping interrelationships in constant reciprocal interaction with personal, environmental, and situational inputs" (Hirschman and Holbrook 1986, 219). On that basis, a crucial task for middle-class consumers was to express and maintain a definition of their social identity and status, and to control the impression they "gave" and the impression they "gave off"—that is, to gain and give face—throughout the entire purchasing process.

As Xiaoli Tian (2018) argued in her research on online shopping in the PRC, the rapid economic transition in modern China led to the lack of consensus on the current status hierarchy, and groups such as the urban middle incomers experiencing a high sense of entitlement. They believed they deserved special consideration and had constantly to justify their social status to non-privileged groups, as when Mr. Qiao asked for more respect from migrant workers when addressing him in the hospital. However, as migrant workers are often reluctant to assume subordinate roles when interacting with middle-class urbanites in service encounters, the latter thus need to spend much emotional energy and affective labour in shopping interactions with sales people (2018, 564). As a result, from a Bourdieusian perspective, the in-store purchasing process becomes a symbolic struggle to impose a legitimate vision of the social world and its structuring divisions.

In these symbolic struggles, as noted earlier, one of the most important forces behind Chinese consumer behaviour is gaining and giving face (*mianzi*), a deeply rooted understanding of social interaction in Chinese society (Zhang 2020, 2). In service encounters, middle-class customers need to show their relative status, power, and face by demonstrating their good taste and "purchasing ability," a performativity closely related to their expected high-*suzhi* (Tian 2018, 564, 549). Here, face "is understood as a desire to gain favourable social self-worth and to be valued in relation to others (Liao and Wang, 2009, in Zhang and Kim 2013, 75). That is why the concept of *mianzi* is also related with the need to buy. Indeed, whereas "westerners' consumption is motivated by their inner self-preference and it is a process of 'want to buy'," Chinese "consumers are mostly motivated by social norms and pressure, and it is a process of 'have to buy'" (Jin et al. 2015,

883). For instance, face is what you can lose if you frequent multiple times the same store without making a purchase, or if you ask about the price of an item and you have to leave because you cannot afford it. Understandably, as much emotional energy is thus involved in shopping experiences in physical stores, Chinese customers prefer to buy online in order to avoid the *mianzi* pressure while fulfilling the need to buy, maintaining social identity, and reinforcing structures of entitlement.

Therefore, online shopping not only reduces horizontal face-to-face interactions but also creates new purchasing processes in which service encounters privilege customers, considerably reduce the *mianzi* pressure and reinforce status hierarchy. The online purchasing process also allows for acquiring goods via a mobile phone in any situation—even when taking the subway—and to receive those products just about anywhere. Rather than going to a pre-determined delivery centre, most prefer the personalized delivery service offered by online shopping platforms such as Taobao or Tmall. Although the former is a cheaper option, it still forces costumers to show up at a certain time. However, the respondents preferred personalized delivery, because they could use GPS to pinpoint the exact location of the deliveryman and proceed with the collection.

On some occasions, during informal conversations with my interviewees at a coffeeshop or restaurant, the informant would stand up, walk to the entrance of the restaurant looking at his mobile, and pick up a purchase after receiving a phone notification from the deliveryman—who was usually, again, a migrant worker. Such practices of surveillance on couriers cultivated a sense of precise and personalized delivery service by reinforcing status hierarchy and reducing the social interaction between the courier (the "low-*suzhi*" subordinated who needs to be monitored) and the customer (the "high-*suzhi*" citizen entitled to self-monitoring and to monitor the courier). Hence, through the online shopping process, the rhetoric of *suzhi* was also internalized and performed as a consumption practice with a social identity marker.

Nevertheless, as mobile consumers before the COVID-19 pandemic, the participants manifested very different consumption practices when travelling abroad such as Mr. Yi, who bought brand products whenever they travel to Europe or the States. As he explained, price remained the main reason for shopping offline when abroad, but not the only one:

> I mostly buy online here [in China], and I usually go shopping when I'm in Europe, like when I buy Armani products because they're cheaper over there … It's so much more expensive here. For example, these Armani Jeans cost almost 1000 RMB in Spain, but here maybe 3000 RMB, two or three times *more costly*! Since I travel frequently, I've been to many countries and tour around. I shop and buy a lot … But in China, going to a shopping mall is expensive and complicated. I have to go there, choose, look around … and there's not much variety.

Similarly, while discussing brand consumption, Mr. Lu explained,

> I go abroad four or five times a year [for work]. Before, I used to buy at tax-free stores like cosmetics, but now I don't have any [brand] preferences … purchasing popular brand products still occurs every now and then when traveling abroad, taking advantage of the cheaper prices.

My findings indicated that while domestic brands were preferred for grocery shopping and home appliances, the respondents chose foreign brands for clothing and health and beauty products. Although foreign products often had higher average selling prices than Chinese brands, non-luxury foreign brands were increasingly priced competitively in the Chinese market and were even moving towards a global pricing standard.

Although some participants such as Mr. Lu did not show much interest in brands, most of them were quite brand conscious by showing high attitudes and shopping behaviour toward foreign retailers. The reasons for our participants' preference of globally shared brands were mainly the result of the growth of global consumer culture in the PRC since market transition (Sun et al. 2020, 862). Well-known brands would provide functional benefits to reduce quality risks and represent symbolic possessions to satisfy consumers' social needs. What is more remarkable, though, is that most of the informants chose unostentatious brand products or, to a lesser extent, discretely unique brand goods.

Indeed, a significant motivation behind their social consumption was what Weiwei Zhang (2020) called "conspicuous frugality," that is, the attempt to differentiate themselves from other groups, such as the new rich, by emphasizing their frugal moral qualities. Conspicuous frugality reflects their attachment to the traditional Chinese values of modesty, humility, thriftiness, self-effacement, and possessing virtue. In fact, Confucian tradition was characterized by the "goodness and simplicity of customs" (*chunhou fengsu*). Also, the Republican middle society was also characterized by a frugal lifestyle, in which frugality was not only a personal behaviour, but also "a way of connecting the individual and society" (Mao 2018, 635). Similarly, by emphasizing such practices, middle-class consumers in the post-reform era essentially stressed their cultural capital, which was a necessary way to secure and perform their position on the hierarchical ladder (Zhang 2020, 16). These distinctive practices showed how the interaction between the economic, the cultural, and the symbolic was established in Chinese society immediately before the pandemic.

Consequently, the purchase of luxury goods without logos and discreet premium items became a class-based practice and high-*suzhi* behaviour of China's urban middle class. This was what happened to Mr. Lu when he travelled abroad on business and took the opportunity to buy Michael Kors handbags for his wife, the ones with small logo, priced between 150 and 1,200 euros. From the normative cultural perspective of global travellers like Mr. Lu, Michael Kors can be defined as an "inconspicuous brand" as it is associated with subtle and delicate products (Eckhardt, Belk, and Wilson 2015, in Greenberg et al. 2020).

Considering design aesthetics, the colours of Michael Kors handbags are usually "sober and muted, as elements of a quiet luxury brand," just what high-*suzhi* consumption represents, as opposed to the loud luxury brands which "have a flashier set of products" (Greenberg et al. 2020) with shocking colours more associated with the ostentatious taste of the new rich.

By buying these *quiet* luxury products from foreign brands, Mr. Lu and most of the participants who went on business trips abroad, primarily sought to meet two consumer needs that distinguish Chinese consumers from their global peers. Firstly, they distinguish themselves from the new rich, who are low in cultural capital, "focus on popular brands, and follow mass taste" by pursuing *loud* luxury products with noticeable logos (Zhang 2020, 15); and, secondly, they emphasize group harmony and individual responsibility to the group by choosing products from "quiet brands" that conform to social norms of modesty and thriftiness (Zhan and He 2012). Such materialist behaviours indicate the tendency among the Chinese middle class to use possessions to attain taste, happiness and self-identification, as is the case in Western societies (Belk 1985). Additionally, and from a social psychology approach, as many of our informants are only children, the rise of materialist values can also be explained by historical reasons such as the one-child policy in (1979–2013) and its implications in promoting a spoiled generation in China. Hence, material parenting practices through which parents use goods to express their love or to shape children's behaviour can foster materialism in adulthood (Richins and Chaplin 2015). These observations confirmed that middle-class consumers embraced not only traditional values, but also Western materialism, individualism, and hedonism.

Simultaneously, other informants who had facility identifying sophisticated brands and new lifestyle trends also sought to meet other consumption needs. For instance, Mr. Qiao sought good value for money, uniqueness, and products that conformed to global middle-class norms. Mr. Qiao not only bought European brands, but also looked for exclusive and non-mainstream fashion brands when travelling abroad. If there was any new brand or item that called his attention, then he would look for more information to decide whether or not he wanted to buy any of their products. This occurred during a visit to Barcelona. "Many people there carried bags from Freitag," he explained. Since he liked the brand, he looked it up online and liked the exclusivity of their merchandise—all designs are different from one another. To avoid carrying it all over Europe until returning to Beijing, he searched for the cheapest way to buy one in China. He explained at length that in Beijing, there were only two stores that sold Freitag's products, but the variety was lacking. The exclusivity of its merchandise and rarity within China motivated Mr. Qiao to buy a backpack (240 euros) and a wallet (65 euros) from the brand's official website. In a matter of days, the items had arrived at his doorstep all the way from Switzerland: "I don't want to wear what everyone else is wearing, I like things that are unique."

These consumer habits were "distinctive" for three reasons. Firstly, the practice and experience of shopping itself was different. What distinguishes the purchased product goes beyond the product itself. In the case of the Freitag brand, the difficulty of finding it in Beijing endowed its products with a double distinction.

Acquiring a premium brand or "volume plus" product in the country of origin for its lower cost compared to Chinese prices, implied that the buyer has travelled to a European or North American country, which meant that she/he possessed high economic capital (when travelling as a tourist or visiting friends/relatives) and/or possessed high cultural and symbolic capital (when travelling for business). Secondly, the impossibility of identifying through direct observation where the item was purchased also gave a double discrete distinction to the practice of acquisition. On the one hand, the buyer's high economic capital that has acquired a premium or luxury brand item in China or abroad and, on the other hand, the act of assuming a consumer habit with high symbolic capital that cannot be transferred.

This quest for uniqueness confers a semantic unity on the practices that warrants reference to coherent "lifestyles" (Weininger 2005, 95). Whereas foreign brands such as Armani or Michael Kors may represent the whole category of luxury products and services—which makes these middle-class items particularly appealing to consumers with a general lack of knowledge about fashion brands, such as Mr. Yi and Mr. Lu—Freitag connotes cosmopolitanism, and a bohemian and affluent European lifestyle. Hence Freitag reflects a more sophisticated knowledge about fashion brands in China. However, Mr. Yi, Mr. Qiao, and Mr. Lu's wife used Armani, Freitag, and Michael Kors to develop and support self-identity by integrating symbolic middle-class meanings of these brands, such as cosmopolitanism, subtlety, frugality, and uniqueness, into their own identity (Wiedmann, Hennigs, and Siebels 2009, in Zhan and He 2012, 1454). Although the taste of our informants was heterogeneous, they manifested a preference for a kind of frugal values and *suzhi* products which converged symbolically to form an entire middle-class disposition that appeared markedly different from that of the dominant and the subordinate classes.

Finally, as brand awareness among middle-class individuals is becoming increasingly sophisticated, consumers such as Mr. Qiao avoided using the popular and best-known brands to express their uniqueness and signalled status through brands that will only be picked up by other connoisseur consumers. At the same time, his brand consciousness alleviated the identity threat by distinguishing himself from others after evaluating positively brands that represent prestige, creative ways of using products and uniqueness (Zhan and He 2012). Indeed, less popular brands such as Freitag allowed these cosmopolitan Chinese middle-class individuals to consolidate a distinctive self-image and feel connected to the global world. As a result, such "well-travelled" and high-*suzhi* consumers stand out not only from the new rich—who only own economic capital and consume items from well-known luxury brands—but also from other local middle incomers with high educational credentials but who had not been able to travel as much and had a lack of knowledge about genuine fashion brands and trendy lifestyles.

High-culture aspirations

Although the mass consumption of cultural products has experienced dramatic growth over the past two decades in the PRC, it is not a new phenomenon. As noted earlier, despite the anti-consumerism rhetoric during the Mao-dominated era, the state developed a "socialist consumerism" to manage demand in every respect and consequently the production of cultural assets was kept under the tight control of the economic and political exigencies (Gerth 2020). However, since the reforms of the 1990s, a new social identity has been constructed and negotiated through political economy, and cultural consumption and its symbolic content. In terms of cultural economy, the Chinese cultural production "transformed from a fully state-funded public sector into a market-oriented, profit-driven commercial industry" (Zhang, Xie, and Huang 2020, 6–7). Consequently, the development and spatial distribution of cultural products have been affected by both market factors and the Party-state's determinant influence on the cultural sector in China today.

Therefore, this section aims to analyse the consumption of cultural products mainly related with the world of arts, culture, and leisure and associated with the post-industrial lifestyle that emerged in the PRC after the reforms of the 1990s. It also evaluates how middlebrow activities operate as signals of class structure (homology thesis) in China today, and how they are used by middle incomers to effect distinction from other urban groups. In doing so, respondents were asked directly not only about visits to movie theatres, museums, art galleries, and book-shops, but also how often they engaged in artistic activities, such as Chinese operas, ballet, theatre plays, dances, concerts, Western operas, musicals, etc. Furthermore, during data collection I also attended with some of my informants some artistic performances at the National Centre for the Performing Arts (NCPA) and other smaller theatres, in order to observe the composition of the public, their reactions, and the interaction established between them and the performance.

The results from the interviews revealed that all respondents who were asked about their consumption practices of cultural contents responded that, to a lesser or greater extent, they consumed cultural products. Among these social consumption practices, the most common was going to the movie theatre (77 per cent of interviewees went at least once a month); next was visiting the theatre or opera (38 per cent), and consuming both digital and print books of poetry, novels, comics, essays, and art (30 per cent). The least common were going to concerts and museums, to which only 23 per cent respondents answered affirmatively. The findings also indicated that those who went to the movie theatre did so on an average of 1.15 times a month and went to the theatre once every eight months, or 1.6 times a year.

Those reading literature did not buy a book within a month, but averaged nine books every year. Those who attended concerts or went to museums did so twice a year and once every three months, respectively. Compared to its counterparts in Western countries and other social classes in China, the Chinese middle class not only spent more time on reading books rather than exposure to television, news-papers, or the Internet, but also, they read more books and journals with more knowledgeable information (Hong and Zhao 2015, 3). Despite the degree of cul-tural fragmentation and heterogeneity rather than homogeneity in the consumption of cultural products among the informants, the consumption of cultural contents is therefore a matter of class in China today.

However, the respondents indicated that the main factors that have diminished their moviegoing and attendance at live performances were ticket prices, the rise of home media, traffic, parking problems, overcrowding, and lack of leisure time. Mrs. Ren was a university professor and not particularly fond of art but had a friend with "a truly elegant lifestyle," which has impressed her a lot. She, speaking of her friend, said: "always invites me to exhibitions, to see art house movies and things like that [and] I go with her when she invites me." She never went to the theatre to watch a play

> if it's far from home because traffic in Beijing is such a hassle … [and using public transportation is no good, either] you have to do transfers. It takes too much time. If you go by car, you won't find anywhere to park. So, I don't even bother and just watch it on the computer.

In addition, although Mrs. Yao enjoyed listening to European classical music, price and crowding were the reasons she brought forth to justify her low attendance at classical music performances. Mrs. Gong also complained about prices at movie theatres, "I go to the movies at least once a week and to the theatre twice a year, but the tickets are very expensive." Such complaints about the price of the tickets may reflect reactions to intergenerational memories of China's impoverished and anti-bourgeois past like the need to be convinced of standardized quality, a positive attitude towards economizing, and, in general, a feeling of guilt about cultural consumption (Maxwell 2001). This suggests that not only class memories but also political heritage, in particular the experience of Mao-dominated era versus the second wave of reform and opening after Deng's southern tour in 1992, influenced in the middle class's materialistic concerns and interest in leisure in China today.

While Mrs. Ren, Mrs. Gong, and Mrs. Yao mentioned material issues when consuming culture, interviewees with young children blamed a lack of spare time as their main reason for low cultural consumption. Mr. Lu explained that when he was single, he and the woman who would eventually become his wife frequently assisted cultural events,

> Almost every weekend, we'd go to the theatre in Beijing, but after getting married we didn't so much (…) [Now] if I've got a chance, I'll go watch some musicals. For example, while making a business trip abroad, I look for theatres to watch some play (…) I used to read more before, but now I normally read my kids to sleep every night.

Also, Mrs. Ai confessed to liking music ("folk and indie rock") and, as is the case with Mr. Lu, after having a son, her cultural consumption has diminished. In Beijing, "most small venues [to listen to live music] have disappeared. They've closed them down or have had to go somewhere else to perform because the authorities wanted to make all buildings physically alike." She explained that now she seldom went to the big concerts, "it has to do with my life, with my son. Nowadays, maybe once every half a year [I go to concerts], but I used to go a lot before, maybe once or twice a month." Despite her family's needs, she consumed cultural products on a regular basis:

> I go to the movies quite often because there's one nearby and my husband likes going there, so we go at least once a month. And I watch plays at the theatre in Dongzhimen, I've seen most plays written by one of my favourite playwrights, Meng Jinghui.

Whereas youngest participants consumed online Hollywood movies, American dramas, Taiwanese mandopop and Western pop music, older informants tended to consume another type of Western culture: classical music. For instance, in the case of Mrs. Kang, she hardly ever went to music concerts, but preferred the theatre, "although I go very few times because everything is for children. We recently went to watch a musical, before this last time we also went at the NCPA to see *Swan Lake*." The NCPA was a very popular place for quite a few of the informants because the tickets prices for performances were not expensive for them but still within the middle-class range, ranging between 150 and 800 RMB.

Also known as "The Giant Egg" or *Judan*, the NCPA was opened in December 2007 and since then, it has become Beijing's great centre of *high-culture* consumption. It is located quite close to Tiananmen Square, and, at the time of the interviews before the COVID-19 pandemic, it maintained an active international cultural schedule, showing self-produced Chinese and Western operas, classical music concerts, Western and contemporary Chinese theatre, and performances from the most renowned ballet companies. Its sumptuous architecture, its strategic proximity to symbolic centres of power—the Great Hall of the People, Tiananmen, The Forbidden City, etc.—and the nature of its activities which were so far from popular Chinese consumption, all of these represented powerfully the Gramscian legitimacy of high culture, which was the hegemonic culture despite being practised by a minority.

In addition, the central role played by foreign authors in the NCPA's programmed events was striking, especially in Beijing, where, unlike Shanghai, the concentration of domestic performing arts events, particularly Chinese folk arts, was higher than that of foreign artistic performances (Zhang, Xie, and Huang 2020, 11). However, rather than resulting in simple cultural homogenization, the NCPA reflected cultural globalization by promoting the coexistence of Chinese and Western genres. Here, therefore, the global joined the local in constituting discourses of cultural legitimization through a state-sponsored upper-class lifestyle.

Similarly, the importance of the local and traditional culture in the construction of gendered meanings in consumption was also obvious. Beyond the personal enjoyment produced by the experience of artistic contemplation, some female interviewees were of the opinion that going to movie theatres, for them, was more of a family activity in terms of quality time. Meanwhile, some male informants consumed mainstream cultural products in allusion to their popularity and media coverage, such as the science fiction trilogy *The Three-Body Problem* (*Santi*) by Liu Cixin that Mr. Cui and Mr. Duan read, or Wes Anderson's film, *Isle of Dogs*, which Mr. Qiao went to watch alone one morning when he had spare time, because the movie "was so well received." This binary perspective reflects the heteronormative gender relations implicit not only in marketization processes established in the PRC in the post-reform era but also in the revival, promoted by the Party-state, of the patriarchal aspects in traditional Chinese culture.

Indeed, Confucian philosophy still has a strong cultural influence in China's urban lifestyle. China's Confucian culture emphasizes the men's role in taking responsibility for the family (honouring the family) in the public sphere (enhancing family face, professional success, increasing the level of luxury consumption), whereas women's role tends to be more risk-averse than men, showing more altruism, more care for others, being more family oriented and more responsive to environmentally friendly concerns (Mo 2020, Li et al. 2019). On the one hand, the narratives of female informants describing cultural consumption practices as an opportunity to spend time with their nuclear families reflected the patriarchal Confucian values. For instance, for Mrs. Ren, going to the movies was mainly a family activity, a time spent with family that still counts as a shared consumer habit. "I don't go often [to the movies], and if I go it's because my husband and my son want to see a film, but I'm usually not really interested in watching it, but [I think]: 'Ah, it's time to spend with the family. I should go'."

On the other, the consumption of mainstream cultural products by male interviewees (not only science fiction literature and Anderson's movies but also watching NBA games online as Mr. Wen and Mr. Yi did) responded to the desire to enhance individual and family face by conforming social norms. This, though, did not contradict Mr. Qiao's disposition towards uniqueness noted earlier. The importance of face in a collective culture like the Chinese manifested in "the need for conforming social norms, whist the need for showing status," also linked to face, is seen in "the need for uniqueness" as expressed by Mr. Qiao when purchasing Freitag products (Sun et al. 2020, 867). Such social norms are defined by influential reference groups which not only reproduce traditional culture's emphasis on group harmony and individual responsibility to the society, but also promote gender division, male-centred hedonism, and heterosexual hegemony. Further, market forces and neoliberal narratives reinforce such links between men and production/essence and between women and consumption/appearance (Craik 1994). As a result, new gender asymmetries and roles are also taking shape in contemporary China by the confluence of Confucian tradition values promoted by the Party-state and modern Western ideals introduced by market forces after the reforms of the 1990s (see also Chapter 5).

Despite the omnivorous preferences of the urban middle class, their leisure practices in Beijing were conditioned by the individuals' marital status and whether they had underage children and/or extended family. For informants with young children, free time was mainly devoted to their children and (elderly) parents. This was consistent with the proliferation in China of cultural products for children and the fact that informants with young children also consumed such cultural products. In fact, "the most popular artistic genres in China are those targeting at mass, especially family-type, consumers, including instrumental concert, family art and theatre" (Zhang, Xie, and Huang 2020, 8). Discussions of relevant literature in both sociologies of childhood and consumption reveal that the economic logic of global marketization may lead to a homogeneous "children's culture" which, in the case of our sample, was quite obvious.

Most of the time, however, the relationships of our informants with their children were often established around not only such shared consumption practices of children's culture but also the acquisition of social and cultural capital. Beyond the desire to spend time together, a coordinated consumption among family members reflected the preeminent assertion of the middle class to make a clear distinction of their positions in social space. Since the sweeping market reforms starting in the 1990s, the formation of social and cultural capital in China has been increasingly created from cultural consumption practices. As a result, Chinese middle-class families have exhibited distinctive practices through class-based consumption while acquiring both social and cultural capital.

In Mrs. He's case, cinema was an educational tool aimed at acquiring cultural capital for her daughter's upbringing while learning the importance of family ties. She explained:

> I go to the movies once a month with my daughter. By going, I get to bond more with her and, since we watch movies in English, she gets to practice her language skills. [That's why] normally I watch movies for kids, but all of them are in English. We never miss the Disney films.

Since Disney is often cited as a defining instance of "cultural imperialism," Mrs. He and her daughter's practice of consuming Disney films in English not only reflected a distinctive way to accumulate cultural capital but also a process of Westernization or Americanization (Adams 2007). In the same line, Mrs. Wu also noted, "I go to dance performances, or musical theatre like that they have children's choirs at the NCPA, or to ballets like *Swan Lake*. I basically join my daughter."

There is considerable evidence to suggest that the aesthetic taste of social agents with high cultural capital under the influence of cultural imperialism is used to secure positions of status and class boundaries in the social hierarchy by highbrow or legitimating culture "through exercising a mark of distinction" (Trigg 2001, 105). Under these conditions, parents like Mrs. He and Mrs. Wu, conscious of cultural hierarchies and taste distinctions, intended their children to behave like the offspring of the dominant class by making them familiar with the upper-class "language" (English), cinema taste (Disney films) and art performances such as *Swan Lake* (Luo and Tebbutt 2019, 363). Therefore, as cultural activities are often extensions of the self, one way to differentiate oneself from others and establish a consumer's uniqueness in China is to consume Western cultural products. Such activities can distinguish its participants from others because this elitist genre of Western performing arts is relatively novel and far removed from the tastes of the subordinate classes and the new rich in terms of economic and cultural capital.

At the time of the survey, Mrs. Gong's weekends were highly representative of the free time spent by the rest of middle-aged couples with children in the sample. While Saturdays were dedicated to the accumulation of cultural capital through a great variety of formative extracurricular activities for the youngest, Sundays were saved for the *accumulation* of another kind of asset: social capital. Parents foster social and familial relationships with their children through various types of activities such as excursions, visiting classmates, family meals, etc. (see also Chapter 5). During weekends, Mrs. Gong said, "I take my daughter to extracurricular activities to study all day on Saturdays and take her out to the park or a friend's house on Sundays." The urgency when acquiring cultural capital revealed that middle-class individuals expressed their class identity through their consumption, ranging from clothes, food, cars, and leisure to housing or extracurricular activities.

Keeping in line with this pattern, the informants' narratives articulated consumerism and cultural capital accumulation with family togetherness and relationship enhancement. Mrs. Kang also explained that "basically all activities during my weekends revolve around our son" and his private supplementary tutoring. Her son

> plays soccer and is learning to play the piano, so we have to take him and pick him up. [On weekends] we also do the shopping for the rest of the week, clean up the house and, if the weather's nice, we'll go outside or see a performance at the NCPA.

Also, as Mr. Lu commented,

> Like many people my age, I spend almost all my time with my kids on weekends, [since] I don't have time during the work week … [on Saturdays] I basically join my kids to their classes, [and] because my wife also works many extra hours [during the week], we normally use weekends to be with the kids. It's also an opportunity to be together and chat with my wife …. If relaxing means doing personal things, then accompanying my children to their extracurricular activities is also a kind of entertainment.

In addition, the defining practices of Beijing's middle class also affected the urban landscape. Not only shopping centres containing music schools for children saw the number of parents and grandparents increase during weekends, but Beijing's traffic was also altered. Mr. Cui recalled his experience a few years ago when his son went to school.

You can see many parents who take their sons to participate in extracurricular activities. It's like a battle, and parents are outside the entire time waiting for them to come back out. The traffic is tremendous because of this, they only go with their kids from one place to another. That's how weekends are spent … [That's why] the typical lifestyle in Beijing is characterized by its traffic, it's something typical of this city. The time one spends in a car is plenty.

However, when the school year was over, the respondents manifested class-based consumption practices and capital accumulation in other ways. Through family consumption of tourism experiences, some informants assigned meaning to places and images in order to turn them into cultural capital for their children. For instance, Mrs. Ren mentioned that every year she spent a few weeks travelling with her family, "The trick is combining tourism and some activity. For example, last time, we went to Japan, visited some places, and we also took a class on Japanese tea culture … We want to educate our son, we want him to have different experiences." Hence, consumption of tourism experiences became not only an educational tool aimed at acquiring a certain non-academic cultural capital, but also a distinctive class practice associated with distinctive lifestyle mobilities, as the next section evaluates.

Lifestyle mobility

Since the second wave of market reforms launched in the 1990s, lifestyle mobility has increasingly become a strategy developed by the Chinese middle class for class reproduction and a way to convert economic capital into social status and prestige. However, lifestyle mobility is a new topic in China studies that has gained increasing attention over the last decade (Sun and Xu 2017; Xu and Wu 2016). As a result of globalization and enhanced commercialization, the recent spatial mobilities of middle-class and wealthy Chinese to the minority world involved both class reproduction procedures and social distinctions. Such practices of "buying status" (*mai shenfen*), as Liu-Farrer (2016) named it, revealed not only a desire to secure their wealth (investment in housing and companies in minority world) and an aspiration for a different education for their children, or concerns with air pollution and food safety, but also involved a strategy for class reproduction and social distinction (e.g., golden visa) and a desire to enjoy the advantages of the global elite.

In the domestic context, middle-class migrants in Chinese large cities, such as some of the informants in Beijing, reproduced these *mai shenfen* (transnational and modernizing) trends while retaining their original local and familial relationships in their hometowns by visiting home at certain times every year (Xu and Wu 2016). Through their narratives, the respondents expressed the representations of themselves in relation not only to their belongings to places both outside and inside China and engagements with these places, but also their mobility practices. This section attempts to understand how place imaginaries and self-identities of the post-reform middle class are constructed through their lifestyle mobility practices. The findings contribute to an understanding of lifestyle migration in contemporary China and the manifestation of class-based consumption practices and discourses of prestige and distinction among middle-class urban subjects in the pre-pandemic period.

In this context, and returning to informants with young children, a significant feature was the difference between the formative activities their children did on weekends and those done during the school vacation period. As noted in the previous section when analysing Mrs. Gong's case, she explained: "I take my daughter abroad to participate in summer or winter camps ... [so that] my daughter can experience a different world and I can experience a different activity." This way, Mrs. Gong's idea of her daughter's education and lifestyle mobility during school vacation was a constant process of capital accumulation through cultural consumption (of activities, experiences, meeting new people, etc.). As a result, such accumulation processes were an investment in her daughter's education at both academic—such as "new formative experiences" abroad—and social level—through practices of social distinction. As Mrs. Gong argued,

> [I want] her to go to a foreign university because for her generation, unlike us, it's no longer difficult to earn a living. The most important thing is that she sees more of the world, and experiments as much as possible. It doesn't matter which university she goes to; the important thing is that it's outside the country ... [Now] there are many people sending their children abroad to study a bachelor's degree, but I don't want that for my daughter. She's still very young; I'm not prepared to let her go abroad.

Mrs. Gong sought out international student mobility for her daughter while gaining mobility capital, i.e., experiences, educational prestige and hence distinction. In China today, lifestyle mobility, as we have seen, is a form of individualized consumption and discourse of prestige and distinction which amplifies powerful social processes that cement existing social inequalities and dynamics (Xu and Wu 2016, 510). Mrs. Gong's desire for her daughter "to go to a foreign university," not a Chinese one, so that she could "see more of the world and experiments as much as possible," underlined the importance of capital accumulation and, therefore, desirability and distinctiveness as main features of the educational experience outside China. International student mobility also refers to privileged, urban, bilingual Chinese students, moving abroad not only for academic purposes but also for reasons which signify for them something loosely defined as quality of life (Benson and O'Reilly 2009, 621), such as seeing more of the world and living new experiences, as Mrs. Gong indicated.

On that basis, international student mobility is also a path to be among the global middle class and the "people like us." It is thus an ideology to fashion oneself as a modern subject (Liu-Farrer 2016). Additionally, the accumulation of cultural and social capital within international student mobility endows students not only with a social mark of distinction by attending a "world-class" university but also with an advantage over peers in the labour market upon return China which ensures class perpetuation (Prazeres et al. 2017). For instance, Mr. Cui and his wife "live now with *kongchao laoren* [empty nest syndrome]," because his son, at the time of the interview, was studying at an American university. As Mr. Cui noted, educational mobility would allow his son "to choose their future" and thus gain cultural capital, build social contacts as resources for future employment, and acquire social capital to enter distinctive and exclusive groups that could benefit his son's future credentials both outside and inside China.

Beyond Mrs. Gong and Mr. Cui's contrasting motivations for their children to study overseas, their mobility expectations manifested *mai shenfen* practices in the sense of converting economic or political capital into social status and prestige when returning to China (Liu-Farrer 2016, 499). In this context, such capital conversions reinforce pre-existing differences and inequalities between young people in the PRC by positioning already privileged students (those with prior cultural, economic, and social capital) ahead of stay-at-home peers (those deprived of the necessary capitals for mobility) (Prazeres et al. 2017, 115). In this way, urban students and their parents acquire thus prestigious educational credentials and embody self-realization and cosmopolitan narratives through consumption practices of international student mobility.

Nonetheless, in an increasingly mobile society such as the Chinese today, not only children and university students devote a considerable part of their spare time to the acquisition of cultural capital but also adults continue their training after work, even moving out of the city to be more focused on the acquisition of cultural capital. Firstly, one interesting feature to come from my conversations in Beijing was the fact that middle-class professionals were increasingly choosing to study for a doctorate degree while working and taking care of their families. For instance, Mr. Lai, 37, was completing his PhD while working, and his wife, who worked in a state agency, also recently finished a doctorate degree at Beiwai University. Similarly, Mr. Yang, a single engineer from Beijing, studied in the afternoon a couple of hours a day to extend his training course portfolio. By the same token, Mr. Qiao, a 35-year-old single professional, changed jobs and during the first months, he spent his weekends alternating between study sessions to learn information required by his new position in the company, with strolls through nature after renting an apartment in a hotel on a mountain outside Beijing. This was a common practice for Mr. Qiao when he had to concentrate on some important professional matter.

Mr. Qiao's relatively privileged position as an "urbanite who was merely 'consuming' the advantages of non-urban lifestyles temporarily but with no lasting commitment to these places" (Xu and Wu 2016) denoted a mobility practice which identifies the lifestyle of the post-reform middle class and a form of consumption that also involved the acquisition of cultural capital. Mr. Qiao's practices seemed similar to those that some informants' children engaged in on Saturdays and during school holidays to accumulate cultural capital that were discussed in the previous section. The making of an autonomous, economically calculative individual, pending the accumulation of different capitals, was one of the multiple dimensions in the reconfiguration of society and culture in urban China (Zhang 2016, 2). In this context, career and cultural capital accumulation became an important part of the leisure time not only of the many households without children, but also most of the households with children.

These informants have incorporated the utility-maximizing calculation of human capital characteristic of what Foucault (2004) called in 1979 "the entrepreneurs of themselves" based on the notion of the human capital production developed by Becker (1976). In this context, the neoliberal narratives of "the entrepreneur of the self" turned individuals into calculating businessmen of their own lives according to values characteristic of the market—investment, benefits, losses, and so on—in which the body is also a site of investment that needs to be cared for in order to be as productive as possible, for example with walks in the mountains in an environment that encourages maximum concentration, as Mr. Qiao did. Therefore, lifestyle mobility also involves aspirations for a more fulfilling and productive life, insofar as they combine a high level of professional activity (production) with leisure such as enjoying rural tourism or sport (leisure and consumption).

Indeed, lifestyle mobility has been attributed not only to a desire to aspire for different education and class reproduction, but also to other post-industrial alternative connections between mobility and lifestyle, such as perceptions of "quality of life." For instance, public concerns and environmental awareness about how food safety and air pollution in cities affected residents' "quality of life" have been observed as a result of environmental degradation and an intense and rapid economic development in contemporary China. In this context, it is significant that three informants used Beijing's air pollution as a reason why they would move from Beijing to another city with cleaner air.

Mrs. Ai and her husband, for instance, once considered moving to Guangzhou, her husband's hometown, but they have ultimately changed their minds, "The air in Beijing now has improved over the last few years in relation to the pollution, so I think we'll be here for a while and see if it gets better or not." Certainly, at the time of conducting the interviews, the air quality improved in Beijing due to central and municipal governments' intensified control strategies. For Mrs. Ai, food safety and air pollution "are a very important part of our life, and the influence is increasing, especially on children." She was mostly concerned about air and water pollution, "Food is fine because you can buy different kinds of food nowadays, like organic products, but water and air are something you can't improve, it's not up to you."

Similarly, Mrs. Tang had seriously considered moving out of Beijing, and not only because of pollution concerns. She worked as an administrative clerk in Beijing, and she was originally from a small town in Liaoning. Mrs. Tang enjoyed spending quality time with her parents and other family members. However, she argued,

My folks don't live here, that's why I don't see them. Sometimes they come to Beijing and we stay together at home. If they don't come then I wait till vacation time and go see them [and then] we are together all the time. We eat together, watch TV, chat, go shopping, or read ... In my hometown, the air quality is better and my parents are there, [and] my whole extended family is there.

Beyond Chinese traditional narratives associated with rural nostalgia, air pollution and homesickness have prompted her to consider leaving her life in Beijing and returning to Liaoning. "I don't know about my future, it's not very clear. Sometimes I want to go back and sometimes I don't," she said. However, Mrs. Tang also cited material reasons when she considered leaving Beijing. "I don't have enough money, that's why it's not easy [living in Beijing], the city is also full of people." Further, the only reason she liked her current job was because of her co-workers. Such disaffection with the urban lifestyle and the thought of returning to one's hometown did not appear in any of the other interviews involving individuals from other provinces. Rather, the tendency among most middle-class migrants in the sample was to be mobile, settle in Beijing, buy a flat, start a heteronormative family, and bring their parents to the capital to be close by.

Regarding leisure, sport practices in general and sport mobilities in particular have become an increasingly important part of the lifestyle of the Chinese middle class that emerged in urban contexts in the 1990s. For instance, before Beijing became the host city for the 2022 Winter Olympics, the popularity and attraction of skiing had been gradually growing among the middle incomers. The Chinese government has promoted the domestic ski and snow industry by building new skiing facilities not only as a part of its pre-Olympics campaign but also as a way to stimulate local tourism and urbanization. Skiing is a "new sport" in China and that is one of the reasons why Beijing's middle class adopted the perception, common in the minority world, that skiing has a distinct class profile and is a sign of individualization.

Three informants declared themselves to be practitioners of this sport. Among them, Mrs. Ai mentioned that "Every Winter we go skiing [near Beijing] for one week, more or less, or we go places like to Japan." Bearing general similarities to post-industrial societies in the minority world, Mrs. Ai expected and welcomed the opportunity to escape from her fast-paced life when travelling with her family by immersing in nature-related activities, including snow sports or simply appreciating the scenery and taking pictures and videos, which contribute to the functionality and sociability of a heteronormative family. Likewise, Mr. San and Mr. Qiao were also snow sports enthusiasts but gave other reasons for their hobby such as connection with nature, well-being, and personal health.

In Mr. Qiao's case, he skied in the winter around Beijing and, at other times of the year, he skied in indoor skiing centres in the city or travelled to other countries. In an informal chat, he said that he had travelled to Georgia, and hired a guide to take him to the mountains and sky, "Nature relaxes me." In conclusion, before the outbreak of the COVID-19 pandemic, Chinese skiers had the privilege to "enjoy a hyper-mobile lifestyle and demonstrate resistance to the mainstream cultural norms of risk-aversion," while sports in nature incorporated therapeutic benefits ("the body–place interactions"), the realization of ideals such as the happy heteronormative family, and "the construction of personal identities" through consumption (Wu and Yang 2021). In general, class origin and symbolic inequalities have contributed decisively to the social construction of an urban identity associated with the post-industrial lifestyle of the middle class in contemporary China. The findings of this section suggest that State interventionism, capitalist categories introduced by market forces, Western cultural aspirations, and Chinese traditional values have articulated new narratives of class distinction in China since the reforms of the 1990s. On that basis, the correspondences between such social imaginary and subjective defining variables, such as the identification with a social figure, the conceptualization of happiness, and romantic love, are analysed in the next chapter.

Bibliography

Adams, Laura L. 2007. "Globalization of Culture and the Arts." *Sociology Compass* 1 (1): 127–142. doi:10.1111/j.1751-9020.2007.00024.x.

Anagnost, Ann. 2008. "From 'Class' to 'Social Strata': Grasping the Social Totality in Reform-era China." *Third World Quarterly* 29 (3): 497–519. doi:10.1080/01436590801931488.

Andreas, Joel. 2009. *Rise of the Red Engineers. The Cultural Revolution and the Origins of China's New Class.* Stanford, CA: Stanford University Press.

Becker, Gary. 1976. *The Economic Approach to Human Behavior.* Chicago: University of Chicago Press.

Belk, Russell. 1985. "Materialism: Trait Aspects of Living in the Material World." *Journal of Consumer Research* 12 (3): 265–280. doi:10.1086/208515.

Benson, Michaela, and Karen O'Reilly. 2009. "Migration and the Search for a Better Way of Life: A Critical Exploration of Lifestyle Migration." *The Sociological Review* 57 (4): 608–625. doi:10.1111/j.1467-954X.2009.01864.x.

Chu, Julie. 2010. *Cosmologies of Credit: Transnational Mobility and the Politics of Destination in China.* Durham, NC: Duke University Press.

Craik, Jennifer. 1994. *The Face of Fashion: Cultural Studies in Fashion.* London: Routledge.

Crompton, Rosemary. 1998. *Class and Stratification.* Cambridge: Polity Press.

de Oliveira, Sandi Michele. 2002. "Discourses of Identity at the Spanish/Portuguese Border: Self-Identification Strategies of Centre and Periphery." *National Identities* 4 (3): 245–256. doi:10.1080/1460894022000026114.

Eckhardt, Giana, Russell Belk, and Jonathan Wilson. 2015. "The rise of inconspicuous consumption." *Journal of Marketing Management* 31 (7–8):807–826. doi:10.1080/0267257X.2014.989890.

Foucault, Michel. 2004. *The Birth of Biopolitics. Lectures at the Collège de France, 1978–79.* Translated by Graham Burchell. New York: Palgrave Macmillan.

Gerth, Karl. 2020. *Unending Capitalism: How Consumerism Negated China's Communist Revolution.* Cambridge: Cambridge University Press.

Goodman, David S.G. 2014. *Class in Contemporary China,* Cambridge: Polity Press.

Greenberg, Daria, Elena Ehrensperger, Michael Schulte-Mecklenbeck, Wayne D. Hoyer, Z. John Zhang, and Harley Krohmer. 2020. *Journal of Brand Management* 27: 195–210. doi:10.1057/s41262-019-00175-5.

He Qinglian. 2000. "China Listing Social Structure." *New Left Review* (5):68–99. https://newleftreview.org/issues/ii5/articles/qinglian-he-china-s-listing-social-structure.

Hirschman, E.C., and M. B. Holbrook. 1986. "Expanding the ontology and methodology of research on the consumption experience." In *Consumer Research*, edited by D. Brinberg and R.J. Lutz, 213–251. New York: Springer-Verlag.

Hong, Yanbi, and Yandong Zhao. 2015. "From Capital to Habitus: Class Differentiation of Family Educational Patterns in Urban China." *The Journal of Chinese Sociology* 2: 18. doi:10.1186/s40711-015-0021-y.

Hu, Anning, and Jacob Hibel. 2014. "Changes in college attainment and the economic returns to a college degree in urban China, 2003–2010: Implications for social equality." *Social Science Research* 44 (March): 173–186. doi:10.1016/j.ssresearch.2013.12.001.

Jin, Xiaotong, Hefeng Wang, TianxinWang, Yang Li, and Shengliang Deng. 2015. "Why Chinese Elites buy what they buy: The signalling value of conspicuous consumption in China." *International Journal of Market Research* 57 (6): 877–908. doi:10.2501/IJMR-2015-041.

Li, Jiajia, Jiang Zhang, DayongZhang and Qiang Ji. 2019. "Does gender inequality affect household green consumption behaviour in China?" *Energy Policy* 135. doi:10.1016/j.enpol.2019.111071.

Liao, Jiangqun, and Lei Wang. 2009. "Face as a mediator of the relationship between material value and brand consciousness." *Psychology and Marketing* 26 (11): 987–1001. doi:10.1002/mar.20309.

Liu-Farrer, Gracia. 2016. "Migration as Class-based Consumption: The Emigration of the Rich in Contemporary China." *The China Quarterly* 226: 499–518. doi:10.1017/S0305741016000333.

Luo, Mengyu, John Tebbut. 2019. "From Cultural Revolution to cultural consumption: forming a contemporary identity through Shanghai Symphony Orchestra." *Continuum* 33 (3): 351–368. doi:10.1080/10304312.2019.1587741.

Mao, Peijie. 2018. "The Cultural Imaginary of "Middle Society" in Early Republican Shanghai." *Modern China* 44 (6): 620–651. doi:10.1177/0097700418766827.

Maxwell, Sarah. 2001. "An Expanded Price/brand Effect Model - A Demonstration of Heterogeneity in Global Consumption." *International Marketing Review* 18 (3): 325–343. doi:10.1108/02651330110695602.

McKinsey and Company. 2021. "China consumer report 2021. Understanding Chinese Consumers: Growth Engine of the World." Accessed 18 January 2022. https://www.mckinsey.com/~/media/mckinsey/featured%20insights/china/china%20still%20the%20worlds%20growth%20engine%20after%20covid%2019/mckinsey%20china%20consumer%20report%202021.pdf.

Mo, Tingting. 2020. ""Income vs. education' revisited – the roles of 'family face' and gender in Chinese consumers' luxury consumption." *Asia Pacific Journal of Marketing and Logistics* 33 (4): 1052–1070. doi:10.1108/APJML-12-2019-0733.

Mok, Ka Ho, and Jiwei Qian. 2018. "Massification of higher education and youth transition: skills mismatch, informal sector jobs and implications for China." *Journal of Education and Work* 31 (4): 339–352. doi:10.1080/13639080.2018.1479838.

Podoshen, Jeffrey, Lu Li, and Junfeng Zhang. 2010. "Materialism and conspicuous consumption in China: a cross-cultural examination." *International Journal of Consumer Studies* 35 (1): 17–25. doi:10.1111/j.1470-6431.2010.00930.x.

Prazeres, Laura, Allan Findlay, David McCollum, Nicola Sanders, Elizabeth Musil, Zaiga Krisjane, and Elina Apsite-Berina. 2017. "Distinctive and comparative places: Alternative narratives of distinction within international student mobility." *Geoforum* 80: 114–122. doi:10.1016/j.geoforum.2017.02.003.

Richins, Marsha, and Lan Nguyen Chaplin. 2015. "Material Parenting: How the Use of Goods in Parenting Fosters Materialism in the Next Generation." *Journal of Consumer Research* 41 (6): 1333–1357. doi:10.1086/680087.

Rocca, Jean-Louis. 2017. *The Making of the Chinese Middle Class: Small Comfort and Great Expectations.* New York: Palgrave Macmillan US.

Rössel, Jörg, Patrick Schenk, and Sebastian Weingartner. 2017. "Cultural Consumption." In *Emerging Trends in the Social and Behavioral Sciences: An Interdisciplinary, Searchable, and Linkable Resource,* edited by Robert Scott and Stephan Kosslyn, 1–14. Hoboken, NJ: Wiley.

Sun, Gong, Jie Li, ZhimingCheng, StevenD'Alessandro, and Lester Johnson. 2020. "Consumer personality factors and iPhone consumption in China." *Journal of Consumer Behaviour* 20 (4): 862–870. doi:10.1002/cb.1899.

Sun, Li. 2019. *Rural Urban Migration and Policy Intervention in China.* Singapore: Palgrave Macmillan.

Sun, Liping et al. 1998. "Trends and Risks of Changes in China's Social Structure in the Near Future." *Strategy and Management* 5.

Sun, Wanning. 2008. "Men, Women and the Maid: at Home with the New Rich." In *The New Rich in China. Future rulers, present lives,* edited by David S. G.Goodman, 213–228. Abingdon: Routledge.

Sun, Xiaoxia, and Honggang Xu. 2017. "Lifestyle tourism entrepreneurs' mobility motivations: A case study on Dali and Lijiang, China." *Tourism Management Perspectives* 24: 64–71. doi:10.1016/j.tmp.2017.06.004.

Tang, Beibei. 2022. "The performance of class: lifestyles and behaviour." In *Class and the Communist Party of China, 1978–2021. Reform and Market Socialism,* edited by Marc Blecher, David S. G. Goodman, Yingjie Guo, Jean-Louis Rocca, and Beibei Tang, 64–80. London: Routledge.

Tian, Xiaoli. 2018. "Escaping the Interpersonal Power Game: Online Shopping in China." *Qualitative Sociology* 41: 545–568. doi:10.1007/s11133-018-9397-8.

Tomba, Luigi. 2004. "Creating an Urban Middle Class. Social Engineering in Beijing." *The China Journal* 51: 1–32. doi:10.2307/3182144.

Tomba, Luigi. 2014. *The Government Next Door: Neighborhood Politics in Urban China.* Ithaca, NY: Cornell University Press.

Trigg, Andrew B. 2001. "Veblen, Bourdieu, and Conspicuous Consumption." *Journal of Economic Issues* 35 (1): 99–115. doi:10.1080/00213624.2001.11506342.

Tsang, Eileen Yuk-ha. 2013. "The quest for higher education by the Chinese middle class: retrenching social mobility?" *Higher Education* 66: 653–668. doi:10.1007/s10734-013-9627-7.

Veblen, Thorstein. 1899. *The Theory of the Leisure Class: An Economic Study in the Evolution of Institutions.* New York: Macmillan.

Wei, Houkai. 2019. *Urbanization in China. The Path to Harmony and Prosperity.* Singapore: Springer Nature and Social Sciences Academic Press.

Weininger, Elliot B. 2005. "Foundations of Pierre Bourdieu's Class Analysis." In *Approaches to Class Analysis,* edited by Erik Olin Wright, 82–118. Cambridge: Cambridge University Press.

Wiedmann, Klaus-Peter, Nadine Hennigs, and Astrid Siebels. 2009. "Value-based segmentation of luxury consumption behaviour." *Psychology & Marketing* 26 (7): 625–651. doi:10.1002/mar.20292.

Wu, Yuefang, and Jingjing Yang. 2021. "Lifestyle skiing contributes to health and eudaimonic well-being: an emergent Chinese lifestyle mobility." *Tourism Geographies.* doi:10.1080/14616688.2021.1955958.

Wynne, Derek. 1998. *Leisure, Lifestyle and the New Middle Class. A Case Study*. London: Routledge.

Xu, Honggang, and Yuefang Wu. 2016. "Lifestyle mobility in China: context, perspective and prospects." *Mobilities* 11 (4): 509–520. doi:10.1080/17450101.2016.1221027.

Zhan, Lingjing, and Yanqun He. 2012. "Understanding luxury consumption in China: Consumer perceptions of best-known brands." *Journal of Business Research* 65 (10): 1452–1460. doi:10.1016/j.jbusres.2011.10.011.

Zhang, Bopeng, and Jung-Hwan Kim. 2013. "Luxury fashion consumption in China: Factors affecting attitude and purchase intent." *Journal of Retailing and Consumer Services* 20 (1): 68–79. doi:10.1016/j.jretconser.2012.10.007.

Zhang, Jun. 2016. "Family Car, Filial Consumer-Citizens: Becoming Properly Middle Class in Post-Socialist South China." *Modern China* 1–30. doi:10.1177/0097700416645138.

Zhang, Li. 2010. *In Search of Paradise: Middle-class Living in a Chinese Metropolis*. Ithaca, NY: Cornell University Press.

Zhang, Weiwei. 2020. "Consumption, taste, and the economic transition in modern China." *Consumption Markets & Culture* 23 (1): 1–20. doi:10.1080/10253866.2018.1467316.

Zhang, Xu, Minghui Xie and Gengzhi Huang. 2020. "Connection Chinese cities with the global performing arts market: the geographies of performing-arts consumption in China." *Urban Geography*: 1–23. doi:10.1080/02723638.2020.1860622.

Zhou, Xiang, and Yu Xie. 2019. "Market Transition, Industrialization, and Social Mobility Trends in Postrevolution China." *American Journal of Sociology* 124 (6): 1810–1847. doi:10.1086/703346.

Zhou, Xiaohong. 2005. *Zhongguo zhongchan jieji diaocha* [*Survey of the Chinese middle class*]. Beijing: Social Sciences Academic Press.

4

CELEBRITIES, HAPPINESS, AND ROMANCE

The reconfiguration of the motivations to achieve

The Chinese middle class is revealed through a combination of aspirations to achieve. Closely connected to the construction of individual and group identity, and the making of social distinctions and inter-group boundaries, aspirations are "part of a normatively evaluative narrative" about who we are and the kind of person we hope to become (Baker 2017). The lifestyle of the middle class has always been considered an example of a society's belief in aspiring and working hard to achieve a positive and comfortable lifestyle (Hsiao and Wan 2013). In this context, this chapter looks at the social representations of success, happiness, and loving relationships as "normatively evaluative narratives" and how they construct social identity and social distinctions in the post-reform era. By evaluating in detail the content of interviews with members of Beijing's middle class in the pre-pandemic period and following more recent contemporary commentators on China's urban society, it is argued that the Chinese middle class exhibits different social representations that in some sense reflect their class position and capital possession. Whereas the assessment of social figures and celebrities reveals the emergence of new social relations between the individual and group identity, the analysis of the narratives about happiness and loving relationships uncovers the emergence of post-material concerns and ideals of long-lasting committed and heteronormative relationships in everyday life in contemporary urban China.

4.1 Celebrities: the new prophets of *suzhi*

Celebrity has become a pervasive aspect of everyday life in present mediatized societies, and a growing field of academic inquiry (Jeffreys and Edwards 2010). It not only "shapes our thought and conduct, style, and manner" (Cashmore 2006, 6), but also it is "a genre of representation that provides us with a semiotically rich body of texts and discourses that fuel a dynamic culture of consumption" (Turner

DOI: 10.4324/9781003299301-5

2010, 13, 14). While some experts still see in celebrities the personification of trivial and deplorable aspects of popular culture, there is an ever-growing interest in comprehending the ways in which cultural and economic changes have created a mass media industry of celebrities, as well as an interest in analysing the celebrities' social functions, particularly their relationship with new forms of individual and community identity. In the case of the PRC, the emergence of middle-class practices and representations went hand in hand with the emergence of new discourses and aspirational values that shape the thought and social practices of Chinese consumers.

By analysing our informants' references of famous personalities, this section aims to understand how social identities are constructed and reinforced in social figures, and explore notions of class, gender, ideology, and nationalism in the PRC in the pre-pandemic period. Celebrities who engage in charitable activities—such as Zhou Runfa and Priscilla Chan—were mentioned by four of the informants, and scientific/academic figures like Stephen Hawking were also put forward by another four, constituting the two groups of famous individuals most admired by the respondents. Some famous sports personalities and athletes were also mentioned. Among the famous figures referenced by the interviewees, those who occupy second position were only mentioned by three individuals, and they consist of: (1) historical figures of the PRC, such as Zhou Enlai, Lei Feng, and Mao Zedong; (2) athletes with a large following, in particular NBA players and "any Olympic athlete"; (3) artists, such as novelists, actors, and the Taiwanese band *Mayday*.

Finally, two of the women interviewed did not give any names at all. One of them mentioned an anonymous woman who was active on the social media app Wechat's timeline, called Moments. The other female informant admired famous people just for their fame and avoided providing any specific names. It should be highlighted that athletes and artists were chosen only by male respondents—representing 50 per cent of the subjects interviewed—while the other 50 per cent were female informants who put forward names of academics and scientists, celebrities who do charity work, and historical figures—all of which were mostly mentioned by women. In this context, and considering the majority opinions, this section first addresses the celebrity philanthropy phenomenon and the statements that mention scientific/academic figures. Later, all other social figures will be evaluated by considering them as products of the cultural, political and historical circumstances in the PRC.

Celebrity philanthropy and intelligentsia

Not surprisingly, celebrities with philanthropic causes and intellectuals constituted the two groups of famous individuals most admired by the informants. On the one hand, philanthropy in China is based on the Buddhist notions of mildness and commiseration or compassion and the Confucian concept of the universal kindness (*ren*) and the feeling that the whole world is like one family. Here, family is related to "the idea of communion between all human beings, and between the human being and heaven" (Solé-Farràs 2014, xxi), "whereby the privileged bear responsibility for the less fortunate" (Jeffreys and Edwards 2010, 18). Additionally, throughout history, scholars have always had a long tradition of enjoying an important role as teachers to the king and advisers to the government. The notion of "to be a scholar is to be the top of society" has long been popular among the Chinese people—even today the modern intellectuals (*zhishifenzi*) still cherish such an important role (social capital) (Li 2015, 3). On the other, philanthropy and the possession of cultural capital (academia and intellectuals) are also part of the state-sponsored discourse of the Chinese middle class and the notion of civilization—particularly, the Party-state's long-term projects of 'building a harmonious socialist society' (middle-class society), the poverty alleviation campaign (2012–2020) and the Dual Circulation strategy (2020–2035).

Despite the absence of a tradition of private philanthropic activities and organizations in the PRC, celebrity philanthropy has expanded in Chinese society since the government encouraged positive media coverage of philanthropy at certain times—e.g., in the event of natural disasters such as the 2004 Indian Ocean tsunami and the catastrophic earthquake that erupted in Sichuan Province in May 2008 (Jeffreys 2015). Over the last two decades, the Chinese government has seen "a potential role for volunteering in addressing social needs and has actively promoted volunteerism through regulations, policies, and program organizing." For instance, mass nonprofit organizations are controlled by the CCP system and aimed to gather most private donations for philanthropic causes while monitoring other forms of volunteerism (Zhao and Lilly 2021). In this sense, celebrity philanthropy "balances widespread public resentment of those who appear to have come by their wealth too easily in the reform period flowing from the former socialist emphasis on egalitarianism and the growing existence of socio-economic inequalities" (Jeffreys and Edwards 2010, 19). In this context, "the Chinese government has initiated various civic service programs to bridge the gate between city and countryside, relieve poverty, promote education, and alleviate unemployment problems" (Xu 2017). All this state-sponsored imaginary created around philanthropy may explain why 20 per cent of participants mentioned celebrities associated with charity.

The respondents were asked to indicate what celebrity they admired most. On the whole, the most cited was the actor from Hong Kong, Chow Yun-Fat (Pinyin: *Zhou Runfa*), who was the only celebrity mentioned by more than one informant—three in total—particularly due to his charity work, his image as a humble and approachable person, and his harmonious relationship with his wife. Actor Zhou Runfa best embodied the paradigm of the Chinese middle class, as Mrs. Kang explained,

> First, he's donated most of his income to a [charitable] foundation. Second, although he doesn't have any children, his relationship with his wife has always been good. As a star, he's never been a yellow journalism celebrity, nor

been involved in any scandals. Third, some of his works are classics, which means he's a great actor … Fourth, when interviewed, he seems to be very clever … I've also read articles that say when he runs around in cities [he's a running enthusiast], he takes pictures with locals, he's very kind, he doesn't put himself on a pedestal.

This way, wealth in the PRC is legitimized by the ideology of the meritocracy and philanthropic ideals. Thus, wealth is presented "as the result of hard work and ingenuity and by ensuring that parts of it are shared with those less fortunate" (Jeffreys and Edwards 2010, 19). Such narratives were present in Mr. Cui's statement. He was a fervent running enthusiast, and alluded to this practice he shared with the Hong Kong actor as a reason for his interest in the celebrity ("He's very well-known among runner communities"), saying:

[Zhou Runfa] ran in Beijing, in the same park that I go to, and in Chaoyang Park … He works hard to earn money, support his family … He has a good relationship with his wife, although they don't have children. On top of that, he does charity work, donates his money to the country and wears sports shoes that only cost 50 RMB. His donations reach 100 million RMB.

Mr. Cui's interest also stemmed from the belief that Zhou Runfa personified his concept of success which consists of three interrelated factors: wealth, prestige, and harmony within the family. The anthropocosmic vision that the harmony of the self with everything that surrounds her or him—which includes harmony in nature, harmony between human beings and nature, social harmony, and individual harmony—is basic to Confucianism. Such values were present in Mr. Cui's statement when arguing that "he [Zhou Runfa] works hard to earn money, support his family" and "he does charity work, donates his money to the country," that is, he contributes to the overall enrichment of the Chinese society. Philanthropy thus is also part of the state-sponsored discourse of the Chinese middle class that includes cultural nationalism and the notions of civilization and *suzhi*.

For instance, the Party-state has promoted philanthropy through a system of prestigious annual charity awards (*Zhonghua cishan jiang*) (Jeffreys 2015), and campaigns to sponsor Chinese children in need to increase educational opportunities— as Mrs. He does, "I provide long-term help for a student who lives in a mountain town. I do it as a public service through an NGO." The promotion of celebrity philanthropy was also in line with the key initiative of eradicating rural poverty that carried out by President Xi. Speaking at a ceremony in Beijing in February 2021, President Xi celebrated "complete victory" in a campaign to eradicate rural poverty that would "go down in history." As we have seen, such a victory is part of Xi's Chinese Dream, "the dream of a strong China" (*qiangguomeng*) that aims to restore optimism and enthusiasm through a national rejuvenation by promoting urbanization, upward social mobility, and middle-class values.

The influence of the philanthropy of the wealthy on NGO development among informants reflected the changes in lifestyle in urban China. Mrs. Yao also seemed to refer to Zhou Runfa when discussing about a famous Hong Kong actor who "has built primary schools in underdeveloped zones to try and help children." She later mentioned the actress, Yuan Li, for similar reasons: "I admire these people, what they do helps people." The fact that Mrs. Yao was a follower of Christianity might relate to why she pointed to "people who do charity work" when prompted to name celebrities she looks up to. Beyond the fact that Christianity was perceived as modern and cosmopolitan within the Chinese context at the turn of the century (Yang 2005), in Mrs. Yao's response, she commented, "for historic figures, I admire Mother Theresa [*laughs*], and now I admire Bill Gates, Zuckerberg and their global charity foundations [and] also stars like wealthy Hong Kong and Taiwan businessmen, as well as some actors who get involved in charity."

Indeed, the Hong Kong actor was not the only personality admired for his charity. Mrs. Ren names Priscilla Chan, the wife of the Facebook co-founder, as a famous person she looks up to:

> She [Priscilla Chan] is a lovely person … She has the ability to love and give love, and is very independent, clever, and very intelligent … She has a very good education and academic achievements and good family relations. I think she never, never bothers others … She's dedicated a lot to social programs; together with her husband [Mark Zuckerberg], they donate 99 per cent of Facebook [to] charity. They give a lot for education development or medicine. They want to make this a better world; it's their mission. I believe she's a wonderful person, people like her are a blessing from God. [smiles] A gift from God to our world … She's the kind of person I can learn a lot from, not because she's rich or because she's well educated, but because of her great heart.

The portrait Mrs. Ren made of Priscilla Chan as a lovely person with a very good education, and an independent, clever woman who "never bothers others," showed the hegemonic representation of woman in middle-class subjects. As Guo (2010) argued, despite the typical model woman as "a skilled and committed worker" and achiever of "a position of eminence in her chosen occupation" during the Mao-dominated era, in the post-1978 era women's liberation "has little place in the construction of a 'harmonious society'" and in the achievement of the Chinese Dream. Hence, women's emancipation "almost inevitably involves rigorous bargaining, confrontation or the transformation of oppressive status orders and value systems, which are not congenial to social harmony" (64), whereas the ideal of social harmony can be achieved through subservience ("never bothers others"), compromise ("She's dedicated a lot to social programs"), self-denial ("very good education") or self-sacrifice. These conservative views on women's role in society and the family have even become integrated into Xi's Chinese Dream (Hird 2017). Gender identity, thus, is significantly constructed through the acts of female "others" such as Priscilla Chan—e.g., her "ability to love and give love"—and whose career interests are largely subordinated to their husband's.

Finally, the findings also indicated that some of the respondents, such as Mrs. Li and Mr. Lu, understood the concept of celebrity as "a quality of individuals" or "the accumulation of attention capital" (Rojek 2015, 1), that is, the capacity to attract, hold, manage, and distribute attention. Hence, Mrs. Li stated, "I've never wanted to live other people's lives," but she admired Stephen Hawking because "he's and optimist and passionate. He communicates with netizens and appears on television." Mrs. Li admired Stephen Hawking for the embodiment of fame that he represented. Mr. Lu refused to name someone famous for similar reasons, "Many stars or well-known figures project kindness because society demands it," and "I don't know any of them in person, I don't know what they're like in private." However, Mr. Lu explained that the first thing he noticed in someone was if she/he transmits good energy (*zhengnengliang*) and admired those who treat others as equals. As a result, cultural capital, attention capital, humility, and the ability to transmit good energy also configure the aspirations of the Chinese middle class that fuel new dynamics of consumption in contemporary urban China.

Sporting celebrities

Following philanthropists and scientists (both mentioned by four interviewees), a group composed of historical figures, sport stars, and artists (each mentioned by three interviewees) ranked second among the most admired celebrities. Regarding athletes, NBA stars were mentioned twice by the informants and Olympic athletes once. Mr. Yi noted that, although basketball star Stephen Curry, "is not physically as good as his teammates, and he's very skinny and short ... he's been named MVP twice thanks to his own effort." Perseverance once again appeared as a constitutive element of an admired public figure.

This applied in a competitive environment such as professional sport in which perseverance, along with flexibility, adaptability, and pro-activeness, was commonly associated not only with self-regulation theories—such as control theory and appraisal theory, which have their origin in cybernetics and engineering applications (Fellenz 1997; Vancouver 2005)—but also with enterprising behaviour (van Gelderen 2012). In addition to perseverance strategies, Mr. Qiao also listed the values he most respected when selecting the Olympic athletes he looked up to the most. "Sports aren't necessarily physical. They require a lot of wisdom, and help people improve both physically and mentally." Moreover, "winning is very good – competing against others and meeting people at competitions – making friends at those games is fantastic." As such, Mr. Qiao's testimony demonstrated the duality between the material and spiritual aspects, between friendship and competition, or physical and mental dimensions, and the willingness to harmonize them.

The ideal of such narratives aimed to develop simultaneously two aspects of the civilization model: the material civilization (*wuzhi*) and the spiritual civilization (*jingshen*). Further, the concept of harmony is an ideal constantly pursued both individually and socially. In fact, although Confucianism attaches equal prominence to both material and spiritual civilization, it methodologically "prioritizes the harmony of the self because it believes that individual harmony is the starting point for attaining all the others" (Solé-Farràs 2014, xix). This double variable of civilization and the key concept of harmony were at the core of the "civilizing process" which has overwhelmed society in the PRC (Rocca 2017; Tomba 2009; Romero-Moreno 2018). Nevertheless, the individual or national civilizing conversion can only be driven if the person (or the nation) can overcome his or her own obstacles through, as Mr. Qiao indicated, "personal perseverance," and be victorious ("winning is very good").

In addition, male sports like soccer and basketball "have not only taken over the playing field but become national symbols of unity" (Burnet 2001, 71) and, in the case of patriarchal societies such as the Chinese, the existing parallelisms between social representations and the ideological lines followed by the Party-state were obvious. The discourse surrounding sports reflected that masculinity has dominated the rules of the game by imposing a binary view, who plays and who wins, and excluding women's participation and marginalizing women's (Cinderella) sports, such as netball or synchronized swimming (Burnet 2001). Hence, sports celebrities in particular and sports competition in general reflect the capitalist paradigms of competition, confrontation, exclusion, and monetary hierarchization, the latter transferred to the logic of "the winners and the losers" in economic terms.

In the same vein, Mr. Wen declared himself an "NBA fan," and emphasized another ideal: "I like Yao Ming, Kobe Bryant, Jason Kidd [*laughs*] … Basketball is a very cool sport, people can work in a team to win the championship. It relies on speed, team spirit." The team spirit he mentioned, the group body-building or group mentality, and the contribution to the formation of national identity were other high-value characteristics explored by some investigations about the culture of celebrities in China and the "narrative of the self" (Combs and Wasserstrom 2013; Xu 2018). For instance, team spirit is a model of organization culture which is also present in values of patriotism (*aiguo*), philanthropy, and public property. Also, group mentality induces productivity by striking a harmonious relationship between two aspects of the civilization model: rivalry (competition) and cooperation.

Artists and memorabilia

Regarding authors and performers, informants put special emphasis on the singing or writing talents of social figures, on their social responsibility, the ability to transmit positive energy, and their role of mediators to establish contact with foreign culture in selecting celebrity endorsers. On the one hand, Mr. San said that Cai Yilin or the Taiwanese singer Jolin Tsai inspired him, "I've been a fan since I was a schoolkid." As "the modern form of popular music began to enter China through Hong Kong and Taiwan," pop musicians from those areas—"that are foreign to the PRC"—still appealed "to the new youth and the post-revolution generations." Pop stars from Hong Kong, Taiwan, and Korea represent desires of modernity in terms of new, middle-class, urban, or even luxurious lifestyles in a positive manner.

Further, Mr. Bai explained that, above all others, he admired several novelists from Sha'anxi province, such as Chen Zhongshi, because "people from Sha'anxi write good novels," and "they have a sense of social responsibility, of passing the baton and their knowledge down to future generations, doing good for mankind and society." According to Mr. Bai, artistic creation implied a social responsibility of doing good for others. Similarly, Mr. Yang also referred to this when commenting about his love for the Taiwanese band, Mayday, because "many of their songs instil something in you, connect with you. They give you positive energy."

Another feature of the PRC's celebrity endorsement was the high value placed on moral and political attributes such as humility, courage, group orientation, ambition, self-cultivation and self-improvement, public propriety, simplicity, patriotism, wisdom, and resilience. The most obvious examples of this preoccupation with moral virtue in China was found in the state-sponsored celebrities such as the military celebrities. In fact, the CCP produced these "heroes" and "models" to stimulate the achievement of "distinct moral and political, as opposed to commercial, goals," and thus "continue to have ideological influence and moral guidance over its vast population" (Edwards 2010, 23). Three participants pointed to three historical figures of the 20th century in the PRC, albeit for different reasons. All three were former soldiers, considered by China's official historiography as people of great importance for the PRC. They embodied stereotypical masculine persona and were often mentioned as examples of military role models of the CCP that have been successfully converted by Party-state into civilian heroes.

Firstly, Mr. Duan admires Lei Feng because "he was a revolutionary of the CCP who helped Mao" and, more importantly, "he helped the people without asking for anything in return." As Edwards (2010) highlighted, Lei Feng (1940–1962) is the paramount "heroic and model serviceman" to the People and the PRC (26). He is the benchmark of all subsequent "soldier celebrities," from the 1960s through to the present, due to "his ordinary everyday acts of service to society and the CCP" (27) "without asking for anything in return," as Mr. Duan noted.

Secondly, Mrs. Yin explained that, although when just a child she had admired her father for being an expert at manufacturing liquor, now she admired Chairman Mao.

> When I read President Mao's biography, I learned that he didn't have any money to make ends meet, but he would say it was fine that way ... they took their dreams very seriously and only focused on that without much help or material wealth. They didn't have anything at that time ... I simply admire those who overcome their personal weaknesses, and the difficulties surrounding them in order for them to do what they have in mind. Maybe that's what spiritual strength is.

As reforms gained speed in the 1990s, "Mao was no longer the threat he had been earlier," as suggested by the regime's mostly tolerant response to the Mao's new status as posthumous celebrity (Dirlik 2012). However, beyond the current popularity of Mao's image due to the emergence of new technologies, new spaces of leisure and tourism, and the so-called "Mao fever" (*Mao Zedong re*), Mrs. Yin's words lay bare the existing discursive spaces in which celebrities and heroes of the Mao-dominated era have scope for overlap and remain compatible with the hegemonic discourses in the PRC. While Maoism is typically associated with the old generations, the underdeveloped and less prosperous era, and the paradigm of the peasant chained to the countryside, narratives of inevitable progress, urbanization, rural migration as a way to "change your destiny," market reforms, industrialization, and social hierarchy have served the Party-state's strategy to maintain its ideological influence, political legitimacy, binary imaginary of society, and moral guidance over the population in China today.

Thirdly, Mrs. He also talked about a national historical character: "I admire Zhou Enlai. He was wise, but also humble and ambitious, which are the most important characteristics," and added "He served important causes." Zhou Enlai, like the other two historical figures mentioned by the informants previously, is the result of personal self-improvement as a lifelong process, and personalizes humility, ambition, resilience, determination to accomplish personal improvement, and self-cultivation, which are central to the representations of the Party-state's soldier celebrities. These role models of the hegemonic culture invoke self-discipline and self-governing behaviours based on a gentle acceptance of the importance of a willingness and ability to change. The Party-state has rocketed these military heroes to celebrity-like visibility by promoting the relationship between the military forces and ordinary Chinese people through the entertainment industry, digital media, and education. Indeed, the techniques of "Education of Quality" (*suzhi jiaoyu*) used in schools in Beijing teach Chinese history through exemplary figures, such as Mao Zedong and Zhu De, not because of their revolutionary fervour, but because of their rigorous self-discipline and the care they expressed towards others (Woronov 2003, 2009). Thus, strategies that seek to get people to be self-improving are introduced by historical figures which reaffirm their proximity to contemporary citizens through discourses of moral virtue and humility.

In addition, military forces are not only examples of a masculine-gendered organization as can be apparent at first glance, but also the assertion of "a nation's identity"—e.g., the People's Liberation Army (PLA) officers are members of a "socialist family," a cohesive and self-disciplining brotherhood—and "the qualities necessary to prosecute war—courage, loyalty, and self-sacrifice" (Hedges 2002, 11). Although these exaggerated and inflated depictions of "heroic and model servicemen" have been popularized by the Party-state in order not to lose relevance as an ideological and moral guide for the Chinese population, they have also served to promulgate the PLA rules. That is, a strict military organization with rigid chain of command, time management methods, and fixed routines. Simultaneously, these historical figures have promoted the pre-eminence of hierarchy of allegiances, patriotism, self-regulation, subordination, the identification of hyper-masculine "worthiness" and warmongering as the supreme virtues of military life and, therefore, of the paradigm of the "hero."

Thus, all the values put forth by the informants fit into a public discourse about civilization and harmony. In this context, the "harmonious society" does not appear to constitute a departure from traditional paternalistic patterns of govern-ance. Nor does it conform to a call to change, or a mere call to order. Rather, the "harmonious society" is essentially different from the simple call for "order." It advocates the conscious and rational removal of any underlying economic, social, or behavioural causes of conflict, rather than its institutionalization and/or repression. It is therefore accompanied by a stress on individual conduct, self-improvement, virtue, and responsibility.

Moreover, state-sponsored discourses have increasingly promoted social representa-tions that envisage the active participation of subjects based on responsibility at the community level (philanthropy), the reproduction of privilege (heteronormativity, social distinctions, gender division), self-discipline (martial values), and the agency of a wide array of players in a virtuous scheme (sporting values). High-*suzhi* representations have been associated with celebrities. They are, as Aschoff (2015) would name them, the "new prophets" of the high-*suzhi* in the post-reform era. As part of China's hegemonic culture, they do charity work to offer guidance, to tell people how to behave and think, and what's wrong with society and how to fix it (Aschoff 2015). Significantly, the most powerful of these celebrities are not the state socialist workers or middle-class individuals, rather they are part of the dominant class. Celebrities in general (and soldier, sporting, and philanthropic celebrities in particular) thus have become a way of normalizing the existence of privileged and unprivileged individuals, promoting the idea that such social asymmetries can benefit the less fortunate and, finally, neutralizing collective visions of change that could challenge economic inequality and the hegemonic culture in contemporary China.

4.2 Happiness

This section discusses the relevance of the concept of happiness from the point of view of social representations. The notion of happiness used in this study stems from Veenhoven (2004), who perceived it as a synonym of subjective well-being (SWB), personal satisfaction, and quality of life. The term SWB is only "a more scientific-sounding term for what people usually mean by happiness" (Seligman and Csikszentmihalyi 2000; in Ludwigs et al. 2017, 2). According to the *Guidelines on Measuring Subjective Well-being*, launched by OECD in 2013, happiness (or SWB) was defined as "Good mental states, including all of the various evaluations, positive and negative, that people make of their lives and the affective reactions of people to their experiences" (OECD 2013, 10). The aim here is to evaluate how Beijing's middle incomers represent happiness by analysing the descriptive process of the social representations of happiness according to two research methods: survey and content analysis.

In order to look at measures of SWB of the informants, and following Veen-hoven's (2007) model, this section addresses two kinds of "subjectivity": subjective substance and subjective assessment. SWB "can be about different domains of life, such as work, family, or leisure" (224). The three main domains of the SWB are objective living conditions, significance of average happiness and/or satisfaction with dimensions of life (this section), and the perceived quality of a society (Veenhoven 1996). With respect to the last item, this section understands, on the one hand, that the perceived quality of a society is seen as generalized social trust. This generalized perception is a crucial component of social capital, not only to a variety of individual-level but also community-level outcomes as the previous section has evaluated and the following chapter analyses—the social space of gender and the community. On the other, and following Jackman and Jackman's (1973) suggestion, this section considers that SWB is also based on the individuals' perceptions about their position within a social hierarchy.

However, since people appraise different aspects of life from numerous approaches and often combine aspects and appreciations, the design of the questionnaire of this study intended to ensure that the informants answered openly and, therefore, avoided any predetermination of concrete domains to facilitate the maximum subjectivity possible. At the same time, during the interviews in Beijing, questions linked to the three domains of the SWB pointed by Veenhoven (1996) were raised, such as "Do you consider yourself happy?" or "Do you feel any pressure in your life?" The answers were coded on a three-category ordinal variable following the Wang and Davis's (2010) model, with 1 representing "happy" (65 per cent of respondents), 2 representing "just so-so" (23 per cent), and 3 representing "unhappy" (12 per cent).

Materialist and post-industrialist concerns

To a greater or lesser extent, the association between happiness and material well-being was mentioned by most of our informants. The most evident expression of happiness comes from Mr. Yi. "I'm very happy [because] I'm satisfied with my circumstances and with myself." He referred to a Chinese idiom which says a person is happy in any situation if she/he does not desire much, "I don't yearn for anything, which is why I think I'm content." Considering that he was equipped with enough economic capital to not have to worry about his economic future, and since he was the informant who expressed himself the happiest ("I'm very happy"), in his case, happiness and economic capital—or lack of "yearning for things"—were two converging variables. According to the theory of post-industrial society and post-materialist culture, after the affluence period, the importance of the post-industrialist concerns for happiness—such as job satisfaction, personal autonomy, environmentalism, and self-expression—relative to that of materialist concerns—for basic needs and income—is greater. However, in transitional economies such as the PRC, post-industrialist values and attitudes may apply only to a small population.

Nevertheless, over the decade from 1990 to 2000, at the time when the PRC experienced a massive improvement in living standards, people's SWB unexpectedly fell considerably. The percentage of the population that described itself as being "very happy" went from 28 per cent in 1990 to 12 per cent in 2000 (Wong, Wong, and Mok 2006). This striking paradox can be explained by the curvilinear model—that is, "at low living standards rising income yields great gains in happiness but these gains level off as incomes continue to rise" (Brockmann et al. 2009, 389). In the case of the PRC, the main reason of such a profound decrease in SWB caused by financial dissatisfaction lay in the rapid transition from a planned subsistence economy. While in the Mao-dominated era money mattered little—the fulfilment of needs depended on family bonds, and, particularly, the political and social capitals—in the post-1978 era money *does* matter, "money is the key to get goods, services, security and also social reputation—in short: for subjective well-being" (Brockmann et al. 2009, 389). As in contemporary urban China money matters more than feelings of powerlessness or political distrust for SWB, new social representations or discourses have emerged from the market-oriented reforms among the urban middle incomers, in particular after the reforms of the 1990s.

Indeed, a sign that financial dissatisfaction showed the greatest negative effect of life satisfaction was the emergence of narratives related to "the winners and the losers in the reform" and personal fulfilment—e.g., the achievement of harmony, tranquillity, well-being, and so on. For instance, Mr. Qiao, who considered himself "happy", also remarked that as "Living in a city like Beijing can be very stressful because there are many people who want to take your place if you slack off." That is why he wanted to apply for a higher position at work, "if you don't apply for this, then you're humiliated by others. So, achieving this will make you feel more at ease, being recognized by others, more money … In the end, you have more options in life." Similarly, Mr. Lai's explanatory statement very clearly set out the reasons why material grounds were the source of his worries, "housing is now an issue; it costs a lot of money, a whole lot." On the one hand, Mr. Lai mentioned material anxieties particular to his generation, since when his parents were young, "The pressure my parents faced was much less! [*bu zouxin*] I think they were happy, they had innocent beliefs just adoring commander Mao, not us."

On the other, Mrs. Tang, whose answer was one of the two assessments coded as "unhappy," explained that "I'm not in a good moment in my life, but I try to be happy." Although she worked as an administrative officer in a public institution, she considered herself poor. She stated that Beijing was a very expensive place if you want to enjoy the food. She hoped to find a partner, get married, and have children. Sometimes, she considered moving back to her hometown and leaving Beijing behind; after all, the only reason she liked her current job was because of her co-workers. Additionally, when she was asked about stress, she responded with apathy, "I don't feel stress in my life because I don't have enough money."

In contrast, the importance of post-material concerns for happiness was also high in the informants' assessments. For instance, the main reasons that Mr. Wen offered to show he felt happy were far from being only materialist:

I'm an optimist ... I'm happy! My parents, my relationship with them is harmonious, I love them and they love me. I have many friends who I communicate with frequently ... and I also have a stable income, which is why I'm not worried about the pressures in life. [*laughs*] There's no huge weight bearing down on me.

Although Mr. Wen mentioned at the end that he did not suffer from stress due to the economic stability he enjoyed, the main causes of his happiness were typical of someone without major materialist anxieties, as he referred to family ties and friendships as the primary source of satisfaction. Not only Mr. Wen, but also Mrs. Ai, and Mrs. Wu, mainly associated happiness with optimism and being a positive person. According to them, happiness depended on one's own personal attitude, meaning the subjective, and not the objective factors such as salary, education, or access to suitable housing. Similarly, Mrs. Wu, Mr. Lai, and Mr. Qiao considered themselves happy people, and indicated that happiness was the result of individual choice that requires responsibility. Mrs. Wu's assessment showed a non-material view when saying that she had reached an equilibrium associated with stability and tranquillity: "I'm a happy person ... Most of the time, I'm a calm person, I don't think about negative things or overreact. I don't think too much, that's why I think I'm happy." Tranquillity, stability, and the lack of material concerns for covering family needs were all features of someone who enjoyed a life "under control" and without uncertainties, in other words, a *xiaokang* life.

Likewise, at the core of the *xiaokang* standard of life is the role of the family as a unit of society, and the importance of social conventions (*li*) to shape the person and "provide each member with a defined place and status within the family and community" (Solé-Farràs 2014, xx). In the case of Mr. Lai, he pointed out that happiness "consists in taking good care of things within those 'concentric circles'" (see also Chapter 5). "A Chinese person's life is like a concentric circle (*tongxinyuan*), meaning that each individual has the responsibility and ability to care for the things in each one of these concentric circles." In the same vein, Mr. Qiao stated that he was happy "most of the time," but "you have to adapt by yourself. If you share an interest with the world, it won't be difficult to be happy because there'll always be things that attract your attention. So, you just do what you want to do, what you like to do." Here, the Confucianist activity of adapting whenever necessary to the world and harmonizing with the social and cultural norms was combined with personal realization in an individualistic fashion ("you just do what you want to do"). That is, the importance of post-industrial concerns for SWB was indeed high among our informants. It clearly indicates that something has changed in the Chinese middle class between the 1990s and 2010s.

Thus, the message here is that if you make the right choices and take the proper attitude you can achieve happiness and personal fulfilment. However, by emphasizing individual strategies for personal and professional success—based on building up enough social and cultural capital, and investing it wisely—such representations "place the burden of success on the individual, in the process disguising societal shortcomings as personal failures" (Aschoff 2015, 14). That is why, achieving this post-industrial ideal was not always easy for the post-reform middle class. They were undergoing a complex process of class crystallization in a transitional economy. Despite the increase in post-industrial concerns among the informants by evaluating SWB, material concerns were still strong factors in depressing life satisfaction. Mrs. He's assessment summarized a general tendency among middle incomers. She focused on the constant accomplishment of her personal objectives, which was the strategic accumulation of different kinds of capital, in order to evaluate her SWB.

> There are different objectives depending on where you are in life. For example, I initially wanted to pass the National Judicial Examination (*sifa kaoshi*) … [and now] I want to familiarize myself with all professional topics and be valued by my colleagues in the profession.

However, when asked if she felt any pressure in her life, the gendered and materialist worries emerged.

> There are two aspects. The first, is work and my family, too. I have to care for them. The second is the economy, because life in Beijing is very expensive, and there's pressure from my studies, too … Pressure from [paying] the mortgage and schooling are the main costs.

This section has observed the mutual reconfiguration of post-industrial concerns such as personal fulfilment on the one hand, and material concerns on the other, in a context of a fast-paced commodification of a growing number of areas in both public and private spheres—rapid industrialization, competitiveness of the labour force, globalization, economically calculative individualization, and urbanization. On that basis, Mrs. He's accumulative aspirations of cultural capital were understood within the context of China's fragmented market environments. After dismantling the redistributive system in the 1990s, the state adopted strategies to develop markets in various economic arenas. Consequently, multiple indicators of economic inequality manifested, specifically income, housing, consumption, and social welfare benefits (Zhao 2012). Simultaneously, these indicators were embedded in distinct market environments and had different allocation processes such as the housing transformative case from public to private property through *danwei*.

As a result of this rapid process of marketization of everyday life, a higher level of contextual inequality, which affected status perceptions and life satisfaction, not only increased status differentiation, but also heightened status competition and status insecurities among social members (Wilkinson and Pickett 2008). Although income become a more salient indicator, after the surge in housing prices due to heated competition in the market, the indicators of social distinction in China were transferred to other areas such as the accumulation of cultural capital and cultural consumption practices. In pre-pandemic China, self-referential narratives of the middle class were built on the assertion that the only effective mechanism to achieve class mobility was educational credentialism, as the following section analyses.

Self-referential narratives and pseudo-happiness

As noted earlier, happiness as a post-industrial social representation in urban China is mostly understood in terms of accumulation of both cultural and symbolic capital—i.e., prestige or personal fulfilment—in multi-dimensional social spaces. It should be noted that cultural capital is the informational capital, primarily legitimate knowledge of one kind or another (Bourdieu 1987, 4; Jenkins 2002, 85), from the completion of a PhD to recognition in the labour market and "enriching" activities. For example, Mrs. Ren, a 46-year-old university professor, explained why she felt happy after accomplishing a series of goals and professional requirements achieved based on effort and sacrifice.

> I'm satisfied with what I have, with what I've received. Now I think that I'm a happy person in this period of time … When I was doing my doctorate … everything was truly difficult, not because of other reasons, but just because of the academic pressure.

However, she stated, "I now believe that I'm enjoying the fruits of what I've paid for [*laughs*] in the past. I worked hard, too much during previous years, and now I'm simply enjoying the sweetness of those fruits [*laughs*]."

These words referred to a self-referential narrative based on personal perseverance as a generating element of well-being. This was also detected in the response of other informants who shared the same condition as relatively privileged migrants. Such self-referential narratives about subjective social status and status change also exerted "a strong impact on subject well-being, even after individuals' economic conditions are controlled" (Zhao 2012, 448). At the same time, factors such as personal income, housing values, and the consumption of lasting goods also contributed to a more positive perception of the general state and of the changing of status, as exemplified by the cases of Mrs. Yin and Mrs. Ai. Furthermore, keeping in mind the results from Chapter 3, people with moderate incomes living in Beijing are characterized more by their geographic, rather than social, mobility. Most of them considered *upward geographic mobility*—that is, migration to *Bei-Shang-Guang-Shen* or Tier-1 cities: Beijing, Shanghai, Guangzhou and Shenzhen—in terms of upward social mobility.

As a result, their testimonies as "successful" migrants in Beijing reinforced their self-referential narratives of SWB. "I come from a small town," said Mr. Bay, alluding to his life course, "I came to Beijing and I appreciate it very much … [I have] a competitive job for most people, but I think I've been successful in a way." Theoretically, a situation in which a perceived inequality was overcome was a reflection itself as a prize for one's effort. Hence, inequality could be positively understood as the manifestation of economic incentive and an opportunity (Jiang et al. 2012, 1191), as explained by Mrs. He when giving an opinion about the wealthy,

> I know many rich people ... their wealth is due to their effort, which motivates me to obtain more wealth in the future through work [because] being rich, I'll be in a better state both in the workplace and at home with my family.

In Mrs. Ren's case, she decided to study a doctorate when working as an English teacher at the university at the end of the 1990s for several reasons such as professional requirements, competition in labour market, personal fulfilment, and

> the fourth reason was that I gave birth to my son in 2001, so you feel that everything is becoming settled, a stable family life. It was as if life was just that: family, teaching, daily life. It gives the impression of being very boring [*laughs*]; life will be like that for the next following years. I didn't want that, I wanted a change in my life.

When Mrs. Ren explained her feeling after having a child and seeing that "everything is becoming settled," it reflected the beginning of the post-material phase that many people with middle incomes had experienced over the last two decades in the PRC. It illustrated that, despite the increase in economic capital, her SWB declined. In a similar vein, clearly the majority of statements coded as "just so-so" seemed to be characterized by the link between the increase in economic capital and the decrease in SWB that Mrs. Ren experienced. Up to this point, Mrs. Ren and the respondents have all shown themselves to be happy despite the pressure that most of them felt for material reasons. However, other participants were not so happy. For instance, Mrs. Kang said:

> To tell you the truth, having a family hasn't really been stressful for me ... My husband actively participates in domestic responsibilities and in the education of our son ... In terms of work, it's given me a little bit of stress, but it's not about whether I'm competent or not, but about knowledge ... I used to feel a lot happier before ... Now, not so much. I don't know if it's because of my age [*laughs*]. When my son was little or when I didn't have any kids, I just focused on my job and was happy.

Mrs. Kang also perceived that when contextual inequality increased, not only the objective difference–economic inequality– increased, but also the competition and insecurity of social actors with regard to their social status. This was evident when she began discussing life in Beijing:

It's not easy, the stress of living is greater than before. You can tell with housing, the pace of work, and in children's education … Beijing is full of smart people … and competition for educational resources is very competitive.

For this reason, some testimonies quantified their happiness around 50 per cent. Although Mr. Bai was conscious of the virtues of his life as a professor, he did not say he was a happy person. The pace of work that he decided for himself has been a burden. "I'm only superficially content. Inside, I have huge pressure; I think I do it to myself, most of all … Nobody has asked me to do anything other than teach classes or do housework, [the rest] is all my choice." Such statements were coded as "just so-so," in other words, "pseudo-happy"—just as it was described in an online article issued by the *People's Daily* (2010) about middle-class families in Beijing and Shanghai. It explored the idea that a higher level of contextual inequality not only increased differences in status, but also competition and insecurity of the social actors. In fact, as the outcome of the investigation undertook by Wilkinson and Pickett (2008) on the association between income inequality and physical and mental health showed, income inequality influences health through psychosocially mediated effects of social comparison.

However, although social comparisons based on income inequality affect the mental health of urban population, there is also a positive relationship between inequality and happiness. As the controversial results of Knight, Song, and Gunatilaka's (2009) analysis showed, higher income inequality within a county "might serve as a proxy for greater diversification in the county, in turn raising the prospect of greater opportunities for economic benefit" (644–645). However, it must be borne in mind that such a "demonstration effect" appeared to be most powerful in the poorest households and areas. While those with wider horizons may experience stronger expectations of the successful development of live chances, those with narrower horizons—such as middle incomers who "have been successful in a way" and enjoyed a *xiaokang* lifestyle—may experience a lower level of motivation; they may feel "only superficially content" or "pseudo-happy."

In the case of Mr. Yang, a 32-year-old Beijinger, he spoke of his dissatisfaction when facing the prospect of unfulfilled expectations and social conventions associated with a certain age, a well-known phenomenon present among the Chinese middle class. Additionally, his words also demonstrated how social pressures to find a partner—traditionally associated with women over 30 years old in China—were also pervasive among single men. He argued,

I used to think I was someone happy, but as the years go by and I get older, I think I'm becoming unhappier [because] I feel that I've lost something … I'm losing my youth, time, and my parents, slowly but surely. My dreams haven't been achieved either and I feel a bit nervous. If I compare myself to a few years ago, I was happier than I am now. I have more money now, but I'm not as motivated as before. I was more positive before … [This is because of] age and time. Sometimes I look at my friends around me and see a whole, and they are those that can't be filled. Like, for example, they all have their own families, which is part of your own dream. It's not easy to have your own family, and I feel a little depressed.

The sensation of emptiness that Mr. Yang brought up was due to the "monetization of happiness" typical of the middle class during the 1990s and at the start of the new millennium. Indeed, the advocacy and encouragement of the new clarion called to "Let one segment of the population get rich first and guide others along the way" as Deng Xiaoping proclaimed, reflected the first manifestations of the new generation of visibly rich Chinese private entrepreneurs, which, in turn led to new social differences based, initially, on the acquisition of economic capital. The "monetization of happiness" was characterized by equating subjective well-being with material well-being. However, the relatively low happiness among the urban population, despite relatively high incomes and expecting higher wages in the future, had to do with the nature of the urban society that had emerged in the 2010s (Knight and Gunatilaka 2010). The feeling of relative privation occurred when individuals believed their achievements, or those of the group, were unjust. It referred, as Ayllón, Mercader, and Ramos (2007) noted, to "the emotional experience" of injustice of post-industrial citizens when comparing their situation with those who surround them and, specifically, with those who find themselves better off.

In the case of the PRC, the pseudo-happiness phenomenon was related to the notion of "frustrated achievers" (Graham and Pettinato 2002). As Brockmann et al. (2009) pointed out, this concept refers to people who have acquired higher incomes in absolute terms, but who are dissatisfied when it comes to their income position relative to the "winners". Further, it should be noted that "negative experiences seem to be more salient than positive ones" when evaluating SWB (391). As we have seen, the economic growth during the 1990s brought with it an increase in inequality that stimulated social comparisons among middle-class citizens. Hence, this provoked many to feel discontented with their financial situation because, although they had increased their economic capital and wages drastically in absolute terms, a growing portion of the Chinese population was placed below the rising national income mean. This confirmed Zhao's (2012) study, which demonstrated that "when social status is controlled, income has little explanatory power on happiness among all indicators of economic well-being" (448). Certainly, the contours of happiness are not well mapped by assuming that the increase in income—or objective living conditions—automatically produce the increase in SWB. In post-industrialist societies, thus, money cannot buy the middle class's happiness.

In short, the findings indicate that, on the one hand, the middle class has always been, and continues to be, a celebrated example of a society's belief in success won from hard work and the quality of "making something of yourself" (Hsiao and Wan 2013, 123; Wheary et al. 2007, 3). On the other, the findings also demonstrate that the group of Beijing's middle incomers was not homogeneous due to the high variance of their material and post-industrialist concerns. The search for happiness produced a set of social practices and representations which were used among the informants to describe new narratives, proving the increasing importance of post-industrialist concerns in the construction of identity in the PRC. From an ideological standpoint, it was also remarkable that the cultural significance of economic success has completely changed in the PRC over the last four decades. There is also growing evidence to suggest that the assorted conceptual features of happiness reflect, in no small part, the codetermination of the post-reform middle class through material concerns and, in particular post-industrial representations, which manifested themselves in everyday practices. Although such post-industrial values are becoming dominant in the politics and mentality of modern populations, they are still fluctuating significantly with market reform and the Party-state's political agenda. However, other variables such as loving relationships or family ties may have a stronger impact on happiness than economic capital. This question will be addressed by analysing informants' assessments on romantic love in the following section.

4.3 Loving relationships

Gender differentiation is an important marker in the loving relationships in the Chinese contemporary scene. Some anthropological studies (Constable 2009; Hansen and Svarverud 2010; Moore 2005; Yan 2009, 2011) have contended that the introduction of Western values after the second stage of the process of marketization in the 1990s has profoundly transformed intimate and personal relations in the private sphere, concluding "that there is a growing individualisation across all sections of Chinese society, from the changing perceptions of the individual to rising expectations for individual freedom, choice and individuality" (Xie 2020, 181). However, as Davis (2014) suggested, the state has regulated couples' most intimate life through the one- and two-child policies, which have stood in contradiction to this turn toward privatization.

These contradictions, though, "have been muted by the CCP's support for expanded autonomy, greater economic freedoms, and minimal constraints on sexual intimacy" (571). In any case, the paradigm of the happy complete heterosexual family (*meiman jiating*) as a basic social unit and institution in the PRC manifests a particular middle-class ideal of monogamy, moralizing representations and non-individualistic values like philanthropy and/or universal kindness (*ren*), filial piety (*xiao*), concentric circles (*tongxinyuan*), and so on. As a result, the state's position toward intimacy is complex, moving between the privatization of the institution of marriage and state interventionism.

As a patriarchal society, gender inequalities of contemporary Chinese society make marriage based on romantic love a struggle for women's pursuit of social success and happiness. Romantic love is typically associated with the modernism of the post-1978 era and the fulfilment of desires and individual choice in conjugal life (Zavoretti 2017, 99). As a global concept, romantic love can be understood as "the idealization of another, within an erotic setting, with the presumption that the feeling will last some time into the future" (Jankowiak and Paladino 2008, 3). While the romantic considerations involved in the social representation of happiness in Western societies aims first to "search" for a romantic partner, or the "right person" (Illouz 2012), and then "to achieve individual fulfilment, realise individual's 'destiny' and accomplish emotional inner balance" (Carter and Arocha 2020, 4–5), romantic love might be less valued by Chinese subjects compared to Westerners (Pimentel 2000).

For instance, Zheng's (2017) study on women's mate selection showed a new generational pattern of intimacy around the term *ganjue* (feelings). This concept includes three defining characteristics: the increased emphasis on the desire for affection, the increased equality between the two gendered partners, and the increased agency in modern Chinese individuals' pursuit of love, in contrast to "the conventional purpose of 'marrying a bread earner' (*jia han jia han, chuan yi chi fan*)." Hence, "marriage is no longer the means of survival as it once was" (65). Therefore, the ideals of romantic love in the PRC are rooted not only in expressing romantic feelings, but, above all, in long-term commitment through marriage.

On that basis, this section analyses the conceptualizations of romantic love as a romantic choice of the informants in Beijing, who were urban university-educated women and men, both married (70 per cent) and unmarried (30 per cent). By looking into their romantic love aspirations, this section uncovers their understandings of class and gender identities by drawing some comparison with the results achieved in Xie's (2020) survey on the marriage aspirations of urban university-educated Chinese women who self-identified as heterosexual; Illouz's (2012) analysis of love's great transformation in minority world; and Rothbaum and Tsang's (1998) comparison study between Chinese and American love songs. Also, considering the previous section on happiness, these questions are addressed below: Is the materialist purpose of "marrying a bread earner" still applicable today among the constituents of Beijing's middle class, or are they in a post-industrial phase in which the *ganjue* equation endures in their lifestyles? Do other variables exist that are outside the normative model?

Romantic love

Loving relationships have been neither free nor equal in China. Regarding romantic love, the "embryonic state" of Western romanticism in China can be placed in the 1920s, when modernizing elites and the Republican middle class "constructed unprecedented conceptual links between modernisation" and "the topics of sex, reproduction, women's liberation and eugenics" in order to make China "a strong and prosperous nation" considering some Western ideals (Aresu 2009, 533). Simultaneously, concepts such as love, desire, and intimacy reliably constituted the narrative about the formation of the modern subject—for instance, romantic love in post-1949 literature adopted the popular revolution-plus-love formula based on the dilemma of negotiating the potential tensions between individuals' erotic desires and the demands of the revolutionary cause (Sun and Yang 2020). In this context, it was the Marriage Law established by the CCP in 1950 that not only outlawed polygamy for the first time in China, but also promoted marriage as a relationship of equals with shared family and children's responsibilities (Evans 1995; Zurndorfer 2016, 13; Sáiz 2009). The aim of this law was to promote freedom of marriage and divorce, but it did not translate to freedom of love and romance, as love remained bound within CCP's nationalistic framework and was subjected to class identity and political revolution in many cases (Wang 2021). The Marriage Law implemented in 1980 by the Chinese state supposedly supported personal independence and equality but in practice gender differences in both private and public spheres increased (see Chapter 5).

In the 1980s, the conceptualization of romantic love *re-emerged* in China as a result of official abandonment of revolution and market-oriented cultural narratives (Zhang 2011). Certainly, as Sun and Yang (2020) highlighted, when China emerged from the Cultural Revolution, the public in general was eager to embrace another way of telling love stories and a new era began in which the individual and the personal started privileging over the collective, and people could "explore the possibilities for a personal life within the broader social transformation (Farquhar 2002, 178)" (11). Under these conditions, in the 1980s and 1990s some well-educated women started in the cities to take romantic love as their major sexual purpose (Pan 1994). Later, although the younger generation seemed "to have fully taken the concept of romantic love on board" (Xie 2020, 183), the lifelong monogamous relationship which harmonized romantic excitement, stability, and companionship is the most desirable loving relationship to obtained among the post-reform middle class in urban China.

Love in China has entered a stage of "crisis" manifested by "the rising number of single individuals struggling to find a partner, an increasing number of registered divorces nationwide," particularly in cosmopolitan cities like *Bei-Shang-Guang-Shen*, and the entangled web of socialist politics, market economy, traditional values, and cultural globalization that make intimacy subject to political, social, and economic changes (Wang 2021, 965, 967, 969). Whereas during the reform era, 50 per cent of couples in the PRC got married not because of romance, but because they were expected to marry (Pan 1994), in China today things do not seem to have changed much. Remarkably, Jankowiak and Moore (2012) and Farrer (2014) found that the ideals of romantic love are rooted not only in expressing "true love" feelings, but, above all, in long-term commitment through marriage between the two members of the couple and their respective families. This is consistent with the results of our study.

For instance, Mrs. Tang expressed the importance of families when personally looking for a partner. She commented that depending on the type of life you want for yourself, it could be easy or difficult to find the right person to marry:

It's not easy for me … Maybe I want it that way [*laughs*], I expect a lot from my marriage … First, I looked for my true love, but at the same time, I wanted there to be harmony between the two families. Meeting these two requirements is difficult.

Thus, when Mrs. Tang spoke of loving relationships, she referred to both individual ("my true love") and non-individual (the "harmony between the two families") motivations.

Indeed, romantic love and its most recognizable romantic manifestations were not their main concerns in most of the informants' narratives about marriage. For example, Mrs. Kang believed that if this kind of love and demonstrations of romance existed in a couple "then even better, but if not, that's fine, too." The way in which Mr. Lai answered a question about love was quite insightful: "complementing economic power between both families means a lot for people of my generation." Mr. Bai showed his class consciousness when discussing romantic love beyond cultural reductionism.

Human beings are all the same … It [romantic love] is important to everyone, but sometimes more so. You don't have any chance, you're not allowed any romantic relationships … Ask construction workers whether they married for love, if they have a romantic partnership. One's romantic life can be different than others, it means to one person can be different to another.

Significantly, the comparative analysis on the nature of romantic love undertaken by Rothbaum and Tsang (1998) between Chinese and American love songs concluded that, although there was a similar level of pervasiveness of intense desires, some well-defined differences also existed that, in our case, coincided with the interviews recorded in Beijing. While North American songs revolved around the individual who was loved and ignored context, in Chinese songs, love appeared as different manifestations of the natural world. The emphasis on interdependence and the concept of *yuan* (contextual forces) were characteristic features rooted in Confucian, Buddhist, and Taoist traditions. *Yuan* emphasized the belief that success or failure in relationships was something predestined and not under our control. The Chinese pessimism about romance may reflect the traditional views of not resisting the greater external (even familial) forces and aligning with nature. Simultaneously, it contrasted sharply with the American assumption that difficulties could be overcome by effort and personal agency (316).

This was evident in Mrs. Kang's testimony and her reference to a poem by Shu Ting about a tree, dealing with ideas of equality, interdependence, and harmony (or "coordination"). She explained what love between partners consists of:

First of all, there's attraction. Otherwise, why choose him? Second: equality. Shu Ting wrote a poem, *To the Oak Tree* (*Zhi Xiangshu*), about equality within a loving relationship. Third, the support between both partners.

Fourth: to compromise… [that] concerns the relationship between love and marriage … It's possible for there to be some coordination or that both people are not truly equal. Maybe one of them has to let go of some things. Compromise is not antithetic to the support that had mentioned before.

Differently, Mrs. Ren was the only participant who clearly associated romantic love with happiness without scepticism in a way very similar to the cultural values associated with the West. It indicated that, on the one hand, her views of love could come from her knowledge of Western cultural references such as Fromm's *The Art of Loving* (1956), and, on the other, negative expectations about the relationship related to the embeddedness of the Chinese view of romantic love. Firstly, this was consistent with the general trend in this study, in which the informants did not equate love with joy or with happiness, except for Mrs. Ren, saying "It [love] is very important [*laughs*] … It's the pillar of the sense of happiness, yes. I think romantic love is: there are two of you in the relationship, but you're both also one single person." Secondly, my outcomes were in line with the conclusions of Rothbaum and Tsang's (1998) study. Chinese love songs transmitted more suffering and present more negative expectations towards romantic goals compared to American ones, in which negative expectations are less an issue, as was noted earlier when discussing the concept of *yuan*.

Moreover, Mrs. Yin and Mrs. Kang mentioned the *feeling* of physical attraction as the greatest difference of the type of love that exists in a couple's relationship. Some informants even remarked about the difference in love they had experienced with their partner when they were merely dating and that experienced after getting married, such as Mrs. Yao and Mr. Lu. For instance, Mrs. Yao pointed out that "building a family is not something romantic [*laughs*]." According to her, romantic love was part of a couple's relationship, "but I think that real life entails managing normal, everyday issues." Likewise, Mr. Lu explained,

Before getting married, I got along with her [my wife], but then the feeling becomes different from friendship … You say "she's attractive," but after getting married, at this moment, I think love is mixed in with family. I still like her, but it's different from when it all started. It's related more with the responsibility for my family, mutual trust, as well as with the kids … In this sense, love is a relationship of responsibilities, it's like a contract.

Certainly, urban middle-class men tended to view sexual attraction in a manner independent of romantic attachment. Mr. Lu's conceptualization of loving relationships seemed to coincide with the patriarchal rhetoric of the modern-day Chinese male (Zurndorfer 2016). According to this, marriage was understood as the realm of responsibility and respectability, while the relationships before getting married, or extramarital relationships with lovers and mistresses, were the true domain of romance and passion (Osburg 2013; in Zurndorfer 2016, 11). In addition, Mr. Lu's assertion that marriage "is like a contract" showed how the Chinese traditional pattern tied the individual to a web of social relationships, responsibilities, and dependencies on others, "like the spider's web" (Hsu 1981, 275, 11), thereby defusing the intensity of romantic passion. In this vein, most informants do not equate love with joy or happiness, but they still showed a high degree of companionship, commitment, and loyalty when describing their partnership. For example, Mrs. Wu also emphasized the companionship shared in her 10 years of marriage, and Mr. Cui stated,

> It [love between partners] consists of *xiangjing rubin* [a relationship in which both partners respect each other, and one treats the other as a guest], which means to be at the same level, no one's superior or inferior to the other.

Indeed, the informants *understood* love mainly through values like equality, respect, or caregiving. However, Mrs. Kang, Mrs. Yin, and Mrs. Ai mentioned communication as a key element in their understanding of love. For instance, Mrs. Ai stated that "Communication is very important ... You have to at least have something to talk about beyond small family issues." That is why "I tend to spend a while with my husband every day after putting my son to bed, talking about things that occurred that day, what's happening in society, and we just talk." Mrs. Ai's conception of love based on communication highlighted a psychological way of thinking—"you have to at least have something to talk about beyond small family issues." In global societies, Illouz (2007) argued, by appealing to individuals looking for new ways of understanding themselves and making sense of their emotional lives, communication transforms emotions into rhetoric objects to be thought about, expressed, discussed, debated, negotiated, justified, and evaluated through guidelines of fairness, equality, and satisfaction of needs, thus being more likely to become interchangeable commodities. To a certain extent, marketization has reshaped intimate relationships established in the private sphere in the post-reform era. Hence, the traditional moral framework based on the socialist family structure upheld by the state co-exists with a clear individualization tendency among the Chinese middle class to apply more subjective criteria in the conceptualization of love.

Monogamy in the market of love and marriage

The paradigm of the happy complete heterosexual family (*meiman jiating*) manifests exclusive monogamous values, gender asymmetries, the commitment to a lifelong relationship certified by marriage, the intergenerational transfer of capital, the reproduction of kinship systems, and intimate and social practices associated with the post-industrial lifestyle of the middle class. Particularly, the state-engineered public determination to marry in synergy with marketization entirely relies on placing patriarchal schemes at the centre of its (self-)disciplinary control in order to "govern from afar" (Zhang and Ong 2008). The Party-state thus has assumed Chinese women's productive and reproductive labour in its policymaking to ensure hierarchical order and intergenerational transfer of privilege within a well-established Confucian patrilineal and patriarchal family tradition. For instance, as Mrs. Tang noted, married women felt pressure to have children, "The pressure I feel comes from society. When I have kids, it'll go away. I also feel pressure coming from this feeling of responsibility, which is why I want to have them."

In fact, media campaigns have sharply criticized "leftover women" and pressured educated middle-class women to marry in their mid-twenties and give birth to improve the "quality" of the nation's next generation of children (Hong-Fincher 2014, 2018). However, as noted earlier, such discourses stood in contraction to Party-state's support for expanded personal autonomy, greater economic freedoms, and minimal constraints on sexual intimacy (Davis 2014). Meanwhile, urban women are "constantly renegotiating" their individual freedom (Xie 2020) not only with traditional gendered aspirations but also with capitalist categories based on gender asymmetries and disempowering mechanisms, in particular *the entrepreneurialization of the self* (Foucault 2004; Gordon 1991). The tension created by these contradicting social representations and narratives is acutely reflected by the stigmatization of single women as "left over" in the marriage market.

However, some middle-class women attempted to overcome such a binary choice model between becoming a happily married woman or a "leftover woman," as Mrs. Ai pointed when explaining that getting married in Beijing was not an easy task. Young people, she noted, still consider marriage as very important, but "people above 30 years of age, I think worry more about quality of life – if it's guaranteed or, as one of my friends said, if she can't achieve a high quality of life after marriage, then she'd prefer not to marry." Indeed, as a friend of Mrs. Ai highlighted, she hoped to settle into fulfilling a romantic relationship in the future, retaining their aspirations, and achieving "a high quality of life." We may consider her psychological narrative as forming part of the idea of a "high-quality" relationship, resulting in a risk-and-rewards rationalization, and interacting with the concept of "equitable exchange" that formed part of processes of intellectualization of intimacy and the *entrepreneurialization of the self*.

The forming of this marriage market was a result of two causes. On the one hand, the dismantling of the *danwei* system and the CCP's endorsement of market transactions in the 1990s meant the transformation of marriage as a "social property" in the *danwei* context to a "personal property" in the market economy as the Marriage Law in 1980 announced (Ocko 1991, 319, in Davis 2014, 554). On the other, the marriage market in the post-reform era caused women to face overt competition with others as in an uncertain market, where different—horizontal and vertical—variables and attributes of a woman could be traded. Significantly, as Mrs. Ai also argued, "Especially for some educated women who've studied a doctorate's degree, … it's very difficult [*laughs*] to marry because I think that in China we still have traditional opinions about women who have a very high education." Indeed, for men who were accustomed to a traditional family, marrying a college-educated woman was a problem. In addition, for young men from Beijing it also stressed materialist concerns, such as "buying a house or a car, which is also another requirement from parents [of prospective bride] to consider if he's the right match or not." That is why, according to Mrs. Ai, "It's easier to get married in small cities. Cost of living is relatively lower and so, people have many friends and parents normally have more *guanxi* and can provide [young married couples] an easier life than in Beijing, for example."

Further, Mrs. Wu indicated another variable to keep in mind. According to her, in smaller cities and

> in towns, it's very difficult for men [to find a partner] because there's a higher number of men in the countryside than women. On the other hand, the number of well-educated women living in Beijing is higher than men, so it's more difficult for women there.

Indeed, while it seemed difficult for heterosexual women in the cities to find a partner because heterosexual men had lower cultural capital, in rural areas the number of women was lower than men and many would not be able to raise "the happy complete heterosexual family." Alternatively, even for privileged middle-class women, ignoring the state-engineered public desire to marry had a price: the loss of social capital.

Nevertheless, fulfilling the public wish to marry and following the reproductive standard came also at a price in terms of social and economic capital. As Mr. Bai, 64, pointed out, having a partner was difficult, "they have different values, both sides' social class must match," since "matching economic power between both families means a lot to people of my generation." However, "It seems that traditions are changing. Young people are getting married later, they don't want to have more children." Although "the government has now shifted policy to allow for a second child," Mr. Bai asked: "if they can't find a roof to put over their head, then where are you going to live? Where can you raise children?" Indeed, most interviewees who were asked about the pressure to commit and have children agreed that, despite their relatively privileged position on the social ladder, they faced material issues in raising "the happy complete heterosexual family" in urban China. As Mrs. Yao indicated,

> They [young couples] nowadays have more things to worry about if they get married, where are they going to live? ... Plus, the cost of raising kids, and younger people today don't really have free time to relax and interact, to associate with other people. They're too busy and most of their time is spent on work ... I think young people have a hard time.

As noted earlier, class background in the Mao-dominated years was the main determinant of an individual's life choices, including the goal to find a suitable marriage partner. Interestingly, class remains central in understanding the mate choice criteria of Chinese youth in the post-1978 era. As Mr. Lai, 37, explained:

My parents worked at a large factory that would manufacture tanks. It was very big, there were 50,000 workers ... My parents were workers at one of them, they were lower middle class ... My wife, my father-in-law was a soldier, an army officer, and my mother-in-law works at the Chinese Academy of Sciences. Maybe we're middle class, so we're compatible, but I'd never choose a woman who's from a higher class than me. It might be difficult for me to accept a woman ... Happiness is not only her and my responsibility, it's also both of our parents' responsibility. It's not just a relationship between the two of us, it's also between two families.

On this point, what equally mattered in these narratives about sentimental relationships was "the importance of matching social ranking (*men dang hu dui*)." Despite individualization and the Party-state's long-time advocacy and support for a communal, conjugal privacy regime, the regulation of filial piety as a part of the withdrawal of the state as a social welfare provider restored earlier traditions that privileged extended family over nuclear family claims (Chapter 5). Additionally, as Mr. Cui stated, marrying "now is more difficult than before. I've gone to several weddings lately, and they're very extravagant. Wedding ceremonies have become very sophisticated." According to him, "In the past—in my day—we'd only put on what we had, and it was easier." Nowadays, however, "people spend a lot on their wedding, and you also need to buy a house and a car. Plus, the man has to give his fiancée's family a *caili*, or money, as a dowry. This makes finding the right partner more difficult." Mr. Cui's testimony reflected how social practices in celebrating wedding ceremonies have changed from a modern industrial society to a post-industrial society in Beijing.

Overall, the findings indicate that the co-existence of a strong group orientation (a responsibility with one's family and community) with certain individualistic aspirations (such as the personal fulfilment way of living) is an inseparable part of the complex processes of social change in contemporary urban China. This can be observed in several testimonies, such as Mr. Lu who said, "After getting married, love mixes with family." Similarly, Mr. Lai explained that happiness in a marriage was not only the responsibility between the two spouses, rather, "It also depends on my parents and her parents." Further, although the loving relationships that could lead to the happy-ever-after were the ones that carry the most powerful allure, the great majority did not consider such romantic excitement as a promise to ensuring a stable future. Rather, most of them associated the concept of love and marriage with aspects of Chinese marital culture that emphasized commitment and, to a certain extent, gender hierarchies. Also, as Chinese culture is characterized by a collectivist spirit, love relationships have a strong commitment with the in-group, including nuclear and extended family. Material difficulty and the desire for affection were the central concerns shown by the middle-aged informants regarding younger citizens in Beijing. In short, all the informants were aware of the difficulty faced by the younger generation to settle down and start a home.

However, coinciding with Xie (2020), the co-existence of such social representations is "[w]hat makes the Chinese case different from its postmodern individualised Western counterparts is the co-existence of the traditional moral framework built within family structures and upheld by the state" (185). Beyond the negative expectations based on the concept of *yuan* in viewing (intense) love with scepticism, and the belief that success or failure in loving relationships is not entirely under control of the individuals—it is thus largely predetermined by class and family—this section has been able to document significant differences in the conception of romantic love and in the public and private spheres of the Chinese middle class immediately before the COVID-19 pandemic. Although the middle class in urban China does not have a homogeneous lifestyle, it has a "coherent" lifestyle. One meaningful feature to come from the conversations carried out in Beijing was the dominant understanding of home as a heterosexualized family space.

Therefore, queer couples, stepfamilies, non-monogamous relationships, divorced, widowers or widows were not mentioned by the informants. They were also lacking in the sample, which could be evidenced at the cultural level. It entailed the understanding of heterosexual monogamy as an organizing system of individual affections and social ties that places "the reproductive nucleus" as the highest expression of social identity (Vasallo 2018). Hence, young women who accumulated cultural capital, developed themselves and earned enough to live independently were condemned for their ambitions as "leftover women," with their consequent loss of social capital.

Consequently, such deeply rooted patriarchal, normative and (self-)disciplinary structure was underpinning gender inequalities in both the public and private spheres. The discourse of marriage and family based on "the happy complete heterosexual family" was part of the paradigm of the Chinese middle class created by the state with its controlled media joined with market institutions and (perhaps unconsciously) the Chinese population. Further, this paradigm encouraged married couples to avoid family breakdown (Wong 2016) and to embrace traditional values of the Confucian culture such as quality, harmony, and filial piety, as the next chapter attempts further to evaluate.

After elucidating the social representations of the urban middle class of their most admired celebrities, examining the descriptive narratives of happiness, in terms of both materialist and post-industrialist concerns, and the in-depth analysis of representations of love discursively, this chapter has set out to identify and define the space in which the most representative narratives about social success, happiness, and loving relationships have been generated in contemporary urban China. This chapter has looked at the aspirations of the Chinese middle class on which the social construction of identity in the post-reform era is based, in order to verify state interventionism and processes of marketization in the formation of the lifestyle of the Chinese middle class. The degree of these aspirations and the influence that class as a potential social force with the capacity to transform society has in contemporary urban China are two of the elements that the next chapter gauges from the data collected in pre-pandemic Beijing.

Bibliography

Aresu, Alessandra. 2009. "Sex Education in Modern and Contemporary China: Interrupted Debates across the Last Century." *International Journal of Educational Development* 29 (5): 532–541. doi:10.0.3.248/j.ijedudev.2009.04.010.

Aschoff, Nicole. 2015. *The New Prophets of Capital*. London: Verso.

Ayllón, Sara, Magda Mercader, and Xavier Ramos. 2007. "Caracterización de la Privación y la Pobreza en Cataluña [Charaterisation of Deprivation and Poverty in Catalonia]." *Revista de Economía Aplicada* 15 (44): 137–175. https://ddd.uab.cat/pub/estudis/2006/hdl_2072_2111/wpdea0410.pdf.

Baker, William. 2017. "Aspirations: the moral of the story." *British Journal of Sociology of Education* 38 (8): 1203–1216. doi:10.1080/01425692.2016.1254540.

Bourdieu, Pierre. 1987. "What Makes a Social Class? On Theoretical and Practical Existence of Groups." *Berkeley Journal of Sociology* 32: 1–17.

Brockmann, Hilke, Jan Delhey, Christian Welzel, and Hao Yuan. 2009. "The China Puzzle: Falling Happiness in a Rising Economy." *Journal of Happiness Studies* 10 (4): 387–405. doi:10.1007/s10902-008-9095-4.

Burnet, Cora. 2001. "Whose Game Is It Anyway? Power, Play and Sport." *Agenda* 16: 71–78. doi:10.1080/10130950.2001.9675975.

Carter, Julia, and Lorena Arocha, eds. 2020. *Romantic Relationships in A Time of 'Cold Intimacies'*. Cham: Palgrave Macmillan.

Cashmore, Ellis. 2006. *Celebrity Culture*. London: Routledge.

Combs, Matthew Tyler, and Jeffrey Nathan Wasserstrom. 2013. "The Guard's Three Bodies: Linsanity, Celebrity and National Identity." *The International Journal of the History of Sport* 30 (11): 1259–1270. doi:10.1080/09523367.2013.806910.

Constable, Nicole. 2009. "The Commodification of Intimacy: Marriage, Sex, and Reproductive Labor." *Annual Review of Anthropology* 38: 49–64. doi:37.081407.085133.

Davis, Deborah S. 2014. "Privatization of Marriage in Post-socialist China." *Modern China* 40 (6): 551–577. doi:10.1177/0097700414536528.

Dirlik, Arif. 2012. "Mao Zedong in Contemporary Chinese Official Discourse and History." *China Perspectives* 2: 17–27. doi:10.4000/chinaperspectives.5852.

Edwards, Louise. 2010. "Military Celebrity in China: The Evolution of 'Heroic and Model Servicemen'." In *Celebrity in China*, edited by Louise Edwards and Elaine Jeffreys, 21–43. Hong Kong: Hong Kong University Press.

Evans, Peter. 1995. *Embedded Autonomy: State and Industrial Transformation*. Princeton, NJ: Princeton University Press.

Farquhar, Judith. 2002. *Appetites: Food and Sex in Post-Socialist China*. Durham, NC: Duke University Press.

Farrer, James. 2014. "Love, Sex, and Commitment: Delinking Premarital Intimacy from Marriage in Urban China." In *Wives, Husbands, and Lovers: Marriage and Sexuality in Hong Kong, Taiwan, and Urban China*, edited by Deborah S. Davis and Sara L. Friedman, 62–96. Stanford, CA: Stanford University Press.

Fellenz, Martin R. 1997. "Control theory in organizational behavior: review, critique and prospects." *SSRN*. doi:10.2139/ssrn.939714.

Foucault, Michel. 2004. *The Birth of Biopolitics. Lectures at the Collège de France, 1978–79*. Translated by Graham Burchell. New York: Palgrave Macmillan.

Fromm, Erich. 1956. *The Art of Loving*. New York: Harper & Brothers.

Gordon, Colin. 1991. "Government Rationality: An Introduction." In *The Foucault Effect: Studies in Governmentality*, edited by Graham Burchell, Colin Gordon and Peter Miller, 1–52. Chicago: University of Chicago Press.

Graham, Carol, and Stefano Pettinato. 2002. "Frustrated Achievers: Winners, Losers and Subjective Well-being in New Market Economies." *Journal of Development Studies* 38 (4): 100–140. doi:10.1080/00220380412331322431.

Guo, Yingjie. 2010. "China's Celebrity Mothers: Female Virtues, Patriotism and Social Harmony." In *Celebrity in China*, edited by Louise Edwards and Elaine Jeffreys, 45–66. Hong Kong: Hong Kong University Press.

Hansen, Mette Halskov, and Rune Svarverud. 2010. *The Rise of the Individual in Modern Chinese Society*. Copenhagen: NIAS Press.

Hedges, Chris. 2002. *War is a Force that Gives Us Meaning*. Oxford: Public Affairs.

Hird, Derek. 2017. "Xi Jinping's Family Values." *China Policy Institute: Analysis.* https://westminsterresearch.westminster.ac.uk/item/q2w43/xi-jinping-s-family-values.

Hong-Fincher, Leta. 2018. *Betraying Big Brother: The Feminist Awakening in China.* New York: Verso Books.

Hong-Fincher, Leta. 2014. *Leftover Women: The Resurgence of Gender Inequality in China.* London: Zed Books Ltd.

Hsiao, Hsin-Huang Michael, and Po-San Wan. 2013. "Comparing Socio-economic Attitudes of the Middle Classes in Taiwan and Hong Kong." In *Chinese Middle Classes. Taiwan, Hong Kong, Macao and China*, edited by Hsin-Huang Michael Hsiao, 110–131. Abingdon: Routledge.

Hsu, Francisillouz L. K. 1981. *Americans and Chinese: Passage to Differences.* Honolulu: University of Hawaii Press.

Illouz, Eva. 2007. *Cold Intimacies: The Making of Emotional Capitalism.* Cambridge: Polity Press.

Illouz, Eva. 2012. *Why Love Hurts: A Sociological Explanation.* Cambridge: Polity Press.

Jackman, Mary R., and Robert W.Jackman. 1973. "An Interpretation of the Relation between Objective and Subjective Social Status." *American Sociological Review* 38 (5): 569–582. doi:10.2307/2094408.

Jankowiak, William, and Robert L.Moore. 2012. "China's Emergent Youth: Gender, Work, Dating, and Life Orientation." In *Adolescent Identity: Evolutionary, Cultural and Developmental Perspectives*, edited by Bonnie L.Hewlett, 285–308. New York: Routledge.

Jankowiak, William, and Thomas Paladino. 2008. "Desiring Sex, Longing for Love: A Tripartite Conundrum." In *Intimacies: Love and sex across cultures*, edited by William Jankowiak, 1–36. New York: Columbia University Press.

Jeffreys, Elaine. 2008. "Advanced Producers or Moral Polluters? China's Bureaucrat entrepreneurs and Sex-related Corruption." In *The New Rich in China*, edited by David S.G. Goodman, 229–249. Abingdon: Routledge.

Jeffreys, Elaine. 2015. "Celebrity Philanthropy in Mainland China." *Asian Studies Review* 39 (4): 571–588. doi:10.1080/10357823.2015.1081871.

Jeffreys, Elaine, and Louise Edwards. 2010. *Celebrity in China*. Hong Kong: Hong Kong University Press.

Jenkins, Richard. 2002. *Pierre Bourdieu*. London: Routledge.

Jiang, Shiqing, Ming Lu, and Hiroshi Sato. 2012. "Identity, Inequality, and Happiness: Evidence from Urban China". *World Development* 40: 1190–1200. doi:10.1016/j.worlddev.2011.11.002.

Knight, John, and Ramani Gunatilaka. 2010. "Great expectations? The Subjective Well-being of Rural–urban Migrants in China." *World development* 38 (1): 113–124. doi:0305750X0900076X.

Knight, John, Lina Song and Ramani Gunatilaka. 2009. "Subjective Well-being and Its Determinants in Rural China." *China Economic Review* 20: 635–649. doi:10.1016/j.chieco.2008.09.003.

Li, He. 2015. *Political Thought and China's Transformation.* Basingstoke and New York: Palgrave Macmillan.

Ludwigs, Kai, Richard Lucas, Martijn Burger, Ruut Veenhoven, and Lidia Arends. 2017. "How Does More Attention to Subjective Well-Being Affect Subjective Well-Being?" *Applied Research in Quality of Life.* doi:10.1007/s11482-017-9575-y.

Moore, Robert. 2005. "Generation Ku: Individualism and China's Millennial Youth." *Ethnology* 44 (4): 357–376. doi:10.2307/3774095.

Ocko, Jonathan. 1991. "Women, property, and law in the People's Republic of China." In *Marriage and Inequality in Chinese Society*, edited by Rubie S. Watson and Patricia Buckley Ebrey, 313–346. Berkeley: University of California Press.

OECD. 2013. "OECD Guidelines on Measuring Subjective Well-being." *OECD Publishing.* doi:10.1787/9789264191655-en.

Osburg, John. 2013. *Anxious Wealth: Money and Morality among China's New Rich.* Stanford, CA: Stanford University Press.

Pan Suiming. 1994. "A Sex Revolution in Current China." *Journal of Psychology & Human Sexuality* 6 (2): 1–14. doi:10.1300/J056v06n02_01.

People's Daily Online. 2010. "Study: Middle Class Families in Beijing and Shanghai Are in Pseudo-happiness." *People's Daily Online*, 17 March. Accessed 18 October 2021. http://en.people.cn/90001/90782/90872/6922601.html.

Pimentel, Ellen Efron. 2000. "Just How Do I Love Thee?: Marital Relations in Urban China." *Journal of Marriage and Family* 62 (1): 32–47. doi:10.1111/j.1741-3737.2000.00032.x.

Rocca, Jean-Louis. 2017. *The Making of the Chinese Middle Class: Small Comfort and Great Expectations.* New York: Palgrave Macmillan US.

Rojek, Chris. 2015. "Celebrity." In *The Wiley Blackwell Encyclopedia of Consumption and Consumer Studies*, edited by J. Michael Ryan and Daniel Thomas Cook, 1–3. Chichester: John Wiley & Sons.

Romero-Moreno, Aran. 2018. "From Process of Civilization to Policy of Civilization: A Holistic Review of the Chinese Concept *wenming.*" *(con) textos: Revista d'Antropologia i Investigació Social* 8: 23–36. https://revistes.ub.edu/index.php/contextos/article/view/31308/31344.

Rothbaum, Fred, and Bill Yuk-Piu Tsang. 1998. "Lovesongs in the United States and China: On the Nature of Romantic Love." *Journal of Cross-Cultural Psychology* 29 (2): 306–319. doi:10.1177/0022022198292003.

Sáiz, Amelia. 2001. *Utopía y Género. Las Mujeres Chinas en el siglo XX* [*Utopia and Gender. Chinese Women in the 20th Century*]. Barcelona: Edicions Bellaterra.

Sáiz, Amelia. 2009. "Mujeres y Género en la Sociedad China Contemporánea [Women and Gender in Contemporary Chinese Society]." In *Visions de la Xina: cultura multimil·lenària* [*Visions of China: A multi-millennial culture*], edited by Joan Julià-Muné, 169–190. Lleida: Institut d'Estudis Ilerdencs.

Seligman, Martin E. P., and Mihaly Csikszentmihalyi. 2000. "Positive Psychology: An Introduction." *American Psychologist* 55 (1): 5–14. doi:10.1007/978-94-017-9088-8_18.

Solé-Farràs, Jesús. 2014. *New Confucianism in Twenty-first Century China.* Abingdon: Routledge.

Sun, Wanning, and Ling Yang. 2020. "Introduction: love stories in contemporary China." In *Love Stories in China. The Politics of Intimacy in the Twenty-First Century*, edited by Wanning Sun and Ling Yang, 1–21. Abingdon: Routledge.

Tomba, Luigi. 2009. "Of Quality, Harmony, and Community: Civilization and the Middle Class in Urban China." *Positions* 17 (3): 591–616. doi:10.1215/10679847-2009-016.

Turner, Graeme. 2010. "Approaching celebrity studies." *Celebrity Studies* 1 (1): 11–20. doi:10.1080/19392390903519024.

van Gelderen, Marco. 2012. "Perseverance strategies of enterprising individuals." *International Journal of Entrepreneurial Behavior & Research* 18 (6): 630–648. doi:10.1108/13552551211268102.

Vancouver, Jeffrey B. 2005. "The depth of history and explanation as benefit and bane for psychological control theories." *Journal of Applied Psychology* 90 (1): 38–52. doi:10.1037/0021-9010.90.1.38.

Vasallo, Brigitte. 2018. *Pensamiento Monógamo, Terror Poliamoroso* [*Monogamous Thinking, Polyamorous Terror*]. Guadalajara: La Oveja Roja.

Veenhoven, Ruut. 1996. "Happy Life Expectancy: A Comprehensive Measure of the Quality-of-Life in Nations." *Social Indicators Research* 39: 1–58. doi:10.1007/BF00300831.

Veenhoven, Ruut. 2004. "Subjective Measures of Well-being." Working Paper, United Nations University UNU-WIDER. Accessed October 18, 2021. https://www.wider.unu.edu/publication/subjective-measures-well-being.

Veenhoven, Ruut. 2007. "Subjective Measures of Well-being." In *Human Well-being*, edited by Mark McGillivray, 214–239. Hampshire: Palgrave Macmillan.

Wang, Pan. 2021. "Love in China (1950-Now)." In *International Handbook of Love*, edited by Claude-Hélène Mayer and Elisabeth Vanderheiden, 955–973. Cham: Springer.

Wang, Jianying, and Deborah S.Davis. 2010. "China's New Upper Middle Classes: The Importance of Occupational Disaggregation." In *China's Emerging Middle Class: Beyond Economic Transformation*, edited by Li Cheng, 157–176. Washington, DC: Brookings Institution Press.

Wheary, Jennifer, Thomas M.Shapiro, and Tamara Draut. 2007. *By A Thread: The New Experience of America's Middle Class*. New York: Dēmos.

Wilkinson, Richard G., and Kate E. Pickett. 2008. "Income Inequality and Socioeconomic Gradients in Mortality." *American Journal of Public Health* 98: 699–704. doi:10.2105/ajph.2007. 109637.

Wong, Chack Kie, Ka Ying Wong, and Bong Ho Mok. 2006. "Subjective Well-being, Societal Condition and Social Policy—the Case Study of a Rich Chinese Society." *Social Indicators Research* 78: 405–428. doi:10.1007/s11205-005-1604-9.

Wong, Day. 2016. "Sexology and the Making of Sexual Subjects in Contemporary China." *Journal of Sociology* 52 (1): 68–82. doi:10.1177/1440783315587799.

Woronov, Terry Ellen. 2003."*Transforming the Future:"Quality" Children and the Chinese Nation*. PhD diss., University of Chicago.

Woronov, Terry Ellen. 2009. "Governing China's Children: Governmentality and 'Education for Quality'." *Positions: East Asia Cultures Critique* 17 (3): 567–589. doi:10.1215/10679847-2009-015.

Xie, Kailing. 2020. "Chasing Happiness: The Role of Marriage in the Aspiration of Success Among China's Middle-Class Women." In *Romantic Relationships in a Time of 'Cold Intimacies'*, edited by Julia Carter and Lorena Arocha, 181–206. Cham: Palgrave Macmillan.

Xu, Janice Hua. 2018. "Transformation of a Celebrity Athlete (Lang Ping): The Journey to Authentic Leadership in Women's Sports." *China Media Research* 14 (1): 11–19.

Xu, Ying. 2017. "Volunteerism and the State: Understanding the Development of Volunteering in China." In *Perspectives on Volunteering. Voices from the South*, edited by Jacqueline Butcher and Christopher J. Einolf, 213–226. Cham: Springer.

Yan, Yunxiang. 2009. *The Individualization of Chinese Society*. Oxford: Berg.

Yan, Yunxiang. 2011. "The Changing Moral Landscape." In *Deep China: The Moral Life of the Person. What Anthropology and Psychiatry Tell Us about China Today*, edited by Arthur Kleinman, Yunxiang Yan, Jing Jun, Sing Lee, Everett Zhang, Pan Tianshu, Wu Fei, and Guo Jinhua, 36–77. Berkeley: University of California Press.

Yang, Fenggang. 2005. "Lost in the Market, Saved at McDonald's: Conversion to Christianity in Urban China." *Journal for the Scientific Study of Religion* 44 (4): 423–441. doi:10.1111/j.1468-5906.2005.00295.x.

Zavoretti, Roberta. 2017. *Rural Origins, City Lives. Class and Place in Contemporary China.* Seattle: University of Washington Press.

Zhang, Everett. 2011. "China's Sexual Revolution." In *Deep China: The Moral Life of the Person. What Anthropology and Psychiatry Tell Us about China Today,* edited by Arthur Kleinman, Yunxiang Yan, Jing Jun, Sing Lee, Everett Zhang, Pan Tianshu, Wu Fei, and Guo Jinhua, 106–152. Berkeley: University of California Press.

Zhang, Li, and Aihwa Ong. 2008. *Privatizing China.* Ithaca, NY and London: Cornell University Press.

Zhao, Rong, and Adam G. Lilly. 2021. "The Role of State Mobilization for Volunteerism in China." *Nonprofit and Voluntary Sector Quarterly.* doi:10.1177/08997640211057458.

Zhao, Wei. 2012. "Economic Inequality, Status Perceptions, and Subjective Well-being in China's Transitional Economy." *Research in Social Stratification and Mobility* 30 (4): 433–450. doi:10.1016/j.rssm.2012.07.001.

Zheng, Jing. 2017. "Mate Selection and Gender Reflexivity." *Asian Women* 33 (1): 49–71. http://e-asianwomen.org/xml/10074/10074.pdf.

Zurndorfer, Harriet. 2016. "Men, Women, Money, and Morality: The Development of China's Sexual Economy." *Feminist Economics* 22 (2): 1–23. doi:10.1080/13545701.2015.1026834.

5

FAMILY, FRIENDS, AND THE COMMUNITY

The reconfiguration of the private and public spheres

This chapter completes the methodological plan of the study of the lifestyle of the post-reform middle class by exploring the interactions between the public and private spheres in Beijing before the COVID-19 pandemic. Over the last three decades, the public and private spheres have become increasingly differentiated in urban China as the country's political economy of privatization implemented by the state has transformed a "socialist centralized economy" into "a productivity-and-efficiency-oriented market economy" (Ji et al. 2017). This chapter identifies two axes or imaginaries to which the two spheres have been contrasted: the private as the individual whose specific space is the household (*jia*), and the public as the collective that is represented in the urban public space of the gated community, the workplace, and the labour market. In doing this, gender asymmetries in both productive and reproductive labour can be observed as well as new manifestations of practices associated with family responsibility and care, emotional ties beyond the hegemony of the "enclosed family," and the participation in the neighbourhood community as the core of urban governance and associationism in contemporary urban China. The boundaries of these new social relations are analysed here alongside the ideologically overlapping nature of state regulations, market forces, and the lifestyle of the post-reform middle class that emerged in urban China after the second wave of market reforms in the 1990s.

5.1 The private and public spheres

The Party-state has attempted to regulate and shape the public and private spheres of the urban population in China today. The establishment of the PRC in 1949 constituted a shift from "the previous feudal-based clanship system" based on large patriarchal families hierarchically arranged and economically self-sufficient to socialist institutions and the *danwei*. In work-units the private sphere was largely

DOI: 10.4324/9781003299301-6

integrated into the public sphere, as the government dominated not only the work-unit but also the family and the individual with a paternalistic approach (Holroyd 2003, 303). With the decline in Marxist gender-egalitarian ideology and the collapse of the *danwei* system in the late 1990s, the private and public spheres separated, and gender asymmetry deteriorated in the later reform in the form of growing gender discrimination, increasing gender wage gap, decreasing female employment rates, and escalating work–family conflicts (Ji et al. 2017). As Siegelbaum (2006) noted, like any other binary approach, the public and the private spheres "are mutable categories that construct each other," and they can be very effective lenses of sociological analysis for understanding how class, gender, and governmentality worked in the post-reform era (2).

Based on the analysis of interviews conducted in Beijing between 2018 and 2019 and previous studies on the changes in private and public spheres in post-reform urban China, this section focuses on the lifestyle of middle-class women and how interlayered forms of governance and domination reconfigure and perpetuate gender asymmetries. Additionally, existing literature is reviewed to contextualize how gender asymmetries in the public and private spheres—in the labour market and within the household—mutually reinforce each other within the lifestyle of the post-reform middle class. In relating the findings to the power relations between men and women in everyday life, this examination is primarily oriented around two aspects: the productive sense following the narrative of gender segregation based on the notion of *haoyong*, ("useful, effective") that imposes a binary social stratification among middle female incomers in the professional sphere, and the intergenerational relationships considering the indigenous concept of filial piety (*xiao*) and the feminist approach developed by Laslett and Brenner (1989) of "social reproduction" toward the practices involved in the maintenance of life on a daily basis and intergenerationally.

Gender asymmetries

Gender differentiation in both productive and reproductive labour has increased over the last three decades in contemporary urban China due to economic and political factors. Since the 1990s, women's disadvantages in the labour market and within the domestic household have been reinforced by the Party-state's decision to implement the second stage of marketization, diminish the promotion of Marxist egalitarian ideology, dismantle the collective *danwei* system and revive the Confucian patriarchal family (Ji et al. 2017). Thus, the changes since the 1990s have indicated a more radical "deinstitutionalization" of group forms such as marriage and *danwei*—as a multi-functional organization which combined productive and reproductive functions—without any clear "reinstitutionalization" around generally accepted new norms for division of labour, household, and family formation (Stockman 1994, in Davis 2014, 569). Additionally, market forces introduced the capitalist paradigms of competition, confrontation, exclusion, and monetary hierarchization, which in turn nurtured the nature of patriarchy as a family-based system of control over women and children (Folbre 2009). In this sense, the Chinese state, market forces, and family have perpetuated and widened the gender gap in both workplace and household in the post-reform era.

The relationship between state regulation, marketization of society, the institution of family and gender asymmetries has stimulated a growing research literature in China studies concerning variations across generations, geographic regions, power relations, Feminist theory, domestic violence, and shifts in role responsibilities (Ji and Wu 2018; Qian and Li 2020; Peng 2022; Song and Wesoky 2022; Song, Zhang, and Zhang 2021; Wallace 2019). In this context, this section aims to consider cultural, political, generational, and economic factors in the reconfiguration of women's participation in both paid work and unpaid care work in urban China before the COVID-19 pandemic.

Regarding our sample, 50 per cent are women. Age is an important variable in this section to contextualize gender asymmetries with respect to the emergence of a middle-class lifestyle following the second stage of market reforms in the 1990s. The female informants aged between 25 and 35 years represent 20 per cent of the sample; those between 35 and 45 are 60 per cent, and 45- to 55-year-olds constitute the remaining 20 per cent. The average profile of the women interviewed was 40 years of age (born in 1978), married, had one child, Beijing resident but native of another province, and her profession was related to the academic world and administrative tasks. One crucial fact was that most female participants were born between 1973 and 1983, during a key period that coincided with the first stage of market reforms in the late 1970s and early 1980s, and the one-child-per-couple fertility policy initially applied in 1980.

Although government family regulations in the PRC were initiated in 1962, the strictest policy that limited urban Chinese families to one child was implemented between 1980 and 2015 (since 1 January 2016, all Chinese couples have been allowed to have two children). As many of the female informants were born in urban contexts, where birth quotas were particularly stringent, they were the first female offspring of the Only Child Generation. The existing literature has indicated that these young women received more educational investment from their parents than their male counterparts and any previous generation of women in China (Lin 2019). They were not only educated with barely any gender differentiation in their education as an only child compared to post-industrialist societies (Tsui and Rich 2002), but also possessed a considerable emancipatory potential, as exemplified by the proliferation of the "white-collar beauty" imaginary associated with China's new millennium.

However, once in the workplace, as Liu Jieyu (2017) highlighted, this urban generation of young women, who benefited from unprecedent economic conditions since 1950, "found their prospect narrowed and dominated by a masculine hierarchy" and standardized gender stereotypes. The legitimization of this gendered division of labour was based on "a biological determinist understanding of gender" established in the countryside during the Cultural Revolution that "naturalized men's physical superiority over women" (143–144). Later, this naturalized division of labour was reinforced in the labour market by capitalist paradigms that the urban population eventually internalized. This was evident when listening to Mr. Qiao, a Beijing-born medical graduate:

> In Beijing, people aren't conscious that if they want to be productive, they have to exercise. You have to be strong in order to work, that's why women work worse than men, they aren't so strong, they're not suited for work. Even in office jobs, you have to sleep, eat and exercise in case you have to work extra hours later and earn more … Women are physically weaker, and if you have to work twelve hours a day or sleep little because of long work hours, women can't handle as much as men; they're weaker, physically speaking. They get tired sooner, they lack concentration, they have to pay attention if they're children get sick, if they're family's fine. Men can focus more on their jobs, but if they don't exercise, neither can they withstand such a tough pace in the workplace, working so many hours at a time.

Nevertheless, narratives of gender discrimination in the private sector were not so evident within the state sector. When being interviewed, many female employees were conscious that gender balance was better in public sector than in private sector, although it was still far from equality. They valued the organizational flexibility in public sector to be able to combine paid work and unpaid care work, even if this facilitates the perpetuation of the unequal distribution of caring responsibilities between men and women. As Mrs. Ren noted, "Within universities … We don't have to work every single day; we can adjust our schedules and work from your home."

Furthermore, some informants manifested gender discrimination in firm recruitment in their narratives, such as Mr. Qiao when referring to female workers' incompatibility due to family duties, or with management positions requiring trips to certain countries since they are not considered safe for women, as Mr. Yang suggested. In this vein, Mrs. Ren confirmed the way entrenched social norms shaped gender segregation in the labour market by giving the example of her husband's company.

> In companies, since my husband operates his own business, when employees are selected, they prefer to hire young men because, first, women don't make good engineers. In technical work, they doubt women's creativity in the engineering field. On the other hand, employees have to go on business trips, so women who have families have to stay and take care of their children … The result is that you are not so *haoyong* [useful, effective]. I don't think it will change soon. Maybe in twenty or thirty years.

This conceptualization of *bu haoyong* women—that is, women who are "not useful" according to Mr. Ren's perception of the market—in the private sector took for granted beliefs that categorize women as less qualified than men for technical, creative, management, and leadership positions, being more suited to "take care of their children," the service sector, and domestic work. In practice, this gendered division in the professional sphere naturalized the imposition of a binary decision, which only women must face, between discriminatory and sexualized workplaces (private sector) versus job positions with lesser female wage penalties (public sector). In any case, masculinity legitimizes its privileged economic and symbolic position in occupational hierarchy in terms of income, status, and power relations.

Additionally, in order to maximize profits, market forces have promoted *new feminized practices* and identities associated with productivity and modernity which not only justified and masked lower remuneration for women (Liu 2017, 18) but also revolved upon processes of "subject making" and the ways female workers internalized discrimination and the gender pay gap (Salzinger 2003). For instance, the Party-state with its controlled media, together with market forces, established a hegemonic paradigm of gender "vision and division" to control social structures by promoting traditional values associated with filial piety (*xiao*), concern for authority, *guanxi*, or the happy complete heterosexual(ized) family (*meiman jiating*). These heteronormative narratives evidenced that gender refers to socially and historically constructed relationships, representations, and identities in social space. Such variables are institutionalized through families, politics, and culture (Laslett and Brenner 1989) to justify male privilege and the most striking gender inequality in the PRC, the so-called gender penalty.

Indeed, from 1995 to 2007, cultural and policy drivers underpinned a progressive widening of gender gaps in the PRC even though the percentage of Chinese women performing productive work was among the highest in the world (Song, Sicular, and Gustafsson 2017). Female wage penalty is a form of symbolic violence which results from the motherhood wage penalty, fatherhood wage premium, and gender wage gap in the childless group (Ma 2022). The gender pay gap between men and women rose from over 13.3 per cent in 1995 to over 15 per cent by 1999, and 29.4 per cent by 2007. In 2013, female employees generally earned on average 25.8 per cent less than their male counterparts. Such social institutionalization of gender asymmetries operated, as noted earlier, in intersection with other crucial institutions in Chinese society such as the family or marriage.

Aware of women's market barriers in contemporary China, Mrs. Gong decided to stop working as a lawyer and stay at home, taking care of her daughter and her parents. Mrs. Gong's testimony highlighted how gender in patriarchal societies differs in women's propensity to engage in domestic labour and care.

> I have my own specialty [Labour Laws] that allowed me to make a living and care for my family, but I think that the responsibilities between women and men are different. My husband spends little time at home, and he has a high salary … For him, it's easy to have a high salary. The reason I left my last job is because the salary wasn't very high, so I thought it wasn't necessary that both of us work … [Additionally,] when my daughter was a child, my parents

would take care of her, but now she's grown up. It's not easy for them to take care of her now, they can't keep up with her needs. My main duty is to take care of my parents and my daughter.

The fact that Mrs. Gong detailed her husband's high salary and successful career as an architect suggested that her condition as a housewife also manifested a practice of distinction, thus navigating shifting positionings of class privilege and gender asymmetry. In the remaining households with young children of the sample (55 per cent), full-time motherhood and caretaker was a remote choice due to the perceived necessity for a dual income in the family. Consequently, female informants shouldered, to a lesser or greater extent, the responsibilities of both paid work and unpaid care work. This was the case for Mrs. Wu, who worked as an administrator and had a fixed schedule that allowed her to dedicate some of her free time to performing household duties after leaving the campus, "I have a daughter who's in second grade. So, after work, I have to go pick her up, cook and help her with homework, and I do all the chores."

However, most informants with young children, although still in charge of their domestic roles, preferred to delegate a large part of the household chores. In this context, day care centres are becoming increasingly affordable to middle-class families, but it is also not the preferred destination for care of young children. So, who oversees both care giving and domestic roles such as cleaning, cooking, and the unpaid domestic labour force? The answer is that in all cases these responsibilities were given to other women whose care work was also unpaid or who worked precariously. For instance, the person in charge of reproductive labour in Mrs. Yin's household was her aunt.

> It's normally a woman's job, but in China, it's the grandparents who do a lot. Grandparents help out a lot. In my case, it's not my mom, but my aunt works for me one way or another, in my home … She helps me with the house and is like a grandmother to my son … It's a norm for the grandparents' generation. They help our families settle in, but there are exceptions, like my neighbours. They don't have a grandparent to help them out. In that case, working mom's do a lot more, but sometimes they hire someone to help them because they work somewhere else and must go to meetings [at work], so they're not always at home … Us working moms don't do much at home, [but] men do even less. My husband doesn't do housework, in general, men do little.

In cases when domestic labour was paid work, it belonged to the informal economy, it was unregistered and did not show up clearly in official employment statistics. Generally, the migrant domestic workers were women who faced additional challenges due to their immigration status, precarity, and lack of labour rights. Mrs. Ai explained her experience with a female migrant worker who worked at her house and offered her opinion about this social group.

> Nowadays, working migrant women live relatively better now than before, like the babysitter I have at home. I pay her 6,000 RMB (770 euros) monthly, which I think is quite a reasonable salary for her, even higher than what some graduates earn [*laughs*]. However, she also has experience to take care of my daughter, so I think that she's paid fairly for both her effort and work duties.

In Mrs. Ai's case, the babysitter who worked in her home was from her hometown and was recommended by a relative, otherwise the presence of the "strange other" in one's home was often a source of anxiety and fear when it comes to the safety of people and the security of middle-class residents (Sun 2008). As a result, the female domestic worker suffered not only from low wages and a low level of public support for care provision (Folbre 2009), but also from social suspicion because of her status as a migrant worker. That is why, some apps have recently emerged within the regulatory framework of the China social credit system to report on trustworthiness of domestic workers in the digital era (Zeuthen, Jiang, and Bislev 2022). In any case, despite the ease and convenience of the household service work performed by migrant workers and the increasing affordability and supply of day care services in urban China, the informants still found that the best people to care for their only child were the grandparents.

At the same time, grandparents were willing to compromise part of their time to help their adult children for periods of time when they were in need. According to the informants, it was the grandmothers who often provided care for children. Certainly, as Goh and her colleagues (2017) indicated, grandmothers are usually "twice as involved in care as grandfathers" (7). In any case, although grandparents did not usually co-reside indefinitely to provide childcare as it was often on a temporary basis, these practices revealed a cultural, gendered, and intergenerational emphasis on in-house childcare.

For instance, Mr. Lu also discussed this phenomenon, saying,

> I'm very grateful for my in-laws and my parents for taking care of our kids. I have two children, the oldest is in a day care and the youngest stays at home [since] my parents and in-laws take turns coming to Beijing to take care of them.

He explained that they helped him and his wife to focus on their careers without worrying about their children's well-being or domestic duties. Grandparents—mostly paternal—tended to assume temporary co-residential childcare responsibility as a voluntary exchange for the help they received from their children. Such practices were validated by the Chinese traditional culture, which has been intensively promoted by the state during the last decades. Childcare by grandparents reflected functional solidarity and Confucian norms like filial piety and the conceptualization of the extended family household as both a common enterprise to ensure *chuang zong jie dai* (pass on the family line) and an exclusive social space for emotional bonding.

Concentric care and filial piety

In the ancient Chinese belief system of Confucianism, roles and duties of each family member were connected through mutual interdependence throughout their life cycles. In the ideal view of a multigenerational family of the Chinese-culture system, for a woman, becoming a mother-in-law and grandmother after overcoming previous stages in life—daughter-in-law and mother—was itself considered a gift for having dedicated herself to a life of care and service towards others (Sáiz 2001, 35–36). However, social paradigms and individual aspirations are mobile and reflect changing processes in political economy and family renegotiations. With the first wave of market reforms, the Party-state implemented the Marriage Law in 1980 and specified the obligations of adult children "to support their parents and further emphasized personal independence and equality, in particular the status of women in family relationships" (Holroyd 2003, 303). However, the one-child policy contradicted such prioritization of personal satisfaction, as couple's most intimate life was regulated by the state since 1980 (Davis 2014, 554). As a result, despite promising women equality and personal independence, the Chinese state maintained patriarchal legacies through the one-child policy and obligations to adult children to support their parents in the knowledge that the care providers would be women.

Within last decade, the Chinese state has benefited the patriarchal extensive family as a major institution and basic societal unit over the individual by promoting certain Chinese cultural traditions such as collectivism and parent centeredness in the social relations. The goal was to develop a new socialist culture that could fit the national conditions for the Party-state's legitimization project, facilitate social control at a basic societal level (the family), and create a model of modernization that differs from the hegemonic Western model (Solé-Farràs 2014, 61). As a result, the Chinese family can be understood not only as an auto-oriented institution that provides care and emotional exchange but also as a basic societal unit with ideological implications in which economic, social, and cultural capital is fostered, converted, and reproduced (Zhang 2016). In this context, this section analyses social change and family responsibility, duty, and reciprocity regarding care in middle-class households in urban China. In addition, based on indigenous concepts such as *guanxi*, face, and "concentric circles," the role of the Chinese state in the deliberate family restructuring is also assessed here.

Indeed, as Jun Zhang (2016) noted, the Chinese state has reconfigured familial practices by adopting a series of policies to revive family responsibility, duty, and reciprocity as a part of the withdrawal of the state as a social welfare provider by shifting the liability of care from the state to the family (21). For instance, the reconfiguration of filial piety resonated with the state agenda and the newly revised Law on the Protection of the Rights and Interests of the Elderly (*Laonianren quanyi baozhang fa*) which took effect in 2013. This law not only "encouraged social support for senior citizens" by "reinstating the centrality of the family and the need for filial piety," but also obliged adult children and their partners to take care of their parents, and "those who live apart from their parents should visit or greet the elderly" (20). It differs greatly from the privilege of the individual and the personal over the collective that characterized urban Chinese society in the early decades of the reform era (1980s, 1990s, and 2000s). The return to some earlier patriarchal traditions that privileged familial over both individual and conjugal claims is simultaneously a break with the socialist past (Davis 2014) and a re-institutionalization of certain traditions and non-individualist values into new ideological forms of governance.

The attacks on filial piety of anti-feudalist campaigns launched by the CCP during the Maoist period and the post-socialist state's subsequent push for an agenda of individualization—highlighted by scholars such as Yan Yunxiang (2003, 2009)—are a thing of the past. The current "rejuvenation" of certain Chinese cultural traditions, including the multigeneration family structure, came in the context of the Chinese Dream, the state's attempt to deal with China's fast-growing ageing population and social control through isolation strategies. Although the Confucian revival began to take shape in the 1990s, it was not until the introduction of President Xi's Chinese Dream that the project of re-sinificating or de-Westernizing China by assimilating key elements of socialism and liberalism coexisted in total harmony with the political agenda (Deng and Smith 2018). Indeed, with Xi Jinping in power, there has been a drive toward a balanced position among the three most influential traditions in China today by recovering the Chinese traditional culture and the Maoist revolutionary tradition and de-emphasizing the tradition of learning from the West (Gao 2018, 7). Furthermore, Xi's ideological programme emphasized the importance of the family over the individual and the promotion of an alternative model based on Chinese values relating to cultural traditions as an international "soft power" strategy that could differ from the capitalist paradigm of the minority world, as noted in Chapter 2.

Additionally, by promoting hierarchical family values, the state legitimizes the family bond and family organization over any other collective association outside the family. As Vasallo (2018) pointed out, the European monogamous family as a "reproductive nucleus" is a social construct which has been institutionalized through schools, the nation-state, politics, culture, and associationism (33). Hence, as is the case in the minority world, when the Chinese state regulates family relationships, it also deregulates and neglects all other relationships, thus "isolating" the individual within the social space of the family and hindering social and political bonds that might challenge the established order (Cano 2020). As a result, this enclosed family promoted by the Chinese state acts as an institution that politically denaturalizes and socially disaffects the individual from other social realities.

Despite the positive stance adopted by the Chinese government to investment across the whole spectrum of ageing policies, the PRC still lacks adequate primary medical services and ordinary social care for the elderly that would make it easier for them to live in their own homes and communities independently (Xie and Fan 2020). In some cases, when adult children cannot fulfil filial values and take care of their aged parents, they send elderly parents to institutions, which is still seen as abandonment (Croll 2006). In this context, taking care of grandchildren can also be seen as a negotiating strategy in the intergenerational contract of reciprocity to guarantee grandparents old-age support.

Traditional literature has documented significant intergenerational disputes and emotional grievances in traditional Chinese extended families due mainly to co-residence and parenting style (Yang and Chandler 1992; Xiao 2016; Zhang 2004). However, the findings indicated that the commitment of middle incomers to self-discipline and family ethics was illustrative of their conceptualization of the *xiao-kang* standard of life (see Section 4.2). Additionally, there was a relational dynamic between filial piety prescription—normative intergenerational support—and maintaining face (*mianzi*), that is, displaying care in socially-accepted forms (Lamas-Abraira 2021a). Anyhow, both female and male informants strived to be filial children by devoting time and returning care and support to their parents.

On the one hand, for participants whose parents lived also in Beijing, spending time with them occupied an important part of their spare time. For instance, at the time of the interview, Mr. Yang was living with his parents, and he explained, "Not only on weekends, also on some weekdays I'm at home. I try to talk to them every day, especially with my mom. I speak with them for half an hour or an hour because my time is very limited." Mr. Yang, a single engineer from Beijing, usually did an hour or two of extra work and studied in the afternoon. Some time after the interview, he moved to a single's apartment near his parents' neighbour-hood in the Drum Tower. He was also planning to travel to Taiwan with them for the Chinese New Year.

On the other hand, participants from other provinces displayed filial behaviour by devoting to their hometown a reasonable period of annual holidays, visiting their aged parents or taking their parents to live in their home in Beijing. The process through which filial piety is renegotiated at a distance can be complex, costly, and emotionally exhausting for informants, since intergenerational obliga-tions need to be managed in tandem with work obligations. It might involve long journeys to their hometowns, increasing marital stress, "gift giving, banquets, intense interaction with family members and distant relatives," and organizing a busy schedule to see all their friends (Zhang 2016, 22). However, filial piety extended beyond its ideal form, which was linked to proximity, and revealed a broader meaning of care through its social dimension and new digital connections, particularly the WeChat app (Lamas-Abraira 2021b). Hence, ageing parents were not regarded as an extra burden or an additional chore for our respondents; they followed the filial piety prescription as an internalized premise of the inter-dependence between the individual and the family and a way to enjoy family harmony. In general, besides marital status and age, filial piety was a fundamental part of the respondents' well-being.

According to Mr. Lai, the sense of *guanxi* was related with Fei Xiaotong's theory of concentric circles (*tongxinyuan*) or social circles (*shehui quanzi*), "A per-son's life is like concentric circles. Meaning that every person has the responsibility and ability to care for what is within each." These concentric circles referred to by

Mr. Lai describe the different structural principles of Chinese society through a metaphor: the most important relationship in Chinese society—kinship—is similar to "the concentric ripples of a pebble hitting water." In this context, kinship is a social relationship weaved by marriage and reproduction, but which extend to innumerable individuals in the past, present and future (Fei 1992, 3). On that basis, every Chinese individual has her or his own social network of relationships which is "particularistic," the first circle being the self; the second the nuclear family; the third the extended family, the fourth closer acquaintances, friends and neighbours; and the fifth is where less familiar acquaintances and others are placed. To maintain harmony, concentric circles do not remain static, they are constantly being reconfigured and negotiated through interactional processes to balance interests inside and outside the circles, that is why *guanxi* plays a decisive role in China.

Thus, *guanxi*, which can be translated as "connections, social relationships, relationships," is still a very influential element for understanding not only filial piety but all other social, economic, and political interactions in contemporary Chinese society. As Mrs. Ren said, "China is a *guanxi shehui* [*guanxi* society], it goes beyond Chinese culture." The current trend among most testimonies coincided with the most cultural dimension of the concept of *guanxi*. Despite the Western moral tendency to simplify the concept of *guanxi* by reducing it to a mere instrumentalization of other individuals to achieve one's goals, it fits within the Chinese tradition which aspires to an individual's harmonious relationships on the familial level (family responsibility) and in a more extensive manner with the rest of society. *Guanxi* therefore becomes a multidimensional mechanism to regulate social harmony through personal interactions.

In fact, the instrumental characteristic of *guanxi* is typical of interpersonal relationships established in modern industrial contexts or early post-industrial societies with institutional deficiencies in certain areas that affect the social and familial spheres, such as the right to free medical care and other public social services provided by state institutions (Davis 1995). Hence, the relationship established with another person requires a reciprocity to return favours because the repeated exchange of favours represents a measurement of confidence between members who form a social network. In this context is where intergenerational reciprocity is negotiated between the logic of filial piety and the profit-driven logic of "the entrepreneurs of themselves." However, the findings of this study indicate that filial piety and family values manifested a certainty and ethical power so strong today that avoiding normative reciprocity would incur serious social sanctions for informants.

However, traditional family ethics coexisted without conflict with the new morality of individualization. Mr. Wen, for instance, considered that while "in Chinese tradition, *guanxi* is important," it was less significant for the younger urbanites:

> I think *guanxi* carries less importance for our generation because people in my age group are independent. We have our way of doing things. We believe we

can depend on our capacities, our knowledge and our skills to be successful, [and] not just on connections.

Mr. Wen's narratives manifested male, urban privilege, meritocratic conceptions, the ideals of "the entrepreneurs of themselves" and the pursuit of individual interests.

This involved what Yunxiang Yan (2009) called "the individualization of the Chinese society," an undergoing process of individualization and erosion of family values due to the transformation of political economy after market reforms. According to Yan, market forces spread widely the perception among China's urban youth that "one could change one's fate through intelligence and hard work" (*xvii*) regardless of her or his capital possession, habitus, gender, and spatial trajectory. However, "the relationship between individualization and family values is not all or nothing" (Zhang 2016, 19) and, despite Mr. Wen's individualized conceptualizations, he also explained that one of the main reasons for his happiness was the harmonious relationship with his family, "I'm happy! My parents, my relationship with them is harmonious, I love them and they love me." In similar vein, Mrs. Gong explained that familial *guanxi*

> are very important ... they can make me happy and feel content. If you don't have good relationships with others, then you end up living with anxiety and pressure. Many things can be gained by this relationship that can't be replaced with money.

Guanxi thus not only measures confidence and reciprocity between members who form a social network, but also makes resources more flexible, minimizes uncertainty, and distributes emotional gains (Wong and Chan 1999). In the same way that filial piety revealed, *guanxi* practices were practices which subjects transform themselves in order to be "happy and feel content." Traditional family values might enter subject's individualistic schemas and negotiate without conflict family responsibility, duty, and reciprocity regarding care. As a result, interpersonal relationships not only imply emotional support and individual rewards but also everyday practices of care, respect, sacrifice, and love. That is why this "concentric ethic" and *guanxi* practices are "of utmost importance" for interpersonal and intergenerational behaviours not only in relatives (either by blood or marriage) but also in friends, as next section evaluates.

5.2 Friendship

Friendship is a multifaceted and complex phenomenon that has played a determinant role in emotional ties and *guanxi* processes across historical times in China. As Huang (2007) pointed out, friendship practised by privileged males was "an ambiguous concept in late imperial Chinese culture" (2). A network of friends was considered "indispensable" for a professional career, whether "for passing the government-sponsored examinations, advancing a career in the bureaucratic world" or finding professional alternatives (3). At the same time, though, friendship was also presented as a potential "threat to the strictly hierarchical Confucian social order" prioritizing state and family (10). Differently, privileged female friendships in late imperial China were cultivated within family circles or through "spirit friendship" (*shen jiao*); two female friends who yearned to meet but would rarely or never meet each other would become "pen-pals" (Widmer 2006; Huang 2007). Instrumentality, however, was only one aspect of social networks, and from personal and ideological dimensions, friendship was seen as sign of moral character in traditional Chinese culture (Shields 2015). In most cases, far from being voluntary, friendship in the past was an internalized moral value, a social obligation, a strong affect attached to sacrifice and voluntary favour giving demonstrated by a strong mutual *bao* (reciprocity).

Friendship practised by middle-class individuals in contemporary urban China is infused with instrumentality, affection, and identity construction (social distinction). Adult interpersonal relations usually start with instrumental purposes and, as a result of repeated exchanges of favours between both parties guided by a principle of equity and mutual benefits, expressivity emerges, and an increasing degree of personal involvement is manifested over time (Zang 2006, 81). In the case of the informants, data analysis showed that middle-class subjects are more likely to make friends with other middle-class subjects than with members of the subordinate classes. Additionally, although the Chinese cultural context influenced the moral quality of close friendship and altruism, privatization processes during the past three decades have emphasized hedonistic interests among urbanites.

On that basis, an assessment is made in this section of the nature of friendship networks, the validity of the concept of *guanxi* between friends, and variations in sociability by asking a series of questions relating to social practices with friends and some of the leisure activities in Beijing. The questions focused on the frequency with which they saw their friends, the activities they did together, how their relationships with co-workers, bosses, and neighbours were, and their appraisal of friendship importance in the social sphere. Additionally, conversations with Beijing's middle-class constituents revealed that many of them have maintained friendships which were created during their university studies—both graduate and post-graduate—and, in the case of those coming from other provinces, with friendships fostered during childhood and, in particular, in late adolescence in their hometowns.

Although in terms of lifestyle and social construction of identity friendly relationships play an important role in the everyday lives of the post-reform middle class, most informants in Beijing explained that they were far too busy most of the time and prioritized dedicating time with family or work, rather than with friends. In this way, the affections of the informants were confined exclusively to the nuclear and extended family, thus disassociating them from any other more comprehensive social and political ties. For instance, Mr. Qiao, a single man who graduated in medicine, worked at a European pharmaceutical company and was very focused on his professional career, spending time with his parents and on sports. When on vacation, Mr. Qiao liked to travel but he did not usually travel with friends, but alone as it allowed him to improvise his leisure trips according to his "quite unpredictable" work schedule.

> On weekends, I play tennis, visit my parents, and have dinner with my family. Sometimes I go skiing in winter and hiking in summer, I watch television, go to the movies, eat at home ... I was born and raised in Beijing and I know many people here, so I don't try to socialize with too many people because I don't know many of them. If everyone wanted to eat with me, I'd be out all month long. Normally, I eat with friends once or twice; twice with one person, that's already four times. Sometimes I have to work at night or some sort of clinical work at home ... That's why going out to eat [with friends] is the easiest option to socialize.

Consequently, friendship networks did not have to imply strong ties among our informants due to time constraints, lifestyle mobility and geographical distance. Mr. Lu, a married professor, had two young children and a pre-determined amount of time spent with friends in order to make it as productive as possible. He tended to compartmentalize their friends based on interests and activities and alluded to his elastic and fluid perception of friendship that moves between space and time, and between private and professional spheres.

> Friends can be divided into two types: the first type are those who existed since before getting a job, the others are friends from work with which I have professional contact and share common study interests. With the first type, I share past experiences, they're former classmates, colleagues from my previous job, family and acquaintances from my hometown, [and with them] we sometimes meet on weekends, especially if they live outside Beijing ... In my daily life, for example, from Monday to Friday, I usually eat with co-workers ... [Although with the first type of friends] we sometimes don't speak during weeks, but afterwards we meet for two or three hours. I'm not particularly sociable ... In total, I think I spend no more than three hours a week with friends.

Similarly, Mr. Lai's trajectory of residential mobility and living now far from his hometown also influenced his understanding of friendship and leisure. Mr. Lai, 37, alluded to the pressure he felt due to his family, professional, and academic responsibilities as a PhD candidate. In fact, his social and spatial trajectory was very similar to that of many others in the middle class and of middle age; having arrived in Beijing from other provinces to study, once they graduated and found a job, they stayed in the capital. He sighed, saying,

> My job consists of visiting clients which are Beijing companies, some are far away and might take two hours to get to, but others only need a short walk to get there. I visit different clients every day to incorporate their demands into

our projects ... At night, I get home at six or seven to have dinner, but my job requires me to answer phone calls at night ... On weekends, during the last four or five years I've basically been studying, busy doing my PhD ... My boy sleeps at ten and then I study till one in the morning. I'm studying for a day or a day and a half ... When I write my thesis, I do what I can to write between seven-thirty and nine-thirty in the morning, and at night, when my son is sleeping, I'll continue since ten to twelve or since twelve to one ... I've never had time. I've spent all my time taking care of my parents, my wife's parents, my son, my wife—while doing her doctorate's degree at Beijing University—our jobs ... I don't have time. I hope to have more time to exercise, read, and be with my son.

These three informants, Mr. Qiao, Mr. Lu, and Mr. Lai, have incorporated the utility-maximizing calculation of human capital characteristic of "the entrepreneurs of themselves" (Foucault 2004). In the wake of the market reforms of the 1990s, market forces and state regulations introduced this neoliberal profit-driven logic which rationally acted upon cost/benefit calculations to maximize the returns on their efforts considering time, space, and human capital (Becker 1976). Thus, the narratives of "the entrepreneur of the self" and the enclosed family form an important part of the middle-class lifestyle and hierarchized the leisure time and affections of Chinese urban dwellers according to the new neoliberal logic introduced in China by market reforms. For instance, Mr. Lai and his wife hailed from Guizhou, and he lamented that their friends in their hometown did not understand that the busy rhythm of Beijing's urban life made it difficult to spend time with them in their hometown. In other words, his friends who lived in a smaller town did not seem to share his distinctive urban "entrepreneurialized" vision, which denoted modernity and high-*suzhi*.

Differently, for some informants, having children had become an important part in the process of making new friends (*jiaoyou*) but also in restoring friendship. For instance, as Mr. Kang explained, "before having children, I dedicated most of my time on work." Although "I would talk with my friends a lot on *Wechat*, we didn't meet much. But once we had kids we started to see each other more often because we could discuss about how to educate them." Likewise, Mrs. Wu, whose parents usually help with childcare, often met with her co-workers and her husband's friends who also had children, "We go out to eat together, play tennis, or go to family gatherings so we can spend time with our children together, like hiking in the mountains." As in post-industrial societies, friendships formed in child-centred settings were similar in homophily for parents who experienced either an increase or an "initial reduction in the size of their ego networks" that soon rebounded as they were drawn into local networks through their children's activities (Thomas 2019). In these cases, friendship was thus subordinated to the hegemony of the enclosed family, which essentially acted as a "reproductive nucleus" that hierarchized affections within the heteronormative and monogamous nuclear and/or extended family over any other affective relationship.

Alternatively, adult social life outside parenting and workplace was structured by interests and activities that vary in their formality. For instance, after becoming mothers, Mrs. Li and Mrs. Ren continued to see their friends often and scheduled adult-only time. In Mrs. Li's case, thanks to her mother who helped her look after her 9-year-old daughter, she could organize separately their activities with other adults on one side, and those concerning motherhood on the other:

> When I am not working, I meet my friends twice a week and chat. We talk about books and films that interest us, and gossip about celebrities and others who we personally know. Often, we go to a cafeteria and go shopping, too.

Meanwhile, Mrs. Ren explained that since her daughter was a teenager she could start to enjoy "hanging out with friends once or twice a month. We go out on excursions. For example, to the Summer Palace, the Botanical Garden or exhibitions. We also see each other on holidays like New Year, before or after." As children grow up, gender inequality in network size reverses as male informants' networks shrink, while female informants' networks flourish.

Interpersonal relationships outside family were also formed, albeit to a lesser extent, by religious activities. Although the policies of the authoritarian, atheistic Chinese state explicitly restrict religious activities, especially if they originated in the culturally invasive West, it often encourages social services and spiritual activities by Christian groups because, in part, it is a pragmatic response to government cuts in welfare provision (Vala, Huang and Sun 2015). This is the case for Mrs. Yao, who had also a teenage son and put time aside for her friends and religious practices. She emphasized her Christian background when talking about her friends, an aspect that exhibited a distinctive middle-class position in social hierarchy in terms of cultural capital.

As noted in Chapter 4, once material necessities have been satisfied, people seem to express a sense of existential emptiness or meaninglessness of life that characterizes post-industrial societies. Thus, Christian practices in China became manifestations that the post-material stage had been reached. In terms of friendship, Mrs. Yao emphasized that the most important thing for her was to serve her relatives and friends. Weekends were spent with her family and church friends since she decided to convert to Christianity fifteen years ago.

> I was searching for a truth, the true meaning of life's value … I began to think about life when I was in my thirties and thought, 'Where do we go after leaving this world? What's the point in repeating one day after the next? If professional or economic success is achieved, what does it mean?' In the end, we will leave this world and I found Jesus. So, I think that the meaning of life is to not continue struggling, combatting. You'll feel fine, that you know where you're going and you already know how to understand life. I understand how to build a family [and] the most important thing for me is that I

serve people, serve others, serve my friends … I try my best to make them feel at home [*smiles*].

Informal activities including hobbies, sports, and similar activities were also primary sources of friendship for informants who were single or had adult children. Since his son went to study in the States, Mr. Cui was able to meet his friends more often, "[My friends and I usually] eat together and I also have friends who I run out with. We can do 10 kilometres together in the park." The importance of highbrow practices in social network formation such as Mrs. Yao's religious habits or Mr. Cui's sporting activities have been a determining factor of attraction in interpersonal relationships. Therefore, friendship was strongly related among the informants to willingness to spend time with other people and homophily, that is, similarity in activity preferences and, above all, in attitudes, as these have direct behavioural implications (Nagel, Ganzeboom, and Kalmijn 2011, 426, 439). As the urban society in the PRC is transforming itself into a post-industrialist society, urban middle incomers have free time and money to spend; friendship thus becomes a well-established sphere for the negotiation of identity, hierarchies, and status through practices of consumption.

Although spaces of encounter in the city such as shopping centres, restaurants, and parks shaped and defined friendship, the space most associated with the middle class is the gated community. However, the gated community was not a place to nurture friendship and make new friends. Most of the respondents not only did not feel themselves integrated into their communities, but also did not intend to establish close links with their neighbours. Hence, geographical proximity coupled with social proximity was not an important indicator of friendship patterns in China's mega-cities such as Beijing. One could say that neighbourliness was not a prominent trait for members of the urban middle class despite the activities organized in communal areas such as "children activities, operas, dances and *taiqi* organized for the elderly," and the "self-servicing"—e.g., restaurants and shops—provided in many gated communities, as Mr. Wen pointed out. None of the informants expressed a close relationship with their neighbours. As Mr. Bai stated, "people who live in residential zones do not know each other, they don't talk to each other. I couldn't say that I know my neighbours well, I know them in a simple way … I don't have time for that."

Everything seemed to indicate that the relationships constructed in the gated communities were privatized and "inattentive," where respondents tended to refuse relations, stay unknown to each other, and keep up strangeness (Goffman 1963). This was what happened to Mr. Qiao, who lived in a rented studio "between the third and fourth ring roads" inside a gated community. His relationship with his neighbours was "as if we were strangers", and he did not know what they were like, or talk to them in the elevator. He also avoided participating in his community's activities because "I don't like public activities with many strangers. I have to manage many events at work, with my family, and so I choose not to do it." In fact, Mr. Qiao said that his lack of interest in socializing was the main reason why he had little communication with his neighbours. "I already have enough relationships with my friends and family, I don't need any new relationship."

Anonymous relationships can be conceptualized in China as "facelessness" (in opposition to "face") that suspends the "particularizing strategies of give-and-take face," avoiding having or losing face in strong mutual commitments and experiencing "being part of a crowd" in which "one's personal relation to the community is not an issue" (Hertz 2001, 291, 280, in Richaud 2018). Mr. Wen justified his "facelessness" attitude towards his neighbours by his tiredness and lack of time. He lived in a Beijing apartment located in the 3rd Ring Road close to Guomao, a 30-minute car ride from his job.

> The community where I live is in the CBD [Central Business District]. It's very convenient for shopping, going out for dinner, go to the movies, and people in my community, most of them are middle class … but I barely see my neighbours, so I don't have an opinion of them, but I'm happy because we don't bother each other [*laughs*] … I don't have a relationship with them because during the day, we're working and return home too late. We barely see each other, that's why we don't have any contact … I don't know them, and they don't know me.

Before the disassembling of the *danwei* system in the late 1990s, communal and shared use of facilities in the *danwei* compounds used to be the converging point for residents' interaction by creating strong social bonds among them (Ye et al. 2021). It was in this context that the indigenous concept of "face" was fully operational in referring to a conglomerate of institutions, services, and values that might be characterized as communitarian (Hertz 2001, 276). However, in the post-reform era, "facelessness" manifested in the lack of interaction with neighbours and it was the main source of satisfaction of the urban middle class regarding their situated experience in the social space of the community. For Mrs. Li, too:

> I live in a community of neighbours, but I don't organize activities with them because I stay at home a lot, I don't usually go down and stroll around the community. My neighbourhood is nice because I don't have to participate in any events … I'm content with my neighbours, we don't see each other a lot.

Many interviewees did not participate in the activities organized in their communities since they were associated with retirees or those with no professional activity. As Mr. Yang explained,

> I think the majority of young people don't have time or don't want to do the same things that older people do. [For example,] my mother is in a dance group, it's free and someone organizes it, but the majority of its members are women over 50 years old. No young person wants to participate.

Likewise, Mrs. Gong mentioned that those who participate in her community's activities were "older members, for example, they'll be taken to a hospital to get a complete health check, play in parks," but "for folks my age, there's barely anything." However, Mrs. He admitted, "Lately, I've been participating in [my community's] activities. I was with my daughter in one of the events organized by the community for Children's Day to draw on the ground (*yinjing hai*). I also attended in an event that promoted recycling."

Overall, the undergoing process of reconfiguration of ties in the public and private sphere has reasserted traditional family values, has spread Western values based on materialism, individualism, and hedonism, while it has re-situated friendship practices across the life course considering homophily, consumption practices, and heteronormativity. Additionally, since the second stage of market reforms in the 1990s, the individual has been detached from her or his everyday local context. While it was clear that relations with neighbours were practically non-existent in middle-class's gated communities, the Chinese state implemented mechanisms of grassroots initiatives in urban neighbourhoods through the lens of deliberation and self-governance in the social space of the community, as the next section evaluates.

5.3 The community

The social space of the neighbourhood community is the core of urban governance in the PRC. In order to achieve the maintaining of social stability, the Chinese government has deployed governance strategies based on authoritarian deliverance and monitoring of the interactions between the Party-state and citizens. This section examines (1) how the informants interacted with state and market actors through the lens of deliberation and conflict resolution in urban middle-class communities; (2) in what ways and to what extent authoritarian deliberation was implemented as an instrumental tool in grassroots governance to achieve the Party-state's goal of maintaining social stability; and (3) whether the informants collaborated with activists, social movements (protests) or self-organization outside of the formal-legal channels. Neighbourhood governance in urban China has become a major vehicle for a wide range of theoretical debates, such as civil society, grassroots democracy, class segregation, and self-governance under the Party-state's authoritarian rule. On that basis, this section examines the main mechanisms of grassroots governance implemented in urban China since the 1990s, namely the residents' committee (*jumin weiyuanhui* or *jueweihui*), the homeowners' association (*yezhu weiyuanhui*), and any non-official, horizontal or self-organizational initiative that may emerge in the community level as a result of public participation.

Apathy in the neighbourhood

As a part of the implementation of the second wave of market reforms in the 1990s, the Ministry of Civil Affairs introduced in the late 1990s the "community building" (*shequ jianshe*) campaign in the urban neighbourhood. It was based on the innovative elections and self-management (*difang zizhi*) policies implemented in rural areas in 1987. The community building campaign led to the reconfiguration of the residents' committee (henceforth referred to as RC), a mass organization tool created in 1954. With the community building campaign, the state attempted to reorganize urban residential communities through a new contract with urban residents' representatives and maintain social stability despite the increases in inequality and social tensions due to market reforms.

In the new administrative scheme, government personnel were assigned into one wide-ranging local governance network that included three levels: district (*qu*), street (*jiedao*), and urban communities (*shequ*) (Tang 2019). Whereas *shequ* (literally, "social area") generally encompasses the territory and people under the administration of a RC and is often translated as "community," *xiaoqu* (literally, "small area") refers to a residential compound, either private or run by a company (Tomba 2014, 4). In practice, new housing development at the scale of *xiaoqu* has predominantly taken a gated community form (Lu, Zhang, and Wu 2019). By following the strategy of "community services" (*shequ fuwu*) implemented in the mid-1980s, the community building campaign transformed the relatively abstract idea of "community" (*shequ*) into "the basic unit of urban, social, political and administrative organization" (Bray 2009, 88). Therefore, the *shequ* became one of many organizational novelties designed to create trust in the system as a response to the erosion, and subsequent elimination in the late 1990s, of the *danwei* system that had hitherto been the fundamental provider of labour and welfare in urban China.

This shift to community services, however, was not just about the reconfiguration of market reforms and housing commodification, but also incorporated a specific governance capable of managing the demographic transformation that Chinese society experienced due to the cumulative factors. Certainly, the development of community services in the 1990s focused, as Bray (2009) highlighted, on addressing a wide range of political, social, ethical, and economic problems and fragmentations: the expansion and adaptation of welfare services to ageing of the population; the increasingly diverse and more mobile urban population due to the gradual ease of former controls on rural population movement; the growing number of unemployment urban residents as a result of the abolition of hiring quotas in state-owned enterprises; the emergence of reduction in the size of the traditional family; and the emergence of new family compositions such as one-parent families because of the rising divorce rates (92). Nevertheless, the new paradigm of *shequ* developed by the community building campaign was no longer confined to the issue of administration (*guanli*) and services (*fuwu*) but was broadened to focus on effective social control.

The Tiananmen Square repression, the dismissal of large numbers of urban workers (which was correlated with an increase in street crimes), protests by the unemployed and the "new underclass," and the rise of Falun Gong placed new challenges for the Party-state and the implementation of practical conflict resolution at local levels (Heberer and Göbel 2011, 3). Therefore, the *shequ* became the core organization of urban self-governance administrated by the RC to address service and welfare administration, social control, deliberation, and conflict resolution. The *shequ*, however, operated vertically, far from an egalitarian structure, since it was shaped by regulations crafted by the Chinese leaders, and it was instilled by Party building development. In this way, the RC re-emerged in the *shequ* as an intermediate institution of government between authoritarianism and deliberative consensus.

In practice, as Beibei Tang (2018a) highlighted, the RCs began to take on the responsibility on behalf of the city government for mediating residents' disputes and providing services such as security and social welfare, especially facilitating the Minimum Livelihood Guarantee (*dibao*) system, China's national financial-support scheme for low-income families. That is why, in middle-class gated communities where security and the *dibao* were not a concern and the management companies oversaw community services, the RC "had a less significant role to play in community governance" (120). Certainly, the organization in charge of representing and defending the rights and claims of middle-class homeowners is the homeowners' association (abbreviated as HOA hereafter).

The convergence of housing marketization and local government in the PRC are based on the idea of the pluralization (*duoyanghua*) of society. Therefore, the types of gated neighbourhoods are very different from each other, and they experience different roles of the state in their development and neighbourhood control (Lu, Zhang, and Wu 2019). Li Zhang's (2010) concept of "the spatialization of class" rightly refers to "the mutually constitutive and transformative relationship among three key aspects of the emerging urban regimes of living: spatial form, class-specific subjects, and modes of community governing" (3). The spatialization of a post-industrial lifestyle associated with the urban middle class in gated communities solidifies social boundaries by representing "the phenomenon of fortress and privatized cities," and keeping the unwanted "other" outside the community (Lama and Martín 2016). As a product of the dominant political–economic order of neoliberal capitalism, what makes gated communities unique is that they "exclude the other by default," thus, "the sign of exclusivity is also a sign of exclusion" (Vasallo 2018, 45–46). In the Chinese social context, low-*suzhi* people such as migrant workers can only gain access to the gated community of the middle class as service members (nannies, delivery men, or domestic workers).

Therefore, the gated community is a distinctive element of the paradigm of the Chinese middle class; it represents the hegemonic aspirations of the Chinese population. In terms of class, Tomba (2014) pointed out, whereas poor and unprivileged neighbourhoods hardly achieve a more participatory governance, middle-class gated communities are allowed to establish self-governing and self-elected bodies such as the HOAs to administer their relationship with service companies and to organize their interests inside the neighbourhoods (9). However, in terms of *suzhi*, while in unprivileged neighbourhoods paternalistic government prevails over social autonomy, in middle-class housing compounds a communitarian self-governance was installed by stimulating the forces of self-discipline, self-administration, and self-service rather than community identity that strengthened interest in participation and feeling of solidarity with co-residents (Heberer and Göbel 2011). Thus, class largely determines the degree of self-government in each community; the more "spatialized" a neighbourhood is, the higher the degree of self-governance—despite the impact that management companies have on these middle-class gated communities.

In any case, in the late 1990s and early 2000s, the CCP extended grassroots elections to urban areas, and officers of the RCs began to be democratically elected (Bing 2012). Although elections in China are fundamentally distinct from the ones in the minority world because there is no party competition, the CCP, as indicated earlier, hoped that elections could solve emerging popular grievance resulted from market reforms. However, in terms of participation, direct elections were not always carried out because members of the RCs were elected overwhelmingly from the top-down, as Mr. Qiao explained when referring to the minimal utility that the RC means to him:

> In some communities they ask you to vote, then indirectly suggest who to vote for because that candidate belongs to the same neighbourhood ... The ballots don't have any impact on me ... I don't vote. Why should I vote for someone who I don't know at all? I'd rather avoid using this right because I might choose the wrong person ... So, if I don't have enough information, I'd prefer not to vote.

The informants were not interested in the RCs elections because the RC's function as a service provider was very distant from their needs. In fact, the RC and Street Office largely influence by internally controlling the elections of board members and monitoring the RC's collective decisions through the approach of political examination (*zheng shen*) (Lu, Zhang, and Wu 2019, 10). As such, the RC's role in the day-to-day community governance was minimal and the respondents perceived that these elections were not clean, fair, and competitive. Understandably, since the RC's elections did not carry policy concession, informants manifested apathy and lack of incentive and did not show an active participation in elections.

Mr. Yang clearly expressed his disaffection with the system when he refused to discuss politics and governance organization, "I'm not interested in politics. In China, it's false." By the same token, Mr. Duan also perceived voting for RC in much the same way as Mr. Yang.

> I once participated in the voting process. Community members arrived with their voting cards, and I had to confirm their identities and hand them to the community officials. Everything took about an hour. It was simply done to familiarize myself with the process, but it's all just theatre. Voting doesn't have any value.

Among our informants, 39 per cent affirmed having participated in elections, another 39 per cent did not tend to vote or had never voted, and 22 per cent did not answer. Many of them had never heard about the candidates for director and Party secretary, which is the office to be elected in the RC elections, or some even were not aware of elections. "I didn't know about voting," Mrs. Tang said. Regarding the impact that RCs have had on their lives, the general trend can be summed up in Mr. Lai's words:

> It's partially useful, more so when you have to do paperwork … It exists, and it works as intended. It's not a matter of whether I like it or not. It's been there since I was a child, and I'm not sure if it will improve or get worse.

The participation of the urban middle class in local elections raises questions about Chinese citizens' perception of democracy. Although most informants refused to discuss political issues, Mr. Lai admitted to voting but questioned a hypothetical voting system like liberal democracies occurring in China.

> We Chinese don't consider voting to be useful. We don't make decisions through voting because it's not a good method. I don't think votes can solve any problems; I prefer talking to voting. Do you know the concept of *benfen* (to fulfill one's own responsibilities)? Society under Confucianism is stable because we all obey our *ben*. However, there are those who approach your door, hand you a paper with several questions, and ask you who you like. I'm a traditional Chinese person. I believe in Confucius and think he was right. If many people are allowed to vote, they could really stir up some problems.

Mr. Lai's narrative was significant for several reasons. First, he doubted the implementation of a democratic system in China such as the current voting system, arguing that Confucian values were best suited for the country. Second, he resorted to talking and the use of rational media to solve problems instead of voting. Third, he did not consider the organizational structure of the regime capable of organizing credible elections or all citizens to be equipped with the ability to choose the most ideal candidate to fulfil everyone's general interests. Paradoxically, despite his criticism towards the ideals espoused by democratic systems, Mr. Lai still admitted to participating in elections. However, Mr. Lai's opinion was not an exception among our informants.

Similarly, and in line with *suzhi* narratives, during an informal chat, Mr. Qiao argued,

> We *do* vote at a local level, but the elected representatives' power isn't much. Why ask if we want to vote if the government has already chosen for us? We don't have any other option. In any case, it's normal that city people don't want those from the countryside to be allowed to choose their future. They're not qualified to vote; they don't know what's good for everyone, for the

country. Look at what's happening in the United States with Trump. That guy is a real problem and was chosen democratically, which is proof that people don't know how to vote.

On the other side of the equation, HOAs were organizations that informants overwhelmingly supported. Beyond the RC's administrative duty, Mr. Cui noted, "it doesn't do much for us most of the time, but the HOA does." Likewise, Mrs. Wu was a professor who lived in a gated community in which most of the residents were employees from the same publicly administered institution—in this case, a university—while the rest of the residents had a different professional background. She also owned a property on the outskirts of Beijing, and pointed out that

> In the neighbourhood where I live, we no longer have an RC. What we have is a homeowner's association, it gets to choose the service company ... I think us professors aren't used to organizing ourselves and participating in such a committee [the RC], but I believe it's better to have one. It's very important. Because we don't have an RC, we never vote, but they [the HOA] tend to organize events that seem like a body of the Party. For example, publishing information about security, water, etc. As professors, we vote in the university. Those who vote in the neighbourhood are mostly the retired.

Therefore, Mrs. Wu's testimony coincided with two clear trends identified in the sample: the lack of motivation to participate in local elections, and the perception that gated neighbourhoods were not linked to self-governance per se or to any form of private governance. The lack of capacity in urban policymaking of RC and the constraints of the HOAs vis-à-vis management companies were the reasons most clearly suggested by the informants, despite their refusal to discuss politics. Moreover, our findings showed that the reconfiguration of local government starting in the early 2000s served primarily to proliferate apathy towards elections participation, and disengagement with governmental administration and official organizations. Additionally, this investigation identified a combination of anti-democratic views with political awareness of non-substantial policy influences in political participation among some of the informants.

Overall, the active and inclusive role and self-confidence and self-determination expected from the middle class contrasted with the manifestation of illiberal, classist, and *suzhi* discourses present in some testimonies regarding political participation of unprivileged groups. This reflects how the hegemonic discourse and social hierarchy reconfigured after the reforms of the 1990s in urban China was imposed by the political and economic elites in collusion with the middle class over the unprivileged groups. It echoes the uncomfortable coexistence at the top of the postrevolutionary social order of the new communist elite and the old Republican educated elite during the Mao-dominated era discussed in Chapter 2.

Remarkably, despite the validity of these considerations, it should be borne in mind that most participants rejected speaking out on political issues related to the

RC's elections, and those who spoke openly about self-governance were mostly male respondents. However, both male and female informants were more likely to share their views and speak freely about HOAs and other initiatives not directly linked to the RC in the community level. Along these lines, the next section evaluates alternative civic involvement in grassroots level and whether beyond the gated social borders of privilege groups, self-organized civic moments can flourish at local level in urban China.

Homeowners' activism in the civic society

As noted earlier, along with the rise of a new and broad class of urban homeowners, disputes in middle-class gated communities emerged. Much of their dissatisfaction was laid at the feet of the misconduct of real-estate development companies (*kaifa gongsi*) or their management companies (*wuye gongsi*), which were often offshoots of the former and operated indefinitely. The discontent among middle-class homeowners was related, firstly, to the infringement of property rights, substandard buildings, and poor services facilities, and secondly, to ill-regulated market and inadequate government policies that allowed the absence of any competition, thus favouring the good positioning of these firms to reap handsome profits from management fees (Yip and Jiang 2011; Tang 2018a, 124). The actualization of owners' rights was impeded by legislative defects, local government corruption or interference, and lack of enforcement and inadequate judicial review (Chen and Kielsgard 2013). In this context, the HOAs emerged as a "bottom-up urban governance" organization that was "therefore conducive in fostering civil engagement by mediating between urban citizens/homeowners, on the one hand, and large-scale bureaucracies as well as developers and other business interests, on the other" (He 2015). Although the capacity of the HOA to represent broad societal interests was very limited, some relatively self-organized associational life has been generated in the last two decades.

Since 1994, only the newly constructed residential areas have been able to undergo self-management and be autonomous through HOAs. Formed by elected representatives through the votes of the owners and residents of the neighbourhood dwellings, the HOA is considered a non-government organization, "but in reality, the government controls it," as Mr. Wen pointed out. He explained that every time his community had important issues to decide such as changing the management company, the HOA organized a vote.

> We vote every three years to decide whether to continue hiring the same [management] company or change it [because] we have public funds to keep the community in good condition, and we voted to decide if we will use public funds. We have a *Wechat* group comprised of the people of our community, the organizer asks the group when we must vote on some issues, and we vote … This is done two or three times a year.

Despite the explicit power assigned to the HOAs, the homeowners' ability to organize and defend their collective rights and claims was diminished and restricted due to local policies and administrative formalities in implementing them (Read 2008). Such features were immediately apparent in Mrs. Yin's testimony reproduced below.

> Sometimes, the HOA does surveys, but I don't vote often. However, lately, as the service and security company [that is, the management company] which is responsible for maintaining our community wants to increase the price of services, they want more money... And so, we're collecting signatures to see if we all agree to pay them more, but we didn't agree because we think they don't offer a good service. It's like a struggle, they ask us for more, but we don't want to pay more ... If they want to raise the price, even if they don't have our signatures, they can do it anyway [and then] the next step will be to ask ourselves what to do: *do we throw them out?* ... I am not sure that we can throw them out. This type of relationship is agreed upon, it is not an open market in which there are different companies, and I can choose... It is not so simple. When you buy the house, this company was already there, I think it cooperated with the builder. We have no choice. The builder told us, '*Oh, this company is very good, and has a lot of maintenance experience.*' Then we wanted to buy the house, if the management company does not have a good reputation, then you say, '*Huh, this community is not so good, I don't want to buy here,*' but now it is a simple management company. As time went on, the builder left because we bought the house more than ten years ago and only the management company has worked with us.

In the event of disputes, as Mrs. Yin foresaw it would happen in her community, the HOA would "act openly and autonomously" to protect homeowners' rights and "engage in protracted conflicts" with the management company (Tomba 2014, 50). Otherwise, the property company and the residents, who were concerned about the possible devaluation of their housing in both economic and symbolic (*suzhi*) terms, would invite the RC to step in and mediate the situation (Tang 2018b). Sometimes management companies avoided conflicts by manipulating the formation of HOAs through their elections in different ways. Other times, on the other side of the equation, residents employed tactics of collective protests to mount their claims and assert control over the administration of their *xiaoqu*.

In the 2000s, scholars believed that these middle-class homeowners' movements could be the spur for the democratization process in the PRC. However, it soon became apparent that these protests were demonstrations to preserve or increase only the personal benefit of the middle class and focused, above all, on perceptions of material injustice rather than a demand for democratization (Ong and Göbel 2012). Although homeowners' movements, and environmental protests associated with them, gathered a great number of citizens, action was generally aimed at non-state entities, and it carried a considerably lower risk compared to actions directed against the government or institutions related to it, "where demonstrators and protesters constantly faced threats of losing their jobs and social status" (Ong and Han 2019, 232). It should be borne in mind that the existence of obvious links between the Chinese middle class and activation of civil society (or class consciousness) is determinant for the binary identification in most Western social theories of class as "a real class" vs. "theorical class." Anyhow, although the findings of this study revealed a tendency towards disaffection and lack of confidence with local governance, there was no sign of direct confrontation with the state legitimacy among the informants' testimonies.

Nevertheless, before the outbreak of COVID-19, it was possible to point out various practices of social organization and solidarity ties in the participants' *xiaoqu*. For instance, Mrs. Ai acted for the collective good in her community's public sphere when she had free time.

> I participate in some activities because sometimes I volunteer teaching English to older people. [*laughs*] [And] that is one of the activities organized by our community because we are all registered. We all have to indicate our work and basic information, so they inform you about those opportunities, but you decide if you want to do them or not. If I have time, I tend to do them.

Mrs. Ai's volunteering practices would fit within Salmenkari's (2018) post-colonial approach of civil society by broadening this concept that originated in the minority world and incorporating indigenous aspects of Chinese traditional culture. Salmenkari defined civil society as "public, open, horizontal, voluntaristic, and done together with others" (29) by referring "to a bigger community, not to individual associative activities," for the common good or based on principles of openness, publicity, and solidarity (202). While the Western approach of civil society creates social spaces that can countervail the state's power, Chinese indigenous concepts such as *minjian shehui* create consensual arenas of interaction where the state is not necessarily confronted, and activities are organized among the people and based on values of civilized sociability, mutual solidarity, and concern for the public good (65). It is a strict civic society rather than a civil society. From this perspective, it is possible to identify some practices of social organization and even solidarity ties among our informants in their gated communities.

However, the presence of the Party-state in every corner of Chinese society should not be underestimated. Mr. Lu also carried out collaborative volunteering practices to organize society, but under the supervision of China's ruling entity.

> I'll tell you about a very interesting activity, I'm a member of the Party! [*laughs*] And now all the members that live in Beijing have to participate in some activities organized by the RC in order to improve the environment of the area ... The activity in which I participated was to organize the shared bicycles, I think it is an activity for the public interest, and it served to

improve the environment of the area ... I have also seen in the group chat that they've helped the elderly to use mobile phones. The activities are varied, and I'm in favour of them, [although] since I don't have much time, I only participated once.

Given China's authoritarian regime and the fact that volunteerism is an expression of *free will* and acting without coercion, the relationship between the Patty-state and volunteering practices is complex in the PRC (Xu 2017). Firstly, both Mrs. Ai and Mr. Lu's supportive practices did not challenge state legitimacy, but enhanced it while also creating social trust and being part of "civic society" groups focused on social problems rather than restrictions (Teets et al. 2021). Hence, beyond the symbolic dimension of volunteering, both informants acted "to improve the environment" of their neighbourhood, "to teach English," "for the public interest," and "help the elderly" rather than change the political regime or fight against social injustice.

Thus, the Chinese government actively promoted volunteerism to be internalized by citizens through both regulations and altruistic discourses such as the celebrity philanthropy (see Section 4.1). Certainly, the government saw a potential role for volunteering in addressing social needs and relieving the state of welfare provision. Additionally, volunteering provided a wider (and monitored) space for the voluntary service organizations, legitimized the grassroots volunteers and voluntary service organizations as a policy executor, created volunteer schemes, and organized top-down movements as a service organizer (Zhao and Lilly 2021; Xu 2017). Consequently, civic participation among middle-class constituents combined the manifestation of distinctive social practices with the willingness to solve social problems and the acquisition of social and political capital.

In conclusion, beyond the social space of the *xiaoqu*, the respondents had not alluded to any form of civil society, or unofficial activism. Hence, associationism is limited to the social space of the gated community in the same way that affections are restricted to the enclosed family and gender, and other factors such as time, space, and human capital are subordinated to the utility-maximizing calculation of "the entrepreneur of the self." Apart from Mrs. Yin's testimony about her HOA's dispute with the management company, there had been no other mention of any type of association that collectively defended certain political interests of citizens, either in the realm of consumers, political subjects or workers, or of any cultural or social movements mobilized for any specific claims for justice or equality that were then expressed in universal terms. Thus, cultural capital is negatively related to involvement in altruistic actions for public good.

Only 10 per cent of the participants (Mr. Ai and Mr. Lu) manifested practices of solidarity. Whereas Mrs. Ai acted for the collective good in her community's public sphere by teaching English to older people, Mr. Lu participated in the CCP's volunteer activities, a top-to-bottom volunteering strategy. In both cases, though, the scope of action did not extend beyond their neighbourhoods. At the same time, a new civic morality is emerging, and solidarity representations are increasingly associated with the paradigm of the Chinese middle class, such as filial piety, celebrity philanthropy, Mrs. Yao's Christian life of service to the common good, or the Dual Circulation encouragement to donate. Despite this awakening of social conscience, Beijing's middle class tended to support hegemonic political values, paternalistic authority, social discipline, and the established order. Although they did not allude to any form of unofficial associationism, their interaction with the reconfiguring networks of governance in China on the micro-level is inconspicuous. In neo-authoritarian China, the urban middle class did not express a desire for social change; they navigated shifting positionings of class privilege and political apathy.

Bibliography

Becker, Gary. 1976. *The Economic Approach to Human Behavior.* Chicago: University of Chicago Press.

Bing, Ngeow Chow. 2012. "The Residents' Committee in China's Political System: Democracy, Stability, Mobilization." *Issues & Studies* 48 (2): 71–126.

Bray, David. 2009. "Building 'community': new strategies of governance in urban China." In *China's Governmentalities. Governing change, changing government,* edited by Elaine Jeffreys, 88–106. London: Routledge.

Cano, Virginia. 2020. "Ego/liberalismo y resistencias afectivas" [Ego/liberalism and affective resistances]. In *Neoliberalismo, hospitalidad, resistencias* [*Neoliberalism, hospitality, resistances*], edited by Vanesa Baur and Sonia López Hana, 10–20. Mar del Plata: Universidad Nacional de Mar del Plata.

Chen, Lei, and Mark D. Kielsgard. 2013. "Evolving Property Rights in China: Patterns and Dynamics of Condominium Governance." *Chinese Journal of Comparative Law*: 1–22. https://ssrn.com/abstract=2340014.

Croll, Elisabeth J. 2006. "The Intergenerational Contract in the Changing Asian Family." *Oxford Development Studies* 34 (4): 473–491. doi:10.1080/13600810601045833.

Davis, Deborah S. 2014. "Privatization of Marriage in Post-socialist China." *Modern China*, 40 (6): 551–577. doi:10.1177/0097700414536528.

Davis, Howard. 1995. *China Business: Context and Issues.* Hong Kong: Longman Asia Ltd.

Deng, Jun, and Craig A. Smith. 2018. "The rise of New Confuciamism and the return of spirituality to politics in mainland China." *China Information* 32 (2): 294–314. doi:10.1177/0920203X18764041.

Fei, Xiaotong. 1992. *From the Soil, the Foundations of Chinese Society.* Berkeley: University of California Press.

Folbre, Nancy. 2009. "Varieties of Patriarchal Capitalism." *Social Politics* 16 (2): 204–209. doi:10.1093/sp/jxp011.

Foucault, Michel. 2004. *The Birth of Biopolitics. Lectures at the Collège de France, 1978–79.* Translated by Graham Burchell. New York: Palgrave Macmillan.

Gao, Mobo. 2018. *Constructing China. Clashing Views of the People's Republic.* London: Pluto Press.

Goffman, Erving. 1963. *Behavior in Public Places. Notes on the Social Organization of Gatherings.* New York: Free Press.

Goh, Esther C. L., Bill Y.P. Tsang, and Srinivasan Chokkanathan. 2016. "Intergenerational Reciprocity Reconsidered: The Honour and Burden of Grandparenting in Urban China." *Intersections: Gender and Sexuality in Asia and the Pacific,* 39: 1–23.

He, Shenjing. 2015. "Homeowner associations and neighborhood governance in Guangzhou, China." *Eurasian Geography and Economics* 56 (3): 260–284. doi:10.1080/15387216.2015.1095108.

Heberer, Thomas, and Göbel, Christian. 2011. *The Politics of Community Building in Urban China.* London: Routledge.

Hertz, Ellen. 2001. "Face in the crowd: The cultural construction of anonymity in urban China." In *China Urban: Ethnographies of Contemporary Cultures*, edited by Nancy N. Chen, Constance D. Clark, Suzanne Gottschang and Lyn Jeffrey, 274–293. Durham, NC: Duke University Press.

Holroyd, Eleanor. 2003. "Chinese Family Obligations Toward Chronically Ill Elderly Members: Comparing Caregivers in Beijing and Hong Kong." *Qualitative Health Research* 3 (3): 302–318. doi:10.1177/1049732302250127.

Huang, Martin W. 2007. "Male Friendship in Ming China: An Introduction." In *Male Friendship in Ming China*, edited by Martin W. Huang, 2–33. Leiden: Brill.

Ji, Yingchun, and Xiaogang Wu. 2018. "New Gender Dynamics in Post-Reform China: Family Education, and Labor Market." *Chinese Sociological Review* 50 (3): 231–239. doi:10.1080/21620555.2018.1452609.

Ji, Yingchun, Xiaogang Wu, Shengwei Sun, and Guangye He. 2017. "Unequal Care, Unequal Work: Toward A More Comprehensive Understanding of Gender Inequality in Post-reform Urban China." *Sex Roles* 77 (11–12):765–778. doi:10.1007/s11199-017-0751-1.

Lama, Arsenio Villar, and Miguel García Martín. 2016. "Ciudad Segregada en España: Urbanizaciones Cerradas en Valencia y Sevilla." *Revista IVNI* 86 (3): 145–177. doi:10.4067/S0718-83582016000100006.

Lamas-Abraira, Laura. 2021a. *Chinese Transational Families. Care Circulation and Children's Life Paths.* Abingdon: Routledge.

Lamas-Abraira, Laura. 2021b. "Care circulation and the so-called 'elderly': exploring care in 4G transnational Zhejianese families." *Journal of Family Studies* 27 (3): 460–478. doi:10.1080/13229400.2019.1641427.

Laslett, Barbara, and Johanna Brenner. 1989. "Gender and Social Reproduction: historical Perspectives." *Annual Review of Sociology* 15: 381–404. doi:10.1146/annurev.so.15.080189.002121.

Lin, Xiaoshan. 2019."'Purchasing hope': the consumption of children's education in urban China." *The Journal of Chinese Sociology* 6, 8. doi:10.1186/s40711-019-0099-8.

Liu, Jieyu. 2017. *Gender, Sexuality and Power in Chinese Companies: Beauties at Work.* London: Palgrave Macmillan.

Lu, Tingting, Fangzhu Zhang, and Fulong Wu. 2019. "The variegated role of the state in different gated neighbourhoods in China." *Urban Studies* 57 (8): 1642–1659. doi:10.1177/0042098019838423.

Ma, Xinxin. 2022. "Parenthood and the gender wage gap in urban China." *Journal of Asian Economics* 80 (Forthcoming). doi:10.1016/j.asieco.2022.101479.

Nagel, Ineke, Harry B.G. Ganzeboom, and Matthijs Kalmijn. 2011. "Bourdieu in the Network: The Influence of High and Popular Culture on Network Formation in Secondary School." *Kölner Zeitschrift für Soziologie und Sozialpsychologie* 51: 424–446.

Ong, Lynette H., and Christian Göbel. 2012. "Social Unrest in China." In *China and the EU in Context. Insights for Business and Investors*, edited by Kerry Brown, 178–213. London: Palgrave Macmillan.

Ong, Lynette H., and Donglin Han. 2019. "What Drives People to Protest in an Authoritarian Country? Resources and Rewards vs Risks of Protests in Urban and Rural China." *Political Studies* 67 (1): 224–248. doi:10.1177/0032321718763558.

Peng, Xinyan. 2022. *Corporate Women in Contemporary China. "We've Always Worked."* Abingdon: Routledge.

Qian, Yue, and Jiaxing Li. 2020. "Separating Spheres: Cohort Differences in Gender Attitudes about Work and Family in China." *The China Review* 20 (2): 19–52. https://www.jstor.org/stable/26915620.

Read, Benjamin. 2008. "Property Rights and Homeowner Activism in New Neighborhoods." In *Privatizing China*, edited by Li Zhang and Aihwa Ong, 41–56. Ithaca, NY: Cornell University Press.

Richaud, Lisa. 2018. "Between 'face' and 'faceless' realtionships in China's public places: Ludic encounters and activity-oriented friendships among middle- and old-aged urbanites in Beijing public parks." *Urban Studies* 55 (3): 570–588. doi:10.1177/0042098016633609.

Sáiz, Amelia. 2001. *Utopía y Género. Las Mujeres Chinas en el siglo XX [Utopia and Gender. Chinese Women in the 20th Century]*. Barcelona: Edicions Bellaterra.

Salmenkari, Taru. 2018. *Civil Society in China and Taiwan. Agency, Class and Boundaries.* Abingdon: Routledge.

Salzinger, Leslie. 2003. *Genders in Production: Making Workers in Mexico's Global Factories.* Berkeley: University of California Press.

Shields, Anna M. 2015. *One Who Knows Me. Friendship and Literary Culture in Mid-Tang China.* Cambridge, MA: Harvard University Asia Center.

Siegelbaum, Lewis H. 2006. "Introduction: Mapping Private Spheres in the Soviet context." In *Borders of Socialism. Private spheres of Soviet Russia*, edited by Lewis H. Siegelbaum, 1–21. New York: Palgrave Macmillan.

Solé-Farràs, Jesús. 2014. *New Confucianism in Twenty-first Century China.* Abingdon and New York: Routledge.

Song, Jin, Terry Sicular, and Bjorn Gustafsson. 2017. "China's Urban Gender Wage Gap: A New Direction?" University of Western Ontario, Centre for Human Capital and Productivity (CHCP) Working Papers 201723. Accessed October 18 2020. https://ideas.repec.org/p/uwo/hcuwoc/201723.html.

Song, Shaopeng, and Sharon R. Wesoky, eds. 2022. *Chinese Modernity and Socialist Feminist Theory.* London: Routledge.

Song, Yueping, Jingwen Zhang, and Xian Zhang. 2021. "Cultural or Institutional? Contextual Effects on Domestic Violence against Women in Rural China." *Journal of Family Violence* 36: 643–655. doi:10.1007/s10896-020-00198-6.

Stockman, Norman. 1994. "Gender Inequality and Social Structure in Urban China." *Sociology* 28 (3): 759–777. doi:10.1177/0038038594028003007.

Sun, Wanning. 2008. "Men, Women and the Maid: at Home with the New Rich." In *The New Rich in China*, edited by David S.G.Goodman, 213–228. Abingdon: Routledge.

Tang, Beibei. 2018a. *China's Housing Middle Class. Changing Urban Life in Gated Communities.* Abingdon and New York: Routledge.

Tang, Beibei. 2018b. "Deliberation and Governance in Chinese Middle-class Neighborhoods." *Japanese Journal of Political Science*, 19: 663–677. doi:10.1017/S1468109918000282.

Tang, Beibei. 2019. "Grid Governance in China's Urban Middle-class Neighbourhoods." *The China Quarterly* 241: 1–19. doi:10.1017/s0305741019000821.

Teets, Jessica C., Reza Hasmath, Timothy Hildebrant, Carolyn L. Hsu and Jennifer Y. Hsu. 2021. "Volunteerism and democratic learning in an authoritarian state: the case of China." *Democratization*. doi:10.1080/13510347.2021.2015334.

Thomas, Reuben J. 2019. "Sources of Friendship and Structurally Induced Homophily across the Life Course." *Sociological Perspectives* 62 (6): 822–843. doi:10.1177/0731121419828399.

Tomba, Luigi. 2014. *The Government Next Door: Neighborhood Politics in Urban China.* Ithaca, NY: Cornell University Press.

Tsui, Ming, and Lynne Rich. 2002. "The Only Child and Educational Opportunity for Girls in Urban China." *Gender & Society* 16 (1): 74–92. doi:10.1177/0891243202016001005.

Vala, Carsten T., Jianbo Huang, and Jesse Sun. 2015. "Protestantism, community service and evangelism in contemporary China." *International Journal for the Study of the Christian Church* 15 (4): 305–319. doi:10.1080/1474225X.2015.1115252.

Vasallo, Brigitte. 2018. *Pensamiento Monógamo, Terror Poliamoroso [Monogamous Thinking, Polyamorous Terror]*. Guadalajara: La Oveja Roja.

Wallace, Claire. 2019. "Between state, market and family: Changing childcare policies in urban China and the implications for working mothers." *International Sociology* 35(3): 336–352. doi:10.1177/0268580919885282.

Widmer, Ellen. 2006. *The Beauty and the Book: Women and Fiction in Nineteenth-Century China*. Cambridge, MA: Harvard University Asia Center.

Wong, Y. H., and Ricky Yee-kwong Chan. 1999. "Relationship Marketing in China: Guanxi, Favouritism and Adaptation." *Journal of Business Ethics* 22: 107–118. doi:10.1023/A:1006077210425.

Xiao, Suowei. 2016. "Intimate power: the intergenerational cooperation and conflicts in childrearing among urban families in contemporary China." *The Journal of Chinese Sociology* 3, 18. doi:10.1186/s40711-016-0037.

Xie, Wenye, and Ruiping Fan. 2020. "Towards Ethically and Medically Sustainable Care for the Elderly: The Case of China." *HEC Forum* 32: 1–12. doi:10.1007/s10730-019-09391-7.

Xu, Ying. 2017. "Volunteerism and the State: Understanding the Development of Volunteering in China. In *Perspectives on Volunteering. Voices from the South*, edited by Jacqueline Butcher and Christopher J. Einolf, 213–226. Cham: Springer.

Yan, Yunxiang. 2003. *Private Life under Socialism: Love, Intimacy, and Family Change in a Chinese Village, 1949–1999*. Stanford, CA: Stanford University Press.

Yan, Yunxiang. 2009. *The Individualization of Chinese Society*. Oxford: Berg.

Yang, Haiou, and David Chandler. 1992. "Intergenerational Relations: Grievances of the Elderly in Rural China." *Journal of Comparative Family Studies* 23 (3): 431–453. doi:10.3138/jcfs.23.3.431.

Ye, Nanqi, Michihiro Kita, Shigeki Matsubara, Seth Asare Okyere, and Motoki Shimoda. 2021. "Socio-Spatial Changes in Danwei Neighbourhoods: A Case Study of the AMS Danwei Compound in Hefei, China." *Urban Science* 5 (2): 35. doi:10.3390/urbansci5020035.

Yip, Ngai-ming, and Yihong Jiang. 2011. "Homeowners United: the attempt to create lateral networks of homeowners' associations in urban China." *Journal of Contemporary China* 20 (72): 735–750. doi:10.1080/10670564.2011.604492.

Zang, Xiaowei. 2006. "Social resources, class habitus and friendship ties in urban China." *Journal of Sociology* 42 (1): 79–92. doi:10.1177/1440783306061354.

Zeuthen, Jesper, Qiuyu Jiang, and Ane Bislev. 2022. *"From Informal Blacklists to Social Credit Apps: Trusting Chinese Domestic Workers in the Digital Era."* Paper presented at the conference Categories, Digital Reconfiguration and Mobility in China, Copenhagen, May 18–20.

Zhang, Jun. 2016. "Family Car, Filial Consumer-Citizens: Becoming Properly Middle Class in Post-Socialist South China." *Modern China* 1–30. doi:10.1177/0097700416645138.

Zhang, Li. 2010. *In Search of Paradise: Middle-class Living in a Chinese Metropolis*. Ithaca, NY: Cornell University Press.

Zhang, Qiang Forrest. 2004. "Economic transition and new patterns of parent-adult child coresidence in Urban China." *Journal of Marriage and Family* 66 (5): 1231–1245. doi:10.1111/j.0022-2445.2004.00089.x.

Zhao, Rong, and Adam G. Lilly. 2021. "The Role of State Mobilization for Volunteerism in China." *Nonprofit and Voluntary Sector Quarterly*. doi:10.1177/08997640211057458.

CONCLUSIONS

New configurations to a post-pandemic future

The global crises of this century have spread the awareness that the present is finite. Our time is the time in which we are wanting to get away from the present. Historical linearity has returned, but it does not point to a light at the end of the tunnel, but rather casts a shadow over a posthumous present, with the extinction of ecosystems, the sterility of life-in-common, and the scarcity of resources, water, oil, gas, and clean air (Garcés 2017). The Global Financial Crisis of 2007/2008 and the COVID-19 pandemic have accentuated the impression that the present is dying and the future "cannot be born" by embodying feelings of powerlessness and claustrophobia, "the feeling that we want to escape the planet because we are now so foreclosed" (Redhead 2009). Amid this "morbid present," as Gramsci (1971) would term it, the study of the lifestyle and social distinctions of the Chinese middle class would seem to be a largely superfluous and self-referential exercise, minority world scholars reflecting from their privileged position on what they find interesting about Chinese society.

However, in many respects, lifestyle is a form of communication, and constitutes the economic, cultural, and symbolic embodiment of the truly colossal challenges currently facing societies in the morbid present. Although minority world scholars cannot escape othering when they analyse Chinese society and its diverse social practices and representations, we need to understand lifestyle as communication on its own terms and question epistemologically the endurance of Orientalist knowledge about China and the Western hegemony over the right to knowledge (Gao 2018). Indeed, the knowledge about China has been constructed within "the Western discourse," that is, with the political and economic interest of the West and the exclusion or de-legitimization of a subaltern voice (Spivak 1988, 271). That is why an equal conversation between China and the West is necessary. However, as Xiaolu Guo (2008) suggested, first China has to "view itself as strong as America, only when the quality of life is equal," and the access to education of

DOI: 10.4324/9781003299301-7

the Chinese population has improved, "can we have a conversation" (50). On that basis, this study has attempted to narrativize the Other, in this case the Chinese middle class, as a participant in a dialogue rather than an object to be scrutinized, from self-reflection and self-positioning.

As the reader has found in the pages of this book, it is on lifestyle and social distinctions, and their processes of reconfiguration, hierarchization, and construction of social identity, that we see the impacts of not only the global crises but also the political economy of privatization implemented by the Chinese state throughout the "reform and openness" after 1978. Under these conditions, class formation is not only about the intergenerational transfer of capital and gender-specific asymmetries, but it is also about state interventionism, Western paradigms and capitalist categories introduced by market forces, culture backgrounds and traditional values, memories of an impoverished past, and China's unique conditions and socio-historical events (Zhang 2020). In the case of the post-reform middle class in Beijing, it has revealed the changing landscape of the urban lifestyle in China from the second stage of reforms of the 1990s to the present.

The lifestyle of the post-reform middle class has transitioned from a production-orientated society to a consumer society in which a new morality has established. New manifestations of a de-individualization of the Chinese society have emerged considering the refocus on the nuclear and extended family and the new imaginary of the common prosperity (volunteering, group mentality, philanthropic representations). The "commercializing society" (Zhang 2008) based on materialism, individualization, capital accumulation, and hedonism that emerged at the beginning of this century as a reaction to the second stage of market reforms implemented in the 1990s, has been replaced by a new civic-minded citizen in a neo-authoritarian regime. This post-reform citizen denotes a non-binary morality in which traditional and Western values, individualism and group mentality, consumerism and frugality, materialism and philanthropy, hedonism and filial commitments go hand in hand without conflict.

The urban middle class, thus, has already become a post-industrial middle class, "a real class" in terms of lifestyle and capital possession, but "a theoretical class" in terms of political expressions of collective goals. However, as we have seen, class is determined by the point of view, by the observer. Class cannot be considered a neutral, homogeneous, static category anymore. Indeed, to avoid Eurocentric conceptualizations of class, class analysis needs to look at intersectionality, positioning, dynamic hierarchies, and agency. In reviewing the intellectual debate on the Chinese middle class, it is clear that despite the use of objective and subjective criteria by Chinese and non-Chinese scholars to measure class in the PRC, they estimate the size and definition of the Chinese middle class differently. All quantifications of the Chinese middle class have an ideological basis and to ignore this is to study social inequality in China uncritically.

Additionally, by analysing class as "a *well-founded historical artefact*" (Bourdieu 1987, 8–9, emphasis in original) this study has assessed the continual reconfiguration of inequalities and capital conversion in China since the late Qing era to the

COVID-19 pandemic. Over the last century, the Nationalist Party and the Communist Party of China have both contributed to the protection of the privileged position of the urban population. However, no 20th century regimes fostered a fully economically or politically independent middle class in China. Since market reforms, political dependence has been the price the Chinese middle class has paid for ensuring class reproduction. In the PRC, class is not only a social construct that facilitates capital transferability, but also a historically specific variable and a powerful discursive tool that regulates political economy and exerts social control, as a product of intellectual and political elite consolidation.

Considering discourse analysis, the *Renmin Wang* is a categorical example of the CCP's nationalist, populist, and paternalist rhetoric in addressing class in digital media. Surprisingly, although the *Renmin Wang* is the online version of *Renmin Ribao*, the mouthpiece of the Central Committee of the CCP, this identified the dominant presence of a pro-market view in the content of articles on middle class published between 2000 and 2015. The Party-sponsored discourse on the middle class went hand in hand with the ideological programmes of the leaders of the Party-state and their power to establish the very things that represented and hegemonic culture in the PRC. The presence of a pan-national discourse that appealed to the shared identity of majority world vis-à-vis minority world is verified (Sánchez-Romera 2021). In addition, nationalist, pro-consumerist, reductionist, and normative narratives have been shown in all the discursive spaces analysed, along with a strong emphasis on the acknowledge of Party-state's legitimacy over both public and private spheres, and on the firm desire of the regime to deliver its discourse to all political dimensions.

Therefore, the diversity of topics, voices, and approaches of this study is significant. Yet the analyses of social practices and representations are unified. We have journeyed from the emergence in the second half of the late Qing era of an industrial middle class to the reconfiguration of a post-industrial middle class in the first decades of the 21st century in urban China. The stops on the way included the Republican middle society, a Communist Revolution, a new political elite and classification, the Cultural Revolution, market reforms, class reproduction, the emergence of a post-industrial lifestyle, digital media, new gender asymmetries, and the building of a civic socialist society. Additionally, the testimonial value of this empirical analysis lies in the fact that it was carried out in the immediate past prior to lockdown, providing testimonies of what life was like in Beijing just before the COVID-19 pandemic.

The analysis of semi-structured interviews collected in Beijing has provided a categorical example of the lifestyle and social distinction of the middle class in contemporary urban China. Data collected have illustrated the basic characteristics of the social construction of identity within the middle class by exploring the social field in Beijing as a multidimensional space of social mobility, new lifestyles, gender divisions, and community organizations. This research has captured class asymmetries by the subalternity or privilege positioning that a subject establishes in each situation in relation to others, that is, by considering social agents not only in economic, cultural, and symbolic terms but also through distinctive practices and the interactive processes with other people in which we participate. New social relations and distinctions based on post-industrial consumption, heteronormativity, cultural heterogeneity, *suzhi* discrimination, philanthropic and civic aspirations, monetary hierarchy, and a revival of family mentality have been revealed here. On that basis, class acts in intersectional relationship with other structures that produce and reproduce inequality, such as ethnicity and gender. Intersectional structuring also involves that inequalities are shaped "dialogically and relationally" by people's points of view and memories, escaping thus from the binary paradigm such as the economic versus the cultural.

New configurations on common prosperity

The 2020s is set to be the decade of the expansion of the Chinese middle class, if the COVID-19 pandemic does not prevent it. On the one hand, the materialization of the Chinese Dream as an alternative aspiration for the middle class to the American Dream could become even more influential around the world, especially in the majority world. On the other, while the "common prosperity" (*gongtong fuyu*) campaign reintroduced in 2021 aims to increase the size of the Chinese middle class by "raising the earnings of low-income groups and reduce excessive incomes," the Dual Circulation strategy for the period 2020 to 2035 encourages donations from business and wealthy individuals, to give back some of what they gained from society (Dunford 2022). In these ideological programmes promoted by the Chinese government, the middle class is the hegemonic system of social practices, discourses, and norms that construct an urban, refined, gendered identity as developed and superior to all other expressions of subjectivity. Additionally, after ending extreme poverty in China, the Party-state plans to sustain regime legitimacy from the common prosperity and the anti-poverty governance effectiveness. Matching such emerging imaginaries, social practices, and policies amid a global crisis involves greater intellectual complexity in theorizing not only these new social phenomena but also social change and inequality in the PRC.

Of special note is the fact that the Chinese middle class is not a "new middle class," rather it is a phenomenon of class reproduction. Despite the informants mentioning their personal trajectories as the result of hard work and credentialism alone, assessment made of their social origins show that nearly 85 per cent of them come from the *danwei* middle-class backgrounds. Therefore, upward social mobility is a minority phenomenon among the Chinese middle class. Further, perseverance and personal effort are not positively related to class formation in China today. Such intergenerational class transmission developed by the Chinese middle class during the market reforms was essentially sponsored by the Party-state as a part of its "strategy for survival" (Dickson 2016) and ensuring its legitimacy after the Tiananmen Square protests. As Lin (2008) suggested, class distinctions "not only depend on the accumulation of economic capital but also gradually depends on the reproduction of cultural capital" in the form of educational attainment, cultural consumption and taste. Certainly, consumption and taste reflect not only symbolic power and class location in the post-reform era, but also the proliferation of hegemonic classifications and discourses, and dominant accounts of *suzhi*, civilization, modernity, and progress.

There is considerable evidence based on the analysis of social representations of happiness and romantic love to suggest that the construction of new social identities in contemporary urban China were the result of capitalist paradigms and Chinese traditional values. The reconfiguration of both material and post-material concerns for happiness must be contextualized in relation to cultural consumption. Urban dwellers experienced a feeling of emptiness that could only be filled by the construct of spiritual well-being and some sort of self-fulfilment narratives. Such representations implied a series of distinctive practices which indicated that those who practice them have disposable time and income to develop them, sensibility to enjoy them, and an emerging habitus to represent them. As the private and public spheres construct each other, the proliferation of post-industrial representations for happiness has accelerated due to the fast-paced commodification of housing, rapid industrialization, competitiveness of the labour force, globalization, economically calculative individualization, and urbanization.

In the case study undertaken here the majority of informants positioned themselves within a concept of loving relationships and marriage associated with aspects of Chinese marital culture which emphasized commitment and heteronormativity rather than romantic love. Loving relationships were imbued with a strong in-group engagement and collectivist spirit based on both nuclear and extended family. Loving relationships were not mainly about romantic love, they were mainly about (extended) family harmonization, equality, respect, and caregiving. Despite the relatively privileged position of middle-class couples on the social ladder, romantic manifestations were not the main concern in terms of loving relationships among the participants of this investigation. In contemporary urban China, life after marriage is based on facing material issues in raising a particular ideal of monogamy: the happy complete heterosexualized family.

The findings on reproductive labour and care in the domestic household have revealed little that was not already observed from previous research. Gender asymmetries in both productive and reproductive labour have been reinforced since the market reforms implemented in the 1990s. It was primarily women rather than their male partners who planned, managed, and accomplished care and the day-to-day work activities in urban households. Additionally, the concept of *bu hayong* woman (useless woman) has been used here to highlight narratives of gendered division of labour associated with precarity, modernity, internalized discrimination, and the gender pay gap. While this study has been able to document significant differences in the lifestyle of men and women, it must be remembered that such differences encroached upon Chinese women quite differently according to class background, human capital, and *suzhi* classification. In any case, as Xie (2020) noted, women have been and remain the ones who face the greatest struggles to reconcile the multiple and often oppositional ideologies arising from the intermingling of traditional and modern discourses of housewife, wife, and productive worker.

This articulation of the professional sphere and private life has reasserted traditional family values such as filial piety and has re-situated friendship beyond the everyday local context of the Chinese middle class. In a similar way to the process of reconfiguration of non-material concerns and loving relationships, traditional Chinese family ethics based on values such as filial piety and *guanxi* have coexisted without great conflict with the new morality of individualization introduced in the 1990s. The coexistence of traditional and Western patriarchal approaches in very large cities has facilitated the normalization of inequality, proliferation of gender asymmetries in both private and public spheres, and depoliticization of collective visions of change that challenge cultural hegemony.

Therefore, traditional Chinese culture still plays a key role for interpersonal and intergenerational behaviours within kinship relations in contemporary society. Clearly, Chinese government has actively promoted filial piety and volunteerism by creating what liberal thought describes as the non-governmental arena to relieve the state of welfare provision and as a mechanism of social control. However, it would be a mistake to think that such civic engagement is the result of uncritical acceptance of government directives by the post-reform middle class. Just as the middle class has showed apathy to local elections, the middle class has showed a growing interest in developing its role as a social mediator by participating in volunteering practices and increasing their participation in associational space in which the state is not necessarily confronted. However, such a trend identified by this research in a significant part of pre-pandemic urban society needs to be further analysed by future research to see if it is a phenomenon that has spread during the COVID-19 pandemic in contemporary urban China.

As a result, despite the urban middle class taking a step back from the individualist tendencies that emerged in the 2000s, community ties are still being elaborated. Paradoxes thus define the Chinese middle class. On the one hand, there is considerable evidence to suggest that the social construction of a middle-class identity is constructed in terms of binary division between opposite categories such as high-*suzhi* versus low-*suzhi*, rural versus urban, traditional Chinese culture versus modern Western values, femininity versus masculinity, and so on. On the other, the conceptualization of class in China studies must be understood from a non-binary perspective because, in some respects the middle class overcomes twofold oppositions between actors, and social practices and structures. The social construction of identity through cultural consumption, individualization, hedonism, and capital accumulation goes hand in hand with a tentative but increasing civic disposition, not only discursively (celebrity philanthropy) but also on a daily basis (filial activities, volunteering). For instance, friendship has become a social sphere for the negotiation of identity, new symbolic and status hierarchies, and a post-industrialist way to enjoy free time by combining emotional ties and consumption practices.

Such syncretic processes of class formation and variety in their practices mean that the Chinese middle class can be considered neither a homogeneous social group nor a social class in the post-reform era. However, their heterogeneity is based on a great diversity of practices of cultural consumption and cultural capital accumulation. And these consumption practices and educational attainment are therefore a matter of class in China today. Nevertheless, beyond material measurements of class, nearly 80 per cent of the informants considered themselves as middle class and they indicated their social status through lifestyle. On the one hand, this broad middle-class consciousness among respondents coincided with their objective social position in terms of educational background, spatial mobility, and professional status. On the other hand, they mentioned that their class location was result of individual perseverance, hard work and knowledge (here, again, due to personal effort). In any case, the findings revealed that the middle class venerated the ideology of meritocracy, which was often transformed into a legitimization of social injustices, depoliticization, and an essentialized and exclusionary notion of "hard work" and "intelligence."

Most notable is that the non-binary recognition of the social construction of the identity of the Chinese middle class challenges the clear distinctions between production and consumption, material and non-material concerns, associationism and state, the individual and the community, tradition and modernity. Therefore, social relations in contemporary urban China are not all or nothing. By the same token, transformative, diverse, and heterogeneous social relations require mobile, non-binary, and inter- and transdisciplinary class analysis. Social distinctions and inequalities are accentuated in China as social identities are constructed away from binary criteria such as objective and subjective definitions.

In the process, the middle-class lifestyle is part of the complex processes of social construction of identity seamlessly integrated into the PRC's own trajectory toward modernity, as if it was a mobile process of civilization that constructs social distinctions as possessing oppositional and complementary identities. As might be expected, the civilized middle class has to live in a civilized city. However, considering the transformation of China's development mode, the National Civilized City program is not only about building civilized cities but also building civilized citizenry. Social credit system and multi-model programmes of "building socialist spiritual civilization" show how government programmes regularize and institutionalize civic practices and transform local governance in China without devolving power to local communities.

That is why the Chinese middle class is not a proxy for democratization, nor is it a synonym for democratization. Neither is it an antonym. It is about civilized citizens and civilizing practices. Under these conditions, the Chinese middle class is an advocate of the status quo and the ideology of self-making. Despite their willingness to solve social problems and act for the common good, political change and democratization may be a disturbance to their achieved social position. Their lifestyle does not challenge social inequality, rather it supports the established order. Those who belong to this group tend to be conservative politically, they encourage heteronormativity, accumulate cultural capital, and have a standardized lifestyle. They combine their responsibilities as attentive parents to their children with striving to be filial children and return care and support to their parents. Remarkably, they consider that social hierarchy and entitlement are based on effort, talent, knowledge, and achievement. Those who work hard, they claim, will be rewarded with success, economic goods, and personal satisfaction. However, the findings of this study were supportive of the class reproduction thesis, that is, class location is inherited and is not the result of personal effort and skills alone.

From an empirical aspect, identifying the economic and symbolic power structures that operate together in class formation in urban China is a sober methodological issue, which should be overcome, especially in the geographical context. Although this book has examined the emergence of a lifestyle associated with a post-industrial middle class in Beijing in the post-reform era, the manifestations of middle-class lifestyles in other Chinese geographic contexts, both urban and rural, have not been covered here. Particularly, the notion of periphery appears as a key element in the production and reproduction of social distinctions and new lifestyles in the PRC in the 2020s. The lifestyle of the post-reform middle class beyond very large and mega-cities such as Beijing, Shanghai, Guangzhou, and Shenzhen, challenges the very concept of class and targets the limits of the new imaginary of the common prosperity that the Party-state aims to develop in the next decade. Once the post-reform middle class in large Chinese cities has become a post-industrial middle class, the middle class in smaller Chinese cities deserves our concern in the future to analyse not only the transfer of lifestyles between the mega-cities and the periphery but also power relations, social inequalities, and symbolic hierarchies in medium-sized Chinese cities in the post-pandemic era.

Through such innovative and interesting discussions of the construction of social identity, class analysis in particular—and intersectional approaches in general—emerges as an urgent need and key tool for understanding accelerated mobilities and the ideology of everyday practices and narratives in neoliberal capitalism and undemocratic regimes such as the PRC. To a large extent, the middle class in neo-authoritarian regimes can be seen as an example of cultural consumption and post-industrial concerns as the primary variables for class identity and class location rather than class consciousness and political action. But, generally, the urban middle-class groups not only, to a lesser or greater extent, consume goods and services, but also can be centrally organized around the symbolic production and reproduction of class differences. Therefore, class distinctions not only depend on the accumulation of capital but above all on how they consume such capital and how quantity can be transformed into quality (or *suzhi*). In other words, in an age where avoiding consumption is a privilege, frugality rather than conspicuous consumption denotes high-*suzhi*.

In the end, given the impacts of global crises currently facing world society, the study of class formation throughout lifestyle and social distinctions "constitutes the cultural embodiment of our dominant political-economic order of neoliberal capitalism" which underpins the meta-uncertainties of these volatile times (Raymen and Smith 2019, 2). Thus, the lifestyle of the post-reform middle class constitutes the cultural embodiment of the Party-state's political-economic order and the "new definition of reality" (Rocca 2017, 234). This paradigm of the Chinese middle class, thus, connotes normative ideals of modernity, civilized citizens, progress, human quality (*suzhi*), gender differences, and a comfortable urban life in the PRC. After the Global Financial Crisis, the Party-state established this new paradigm as a key aspect in stimulating domestic demand, accelerating the transformation of the economic growth model, seeking new resources to increase the innovative potential, and promoting sustained long-term development (Beltrán Antolín 2018, 140). Later, during the COVID-19 pandemic, the Chinese leadership did not dwell on this paradigm in a finite present; it drew upon understandings of both the recent past and aspirations of the future to implement a new development strategy based on domestic demand and innovation. Hence, the Chinese government has set the year 2035 as the target date to attain the common prosperity in order to become, by 2050, a great modern socialist country. China's common prosperity initiative implies the achievement of a middle-class society that will not only act as the main generator of domestic demand but it will also reduce income inequality, promote a comfortable lifestyle among the Chinese population, balance regional development, focus on the common good, and encourage wealthy people and enterprises to return more to society. In practice, though, the Chinese middle class is becoming a promise of prosperity, an old promise in an infinite present.

Bibliography

Beltrán Antolín, Joaquín. 2018. "El Partido ante la sociedad: La erradicación de la pobreza" [The Party facing society: Poverty eradication]. In *Viaje al Centro. El XIX Congreso del Partido Comunista Chino* [*Journey to the Centre: The 19th Congress of the Communist Party of China*], edited by Joaquín Beltrán Antolín, 137–158. Barcelona: Edicions Bellaterra.

Bourdieu, Pierre. 1987. "What Makes a Social Class? On Theoretical and Practical Existence of Groups." *Berkeley Journal of Sociology* 32: 1–17.

Dickson, Bruce. 2016. *The Dictator's Dilemma: The Chinese Communist Party's Strategy for Survival*. Oxford: Oxford University Press.

Dunford, Michael. 2022. "The Chinese Path to Common Prosperity." *International Critical Thought* 12 (1): 35–54. doi:10.1080/21598282.2022.2025561.

Gao, Mobo. 2018. *Constructing China. Clashing Views of the People's Republic*. London: Pluto Press.

Garcés, Marina. 2017. *Nova il·lustració radical* [*A new radical enlightenment*]. Barcelona: Anagrama.

Gramsci, Antonio. 1971. *Selections from the Prison Notebooks of Antonio Gramsci*. Translated by Quintin Hoare and Geoffrey Nowell-Smith. London: Lawrence & Wishart.

Guo, Xiaolu. 2008. "China's Youth: Ravenous for the West, With No Memory of the Past." *New Perspectives Quarterly* 25 (3): 48–52. doi:10.1111/j.1540-5842.2008.01005.x.

Lin, Thung-hong. 2008. *Social Classes in China: An Analysis of China's Transition to Capitalism*. PhD diss., Hong Kong University of Science and Technology.

Raymen, Thomas, and Oliver Smith. 2019. "Introduction: Why Leisure?" In *Deviant Leisure. Criminological Perspectives on Leisure and Harm*, edited by Thomas Raymen and Oliver Smith, 1–13. Cham: Palgrave Macmillan.

Redhead, Steven. 2009. "Towards a theory of claustropolitanism: jacking into the trajectories of the catastrophic." *Left Curve* 33: 126–133.

Rocca, Jean-Louis. 2017. *The Making of the Chinese Middle Class: Small Comfort and Great Expectations*. New York: Palgrave Macmillan US.

Sánchez-Romera, Alfonso. 2021. "The Official Discourse of the Chinese Middle Class: Anxiety, Nationalism and Populism." *Revista Española de Investigaciones Sociológicas* 176: 141–156. doi:10.5477/cis/reis.176.141.

Spivak, Gayatri Chakravorty. 1988. "Can the Subaltern Speak?" In *Marxism and the Interpretation of Culture*, edited by Cary Nelson and Lawrence Grossberg, 271–313. Chicago: University of Illinois Press.

Xie, Kailing. 2020. "Chasing Happiness: The Role of Marriage in the Aspiration of Success Among China's Middle-Class Women." In *Romantic Relationships in a Time of 'Cold Intimacies*, edited by Julia Carter and Lorena Arocha, 181–206. Cham: Palgrave Macmillan.

Zhang, Weiwei. 2020. "Consumption, taste, and the economic transition in modern China." *Consumption Markets & Culture* 23 (1): 1–20. doi:10.1080/10253866.2018.1467316.

Zhang, Yi. 2008. "Political Attitudes of the Middle Social Stratum in Today's China." *Chinese Social Science* 2: 117–131 [in Chinese].

INDEX

Printed in Great Britain
by Amazon

39709722R00110